W9-CIP-781

PEARSON CUSTOM SOCIOLOGY
WITH READINGS FROM THE INTERSECTIONS COLLECTION

Formerly published as Intersections, Crossroads & Inequalities

EDITORS

KATHLEEN A. TIEMANN
University of North Dakota
Introduction to Sociology, Social Problems & Issues, Inequalities & Diversity

RALPH B. MCNEAL, JR.
University of Connecticut
Introduction to Sociology

BETSY LUCAL
Indiana University South Bend
Inequalities & Diversity

MORTEN G. ENDER
United States Military Academy, West Point
Inequalities & Diversity

COMPILED BY:

Wayne Brekhus
Queer Theories/Identities
Sociology

PEARSON

Cover Art: "Figures," courtesy of Eugenie Lewalski Berg; "Abstract Crowd," courtesy of Diana Ong/Superstock; "R&B Figures," courtesy of Diana Ong/Superstock; "Bramante's Staircase," courtesy of Veer/Photodisc Photography; "Hand Prints," courtesy of Veer/Photodisc Photography; "People Running-Falling," courtesy of Veer/Campbell Laird; "Sunbathers on Beach," courtesy of Veer/Scott Barrow; "Parada Gay, Florianapolis_25 (colorful balloons being set free)," courtesy of Paul Mansfield Photography/Getty Images; "Family Tree, Relatives," courtesy of Kudryashka/iStockphoto.com.

Copyright © 2013 by Pearson Learning Solutions

Printed in the United States of America.

V092

Please visit our website at *www.pearsonlearningsolutions.com*.

Attention bookstores: For permission to return any unsold stock, contact us at *pe-uscustomreturns@pearson.com*.

Pearson Learning Solutions, 501 Boylston Street, Suite 900, Boston, MA 02116
A Pearson Education Company
www.pearsoned.com

ISBN 10: 0-558-45680-4
ISBN 13: 978-0-558-45680-1

Table of Contents

II

The Heterosexual Questionnaire

M. Rochlin

Many people take their sexuality for granted. For example, it never occurs to them to question what caused their particular type of sexuality. However, there are some people who do not get to take their sexuality for granted: lesbians and gay men. Members of sexual minority groups are often asked questions about what they think caused their sexuality or how they know for sure what their sexual identity is. In this questionnaire, M. Rochlin turns the tables on heterosexuals, asking them the kinds of questions gay men and lesbians are often asked.

1. What do you think caused your heterosexuality?

2. When and how did you decide you were a heterosexual?

3. Is it possible that your heterosexuality is just a phase you may grow out of?

4. Is it possible that your heterosexuality stems from a neurotic fear of others of the same sex?

5. If you have never slept with a person of the same sex, is it possible that all you need is a good Gay lover?

6. Do your parents know that you are straight? Do your friends and/or roommate(s) know? How did they react?

7. Why do you insist on flaunting your heterosexuality? Can't you just be who you are and keep it quiet?

8. Why do heterosexuals place so much emphasis on sex?

9. Why do heterosexuals feel compelled to seduce others into their lifestyle?

Reprinted from *Changing Men*, (1982), by permission of the Martin Rochlin Estate.

10. A disproportionate majority of child molesters are heterosexual. Do you consider it safe to expose children to heterosexual teachers?

11. Just what do men and women *do* in bed together? How can they truly know how to please each other, being so anatomically different?

12. With all the societal support marriage receives, the divorce rate is spiraling. Why are there so few stable relationships among heterosexuals?

13. Statistics show that lesbians have the lowest incidence of sexually transmitted diseases. Is it really safe for a woman to maintain a heterosexual lifestyle and run the risk of disease and pregnancy?

14. How can you become a whole person if you limit yourself to compulsive, exclusive heterosexuality?

15. Considering the menace of overpopulation, how could the human race survive if everyone were heterosexual?

16. Could you trust a heterosexual therapist to be objective? Don't you feel s/he might be inclined to influence you in the direction of her/his own leanings?

17. There seems to be very few happy heterosexuals. Techniques have been developed that might enable you to change if you really want to. Have you considered trying aversion therapy?

18. Would you want your child to be heterosexual, knowing the problems that s/he would face?

☻ ☻ ☻

Questions

1. Which of these questions do you find most interesting? Surprising? Insightful?

2. What do these questions tell us about the comparable questions asked of gay men and lesbians?

3. Do you think most heterosexuals have thought about these questions in relationship to their own sexuality? Why or why not?

4. What other questions might be added to this questionnaire?

5. Find a willing heterosexual and ask her/him some of these questions. How did your interviewee react to the questions?

6. Is this questionnaire an effective tool for helping people understand sexuality? Explain.

Doing Gender

Candace West
Don H. Zimmerman

Is gender simply something that exists in people's heads and forms part of their identity as an individual? Then how do we explain the gendering of institutions, organizations, and even societies? This classic article by Candace West and Don H. Zimmerman helped to pave the way for a fundamentally different understanding of the way gender operates in contemporary society. Rather than locating gender in individuals, West and Zimmerman recast gender as a property of the interactional context. It is in their interactions with others (and themselves) that individuals are held "accountable" to gender: Everything they do can be interpreted in light of gender assumptions. One of the implications of West and Zimmerman's conceptualization is that even if individuals might not be "doing gender," other people "do it" for them. Think about what this means in the course of day-to-day interaction.

In the beginning, there was sex and there was gender. Those of us who taught courses in the area in the late 1960s and early 1970s were careful to distinguish one from the other. Sex, we told students, was what was ascribed by biology: anatomy, hormones, and physiology. Gender, we said, was an achieved status: that which is constructed through psychological, cultural, and social means. To introduce the difference between the two, we drew on singular case studies of hermaphrodites (Money 1968, 1974; Money and Ehrhardt 1972) and anthropological investigations of "strange and exotic tribes" (Mead 1963, 1968).

Inevitably (and understandably), in the ensuing weeks of each term, our students became confused. Sex hardly seemed a "given" in the context of research that illustrated the sometimes ambiguous and often conflicting criteria for its ascription. And gender seemed much less an "achievement" in the context of the anthropological, psychological, and social imperatives we studied—the division of labor, the formation of gender identities, and the social subordination of women by men. Moreover, the received doctrine of gender socialization theories conveyed the strong message that while gender may be "achieved," by about age five it was certainly fixed, unvarying, and static—much like sex.

Since about 1975, the confusion has intensified and spread far beyond our individual classrooms. For one thing, we learned that the relationship between biological and cultural processes was far more complex—and reflexive—than we previously had supposed (Rossi 1984, especially pp. 10–14). For another, we discovered that certain structural arrangements, for example, between work and family, actually produce or enable some capacities, such as to mother, that we formerly associated with biology (Chodorow 1978 versus Firestone 1970). In the midst of all this, the notion of gender as a recurring achievement somehow fell by the wayside.

Our purpose in this article is to propose an ethnomethodologically informed, and therefore distinctively sociological, understanding of gender as a routine, methodical, and recurring accomplishment. We contend that the "doing" of gender is undertaken by women and men whose competence as members of society is hostage to its production. Doing gender involves a complex of socially guided perceptual, interactional, and micropolitical activities that cast particular pursuits as expressions of masculine and feminine "natures."

When we view gender as an accomplishment, an achieved property of situated conduct, our attention shifts from matters internal to the individual and focuses on interactional and, ultimately, institutional arenas. In one sense, of course, it is individuals who "do" gender. But it is a situated doing, carried out in the virtual or real presence of others who are presumed to be oriented to its production. Rather than as a property of individuals, we conceive of gender as an emergent feature of social situations: both as an outcome of and a rationale for various social arrangements and as a means of legitimating one of the most fundamental divisions of society.

To advance our argument, we undertake a critical examination of what sociologists have meant by *gender,* including its treatment as a role enactment in the conventional sense and as a "display" in Goffman's (1976) terminology. Both *gender role* and *gender display* focus on behavioral aspects of being a woman or a man (as opposed, for example, to biological differences between the two). However, we contend that the notion of gender as a role obscures the work that is involved in producing gender in everyday activities, while the notion of gender as a display relegates it to the periphery of interaction. We argue instead that participants in interaction organize their various and manifold activities to reflect or express gender, and they are disposed to perceive the behavior of others in a similar light.

To elaborate our proposal, we suggest at the outset that important but often overlooked distinctions be observed among *sex, sex category,* and *gen-*

der. *Sex* is a determination made through the application of socially agreed upon biological criteria for classifying persons as females or males.[1] The criteria for classification can be genitalia at birth or chromosomal typing before birth, and they do not necessarily agree with one another. Placement in a *sex category* is achieved through application of the sex criteria, but in everyday life, categorization is established and sustained by the socially required identificatory displays that proclaim one's membership in one or the other category. In this sense, one's sex category presumes one's sex and stands as proxy for it in many situations, but sex and sex category can vary independently; that is, it is possible to claim membership in a sex category even when the sex criteria are lacking. *Gender,* in contrast, is the activity of managing situated conduct in light of normative conceptions of attitudes and activities appropriate for one's sex category. Gender activities emerge from and bolster claims to membership in a sex category.

We contend that recognition of the analytical independence of sex, sex category, and gender is essential for understanding the relationships among these elements and the interactional work involved in "being" a gendered person in society. While our primary aim is theoretical, there will be occasion to discuss fruitful directions for empirical research following from the formulation of gender that we propose.

We begin with an assessment of the received meaning of gender, particularly in relation to the roots of this notion in presumed biological differences between women and men.

◉ Perspectives on Sex and Gender

In Western societies, the accepted cultural perspective on gender views women and men as naturally and unequivocally defined categories of being (Garfinkel 1967, pp. 116–18) with distinctive psychological and behavioral propensities that can be predicted from their reproductive functions. Competent adult members of these societies see differences between the two as fundamental and enduring—differences seemingly supported by the division of labor into women's and men's work and an often elaborate differentiation of feminine and masculine attitudes and behaviors that are prominent features of social organization. Things are the way they are by virtue of the fact that men are men and women are women—a division perceived to be natural and rooted in biology, producing in turn profound psychological, behavioral, and social consequences. The structural arrangements of a society are presumed to be responsive to these differences.

Analyses of sex and gender in the social sciences, though less likely to accept uncritically the naïve biological determinism of the view just presented, often retain a conception of sex-linked behaviors and traits as essential properties of individuals (for good reviews, see Hochschild 1973; Tresemer 1975; Thorne 1980; Henley 1985). The "sex differences approach" (Thorne 1980) is more commonly attributed to psychologists than to sociologists, but the survey researcher who determines the "gender" of respondents on the basis of the sound of their voices over the telephone is also making trait-oriented assumptions. Reducing gender to a fixed set of psychological traits or to a unitary "variable" precludes serious consideration of the ways it is used to structure distinct domains of social experience (Stacey and Thorne 1985, pp. 307–8).

Taking a different tack, role theory has attended to the social construction of gender categories, called "sex roles" or, more recently, "gender roles" and has analyzed how these are learned and enacted. Beginning with Linton (1936) and continuing through the works of Parsons (Parsons 1951; Parsons and Bales 1955) and Komarovsky (1946, 1950), role theory has emphasized the social and dynamic aspect of role construction and enactment (Thorne 1980; Connell 1983). But at the level of face-to-face interaction, the application of role theory to gender poses problems of its own (for good reviews and critiques, see Connell 1983, 1985; Kessler, Ashendon, Connell, and Dowsett 1985; Lopata and Thorne 1978; Thorne 1980; Stacey and Thorne 1985). Roles are *situated* identities—assumed and relinquished as the situation demands—rather than *master identities* (Hughes 1945), such as sex category, that cut across situations. Unlike most roles, such as "nurse," "doctor," and "patient" or "professor" and "student," gender has no specific site or organizational context.

Moreover, many roles are already gender marked, so that special qualifiers—such as "female doctor" or "male nurse"—must be added to exceptions to the rule. Thorne (1980) observes that conceptualizing gender as a role makes it difficult to assess its influence on other roles and reduces its explanatory usefulness in discussions of power and inequality. Drawing on Rubin (1975), Thorne calls for a reconceptualization of women and men as distinct social groups, constituted in "concrete, historically changing—and generally unequal—social relationships" (Thorne 1980, p. 11).

We argue that gender is not a set of traits, nor a variable, nor a role, but the product of social doings of some sort. What then is the social doing of gender? It is more than the continuous creation of the meaning of gender through human actions (Gerson and Peiss 1985). We claim that gender itself is constituted through interaction.[2] To develop the implications of our claim, we turn to Goffman's (1976) account of "gender display." Our object here is to explore how gender might be exhibited or portrayed through interaction, and thus be seen as "natural," while it is being produced as a socially organized achievement.

● Gender Display

Goffman contends that when human beings interact with others in their environment, they assume that each possesses an "essential nature"—a nature that can be discerned through the "natural signs given off or expressed by them" (1976, p. 75). Femininity and masculinity are regarded as "prototypes of essential expression—something that can be conveyed fleetingly in any social situation and yet something that strikes at the most basic characterization of the individual" (1976, p. 75). The means through which we provide such expressions are "perfunctory, conventionalized acts" (1976, p. 69), which convey to others our regard for them, indicate our alignment in an encounter, and tentatively establish the terms of contact for that social situation. But they are also regarded as expressive behavior, testimony to our "essential natures."

Goffman (1976, pp. 69–70) sees *displays* as highly conventionalized behaviors structured as two-part exchanges of the statement-reply type, in which the presence or absence of symmetry can establish deference or dominance. These rituals are viewed as distinct from but articulated with more consequential activities, such as performing tasks or engaging in discourse. Hence, we have what he terms the "scheduling" of displays at junctures in activities, such as the beginning or end, to avoid interfering with the activities themselves. Goffman (1976, p. 69) formulates *gender display* as follows:

> If gender be defined as the culturally established correlates of sex (whether in consequence of biology or learning), then gender display refers to conventionalized portrayals of these correlates.

These gendered expressions might reveal clues to the underlying, fundamental dimensions of the female and male, but they are, in Goffman's view, optional performances. Masculine courtesies may or may not be offered and, if offered, may or may not be declined (1976, p. 71). Moreover, human beings "themselves employ the term 'expression', and conduct themselves to fit their own notions of expressivity" (1976, p. 75). Gender depictions are less a consequence of our "essential sexual natures" than interactional portrayals of what we would like to convey about sexual natures, using conventionalized gestures. Our *human* nature gives us the ability to learn to produce and recognize masculine and feminine gender displays—"a capacity [we] have by virtue of being persons, not males and females" (1976, p. 76).

Upon first inspection, it would appear that Goffman's formulation offers an engaging sociological corrective to existing formulations of gender. In his view, gender is a socially scripted dramatization of the culture's *idealization* of feminine and masculine natures, played for an audience that is well schooled in the presentational idiom. To continue the metaphor, there are scheduled performances presented in special locations, and like plays, they constitute introductions to or time out from more serious activities.

There are fundamental equivocations in this perspective. By segregating gender display from the serious business of interaction, Goffman obscures the effects of gender on a wide range of human activities. Gender is not merely something that happens in the nooks and crannies of interaction, fitted in here and there and not interfering with the serious business of life. While it is plausible to contend that gender displays—construed as conventionalized expressions—are optional, it does not seem plausible to say that we have the option of being seen by others as female or male.

It is necessary to move beyond the notion of gender display to consider what is involved in doing gender as an ongoing activity embedded in everyday interaction. Toward this end, we return to the distinctions among sex, sex category, and gender introduced earlier.

◉ Sex, Sex Category, and Gender

Garfinkel's (1967, pp. 118–40) case study of Agnes, a transsexual raised as a boy who adopted a female identity at age 17 and underwent a sex reassignment operation several years later, demonstrates how gender is created through interaction and at the same time structures interaction. Agnes, whom Garfinkel characterized as a "practical methodologist," developed a number of procedures for passing as a "normal, natural female" both prior to and after her surgery. She had the practical task of managing the fact that she possessed male genitalia and that she lacked the social resources a girl's biography would presumably provide in everyday interaction. In short, she needed to display herself as a woman, simultaneously learning what it was to be a woman. Of necessity, this full-time pursuit took place at a time when most people's gender would be well-accredited and routinized. Agnes had to consciously contrive what the vast majority of women do without thinking. She was not "faking" what "real" women do naturally. She was obliged to analyze and figure out how to act within socially structured circumstances and conceptions of femininity that women born with appropriate biological credentials come to take for granted early on. As in the case of others who must "pass," such as transvestites, Kabuki actors, or Dustin Hoffman's "Tootsie," Agnes's case makes visible what culture has made invisible—the accomplishment of gender.

Garfinkel's (1967) discussion of Agnes does not explicitly separate three analytically distinct, although empirically overlapping, concepts—sex, sex category, and gender.

Sex

Agnes did not possess the socially agreed upon biological criteria for classification as a member of the female *sex*. Still, Agnes regarded herself as a female, albeit a female with a penis, which a woman ought not to possess. The penis, she insisted, was a "mistake" in need of remedy (Garfinkel 1967, pp. 126–27, 131–32). Like other competent members of our culture, Agnes honored the notion that there *are* "essential" biological criteria that unequivocally distinguish females from males. However, if we move away from the commonsense viewpoint, we discover that the reliability of these criteria is not beyond question (Money and Brennan 1968; Money and Erhardt 1972; Money and Ogunro 1974; Money and Tucker 1975). Moreover, other cultures have acknowledged the existence of "cross-genders" (Blackwood 1984; Williams 1986) and the possibility of more than two sexes (Hill 1935; Martin and Voorhies 1975, pp. 84–107; but see also Cucchiari 1981, pp. 32–35).

More central to our argument is Kessler and McKenna's (1978, pp. 1–6) point that genitalia are conventionally hidden from public inspection in everyday life; yet we continue through our social rounds to "observe" a world of two naturally, normally sexed persons. It is the *presumption* that essential criteria exist and would or should be there if looked for that provides the basis for sex categorization. Drawing on Garfinkel, Kessler and McKenna argue that "female" and "male" are cultural events—products of what they term the "gender attribution process"—rather than some collection of traits, behaviors, or even physical attributes. Illustratively they cite the child who, viewing a picture of someone clad in a suit and tie, contends, "It's a man, because he has a pee-pee" (Kessler and McKenna 1978, p. 154). Translation: "He must have a pee-pee [an essential characteristic] because I see the *insignia* of a suit and tie." Neither initial sex assignment (pronouncement at birth as a female or male) nor the actual existence of essential criteria for that assignment (possession of a clitoris and vagina or penis and testicles) has much—if anything—to do with the identification of sex category in everyday life. There, Kessler and McKenna note, we operate with a moral certainty of a world of two sexes. We do not think, "Most persons with penises are men, but some may not be" or "Most persons who dress as men have penises." Rather, we take it for granted that sex and sex category are congruent—that knowing the latter, we can deduce the rest.

Sex Categorization

Agnes's claim to the categorical status of female, which she sustained by appropriate identificatory displays and other characteristics, could be *discredited* before her transsexual operation if her possession of a penis became known and after by her surgically constructed genitalia (see Raymond 1979, pp. 37, 138). In this regard, Agnes had to be continually alert to actual or potential threats to the security of her sex category. Her problem was not so much living up to some prototype of essential femininity but preserving her categorization as female. This task was made easy for her by a very powerful resource, namely, the process of commonsense categorization in everyday life.

The categorization of members of society into indigenous categories such as "girl" or "boy," or "woman" or "man," operates in a distinctively social way. The act of categorization does not involve a positive test, in the sense of a well-defined set of criteria that must be explicitly satisfied prior to making an identification. Rather, the application of membership categories relies on an "if-can" test in everyday interaction (Sacks 1972, pp. 332–35). This test stipulates that if people *can be seen* as members of relevant categories, *then categorize them that way*. That is, use the category that seems appropriate, except in the presence of discrepant information or obvious features that would rule out its use. This procedure is quite in keeping with the attitude of everyday life, which has us take appearances at face value unless we have special reason to doubt (Schutz 1943; Garfinkel 1967, pp. 272–77; Bernstein 1986).[3] It should be added that it is precisely when we have special reason to doubt that the issue of applying rigorous criteria arises, but it is rare, outside legal or bureaucratic contexts, to encounter insistence on positive tests (Garfinkel 1967, pp. 262–83; Wilson 1970).

Agnes's initial resource was the predisposition of those she encountered to take her appearance (her figure, clothing, hair style, and so on), as the undoubted appearance of a normal female. Her further resource was our cultural perspective on the properties of "natural, normally sexed persons." Garfinkel (1967, pp. 122–28) notes that in everyday life, we live in a world of two—and only two—sexes. This arrangement has a moral status, in that we include ourselves and others in it as "essentially, originally, in the first place, always have been, always will be, once and for all, in the final analysis, either 'male' or 'female'" (Garfinkel 1967, p. 122).

Consider the following case:

> This issue reminds me of a visit I made to a computer store a couple of years ago. The person who answered my questions was truly a *salesperson*. I could not categorize him/her as a woman or a man. What did I look for? (1) Facial hair: She/he was smooth skinned, but some men have little or no facial hair. (This varies by race, Native Americans and Blacks often have none.) (2) Breasts: She/he was wearing a loose shirt that hung from his/her shoulders. And, as many women who suffered through a 1950's adolescence know to their shame, women are often flat-chested. (3) Shoulders: His/hers were small and round for a man, broad for a woman. (4) Hands: Long and slender fingers, knuckles a bit large for a woman, small for a man. (5) Voice: Middle range, unexpressive for a woman, not at all the exaggerated tones some gay males affect. (6) His/her treatment of me: Gave off no signs that would let me know if I were of the same or different sex as this person. There were not even any signs that he/she knew his/her sex would be difficult to categorize and I wondered about that even as I did my best to hide these questions so I would not embarrass him/her while we talked of computer paper. I left still not knowing the sex of my salesperson, and was disturbed by that unanswered question (child of my culture that I am). (Diane Margolis, personal communication)

What can this case tell us about situations such as Agnes's (cf. Morris 1974; Richards 1983) or the process of sex categorization in general? First, we infer from this description that the computer salesclerk's identificatory display was ambiguous, since she or he was not dressed or adorned in an unequivocally female or male fashion. It is when such a display *fails* to provide grounds for categorization that factors such as facial hair or tone of voice are assessed to determine membership in a sex category. Second, beyond the fact that this incident could be recalled after "a couple of years," the customer was not only "disturbed" by the ambiguity of the salesclerk's category but also assumed that to acknowledge this ambiguity would be embarrassing to the salesclerk. Not only do we want to know the sex category of those around us (to see it at a glance, perhaps), but we presume that others are displaying it for us, in as decisive a fashion as they can.

Gender

Agnes attempted to be "120 percent female" (Garfinkel 1967, p. 129), that is, unquestionably in all ways and at all times feminine. She thought she could protect herself from disclosure before and after surgical intervention by comporting herself in a feminine manner, but she also could have given herself away by overdoing her performance. Sex categorization and the accomplishment of gender are not the same. Agnes's categorization could be secure or suspect, but did not depend on whether or not she lived up to some ideal conception of femininity. Women can be seen as unfeminine, but that does not make them "unfemale." Agnes faced an ongoing task of *being* a woman—something beyond style of dress (an identificatory display) or allowing men to light her cigarette (a gender display). Her problems was to produce configurations of behavior that would be seen by others as normative gender behavior.

Agnes's strategy of "secret apprenticeship," through which she learned expected feminine decorum by carefully attending to her fiancé's criticisms of other women, was one means of masking incompetencies and simultaneously acquiring the needed skills (Garfinkel 1967, pp. 146–147). It was through her fiancé that Agnes learned that sunbathing on the lawn in front of her apartment was "offensive" (because it put her on display to other men). She also learned from his critiques of other women that she should not insist on having things her way and that she should not offer her opinions or claim equality with men (Garfinkel 1967, pp. 147–148). (Like other women in our society, Agnes learned something about power in the course of her "education.")

Popular culture abounds with books and magazines that compile idealized depictions of relations between women and men. Those focused on the etiquette of dating or prevailing standards of feminine comportment are meant to be of practical help in these matters. However, the use of any such source *as a manual of procedure* requires the assumption that doing gender merely involves making use of discrete, well-defined bundles of behavior that can simply be plugged into interactional situations to produce recognizable enactments of masculinity and femininity. The man "does" being masculine by, for example, taking the woman's arm to guide her across a street, and she "does" being feminine by consenting to be guided and not initiating such behavior with a man.

Agnes could perhaps have used such sources as manuals, but,we contend, doing gender is not so easily regimented (Mithers 1982; Morris 1974). Such sources may list and describe the sorts of behaviors that mark or display gender, but they are necessarily incomplete (Garfinkel 1967, pp. 66–75; Wieder 1974, pp. 183–214; Zimmerman and Wieder 1970, pp. 285–98). And to be successful, marking or displaying gender must be finely fitted to situations and modified or transformed as the occasion demands. Doing gender consists of managing such occasions so that, whatever the particulars, the outcome is seen and seeable in context as gender-appropriate or, as the case may be, gender-inappropriate, that is, *accountable*.

◉ Gender and Accountability

As Heritage (1984, pp. 136–37) notes, members of society regularly engage in "descriptive accountings of states of affairs to one another," and such accounts are both serious and consequential. These descriptions name, characterize, formulate, explain, excuse, excoriate, or merely take notice of some circumstance or activity and thus place it within some social framework (locating it relative to other activities, like and unlike).

Such descriptions are themselves accountable, and societal members orient to the fact that their activities are subject to comment. Actions are often designed with an eye to their accountability, that is, how they might look and how they might be characterized. The notion of accountability also encompasses those actions undertaken so that they are specifically unremarkable and thus not worthy of more than a passing remark, because they are seen to be in accord with culturally approved standards.

Heritage (1984, p. 179) observes that the process of rendering something accountable is interactional in character:

> [This] permits actors to design their actions in relation to their circumstances so as to permit others, by methodically taking account of circumstances, to recognize the action for what it is.

The key word here is *circumstances*. One circumstance that attends virtually all actions is the sex category of the actor. As Garfinkel (1967, p. 118) comments:

[T]he work and socially structured occasions of sexual passing were obstinately unyielding to [Agnes's] attempts to routinize the grounds of daily activities. This obstinacy points to the *omnirelevance* of sexual status to affairs of daily life as an invariant but unnoticed background in the texture of relevances that compose the changing actual scenes of everyday life. (italics added)

If sex category is omnirelevant (or even approaches being so), then a person engaged in virtually any activity may be held accountable for performance of that activity as a *woman* or a *man,* and their incumbency in one or the other sex category can be used to legitimate or discredit their other activities (Berger, Cohen, and Zelditch 1972; Berger, Conner, and Fisek 1974; Berger, Fisek, Norman, and Zelditch 1977; Humphreys and Berger 1981). Accordingly, virtually any activity can be assessed as to its womanly or manly nature. And note, to "do" gender is not always to live up to normative conceptions of femininity or masculinity; it is to engage in behavior *at the risk of gender assessment.* While it is individuals who do gender, the enterprise is fundamentally interactional and institutional in character, for accountability is a feature of social relationships and its idiom is drawn from the institutional arena in which those relationships are enacted. If this be the case, can we ever *not* do gender? Insofar as a society is partitioned by "essential" differences between women and men and placement in a sex category is both relevant and enforced, doing gender is unavoidable.

● Resources for Doing Gender

Doing gender means creating differences between girls and boys and women and men, differences that are not natural, essential, or biological. Once the differences have been constructed, they are used to reinforce the "essentialness" of gender. In a delightful account of the "arrangement between the sexes," Goffman (1977) observes the creation of a variety of institutionalized frameworks through which our "natural, normal sexedness" can be enacted. The physical features of social setting provide one obvious resource for the expression of our "essential" differences. For example, the sex segregation of North American public bathrooms distinguishes "ladies" from "gentlemen" in matters held to be fundamentally biological, even though both "are somewhat similar in the question of waste products and their elimination" (Goffman 1977, p. 315). These settings are furnished with dimorphic equipment (such as urinals for men or elaborate grooming facilities for women), even though both sexes may achieve the same ends through the same means (and apparently do so in the privacy of their own homes). To be stressed here is the fact that:

> The *functioning* of sex-differentiated organs is involved, but there is nothing in this functioning that biologically recommends segregation; *that* arrangement is a totally cultural matter . . . toilet segregation is presented as a natural consequence of the difference between the sex-classes when in fact it is a means of honoring, if not producing, this difference. (Goffman 1977, p. 316)

Standardized social occasions also provide stages for evocations of the "essential female and male natures." Goffman cites organized sports as one such institutionalized framework for the expression of manliness. There, those qualities that ought "properly" to be associated with masculinity, such as endurance, strength, and competitive spirit, are celebrated by all parties concerned—participants, who may be seen to demonstrate such traits, and spectators, who applaud their demonstrations from the safety of the sidelines (1977, p. 322)

Assortative mating practices among heterosexual couples afford still further means to create and maintain differences between women and men. For example, even though size, strength, and age tend to be normally distributed among females and males (with considerable overlap between them), selective pairing ensures couples in which boys and men are visibly bigger, stronger, and older (if not "wiser") than the girls and women with whom they are paired. So, should situations emerge in which greater size, strength, or experience is called for, boys and men will be ever ready to display it and girls and women, to appreciate its display (Goffman 1977, p. 321; West and Iritani 1985).

Gender may be routinely fashioned in a variety of situations that seem conventionally expressive to begin with, such as those that present "helpless" women next to heavy objects or flat tires. But, as Goffman notes, heavy, messy, and precarious concerns can be constructed from *any* social situation, "even though by standards set in other settings, this may involve something that is light, clean, and safe" (Goffman 1977, p. 324). Given these resources, it is clear that *any* interactional situation sets the stage for depictions of "essential" sexual natures. In sum, these situations "do not so much allow for the expression of natural differences as for the production of that difference itself" (Goffman 1977, p. 324).

Many situations are not clearly sex categorized to begin with, nor is what transpires within them obviously gender relevant. Yet any social encounter can be pressed into service in the interests of doing gender. Thus, Fishman's

(1978) research on casual conversations found an asymmetrical "division of labor" in talk between heterosexual intimates. Women had to ask more questions, fill more silences, and use more attention-getting beginnings in order to be heard. Her conclusions are particularly pertinent here:

> Since interactional work is related to what constitutes being a woman, with what a woman *is*, the idea that it *is* work is obscured. The work is not seen as what women do, but as part of what they are. (Fishman 1978, p. 405)

We would argue that it is precisely such labor that helps to constitute the essential nature of women *as* women in interactional contexts (West and Zimmerman 1983, pp. 109–11; but see also Kollock, Blumstein, and Schwartz 1985).

Individuals have many social identities that may he donned or shed, muted or made more salient, depending on the situation. One may be a friend, spouse, professional citizen, and many other things to many different people—or, to the same person at different times. But we are always women or men—unless we shift into another sex category. What this means is that our identificatory displays will provide an ever-available resource for doing gender under an infinitely diverse set of circumstances

Some occasions are organized to routinely display and celebrate behaviors that are conventionally linked to one or the other sex category. On such occasions, everyone knows his or her place in the interactional scheme of things. If an individual identified as a member of one sex category engages in behavior usually associated with the other category, this routinization is challenged. Hughes (1945, p. 356) provides an illustration of such a dilemma:

> [A] young woman . . . became part of that virile profession, engineering. The designer of an airplane is expected to go up on the maiden flight of the first plane built according to the design. He [sic] then gives a dinner to the engineers and workmen who worked on the new plane. The dinner is naturally a stag party. The young woman in question designed a plane. Her co-workers urged her not to take the risk—for which, presumably, men only are fit—of the maiden voyage. They were, in effect, asking her to be a lady instead of an engineer. She chose to be an engineer. She then gave the party and paid for it like a man. After food and the first round of toasts, she left like a lady.

On this occasion, parties reached an accommodation that allowed a woman to engage in presumptively masculine behaviors. However, we note that in the end, this compromise permitted demonstration of her "essential" femininity, through accountably "ladylike" behavior.

Hughes (1945, p. 357) suggests that such contradictions may be countered by managing interactions on a very narrow basis, for example, "keeping the relationship formal and specific." But the heart of the matter is that even—perhaps, especially—if the relationship is a formal one, gender is still something one is accountable for. Thus a woman physician (notice the special qualifier in her case) may be accorded respect for her skill and even addressed by an appropriate title. Nonetheless, she is subject to evaluation in terms of normative conceptions of appropriate attitudes and activities for her sex category and under pressure to prove that she is an "essentially" feminine being, despite appearances to the contrary (West 1984, pp. 97–101). Her sex category is used to discredit her participation in important clinical activities (Lorber 1984, pp. 52–54), while her involvement in medicine is used to discredit her commitment to responsibilities as a wife and mother (Bourne and Wikler 1978, pp. 435–37). Simultaneously, her exclusion from the physician colleague community is maintained and her accountability *as a woman* is ensured.

In this context, "role conflict" can be viewed as a dynamic aspect of our current "arrangement between the sexes" (Goffman 1977), an arrangement that provides for occasions on which persons of a particular sex category can "see" quite clearly that they are out of place and that if they were not there, their current troubles would not exist. What is at stake is, from the standpoint of interaction, the management of our "essential" natures, and from the standpoint of the individual, the continuing accomplishment of gender. If, as we have argued, sex category is omnirelevant, then any occasion, conflicted or not, offers the resources for doing gender.

We have sought to show that sex category and gender are managed properties of conduct that are contrived with respect to the fact that others will judge and respond to us in particular ways. We have claimed that a person's gender is not simply an aspect of what one is, but, more fundamentally, it is something that one *does,* and does recurrently, in interaction with others.

What are the consequences of this theoretical formulation? If, for example, individuals strive to achieve gender in encounters with others, how does a culture instill the need to achieve it? What is the relationship between the production of gender at the level of interaction and such institutional arrangements as the division of labor in society? And, perhaps most important, how does doing gender contribute to the subordination of women by men?

◉ Research Agendas

To bring the social production of gender under empirical scrutiny, we might begin at the beginning, with a reconsideration of the process through which societal members acquire the requisite categorical apparatus and other skills to become gendered human beings.

Recruitment to Gender Identities

The conventional approach to the process of becoming girls and boys has been sex-role socialization. In recent years, recurring problems arising from this approach have been linked to inadequacies inherent in role theory *per se*—its emphasis on "consensus, stability and continuity" (Stacey and Thorne 1985, p. 307), its ahistorical and depoliticizing focus (Thorne 1980, p. 9; Stacey and Thorne 1985, p. 307), and the fact that its "social" dimension relies on "a general assumption that people choose to maintain existing customs" (Connell 1985, p. 263).

In contrast, Cahill (1982, 1986a, 1986b) analyzes the experiences of preschool children using a social model of recruitment into normally gendered identities. Cahill argues that categorization practices are fundamental to learning and displaying feminine and masculine behavior. Initially, he observes, children are primarily concerned with distinguishing between themselves and others on the basis of social competence. Categorically, their concern resolves itself into the opposition of "girl/boy" classification versus "baby" classification (the latter designating children whose social behavior is problematic and who must be closely supervised). It is children's concern with being seen as socially competent that evokes their initial claims to gender identities:

> During the exploratory stage of children's socialization . . . they learn that only two social identities are routinely available to them, the identity of "baby," or, depending on the configuration of their external genitalia, either "big boy" or "big girl." Moreover, others subtly inform them that the identity of "baby" is a discrediting one. When, for example, children engage in disapproved behavior, they are often told "You're a baby" or "Be a big boy." In effect, these typical verbal responses to young children's behavior convey to them that they must behaviorally choose between the discrediting identity of "baby" and their anatomically determined sex identity. (Cahill 1986a, p. 175)

Subsequently, little boys appropriate the gender ideal of "efficacious-ness," that is, being able to affect the physical and social environment through the exercise of physical strength or appropriate skills. In contrast, little girls learn to value "appearance," that is, managing themselves as orna-mental objects. Both classes of children learn that the recognition and use of sex categorization in interaction are not optional, but mandatory (see also Bem 1983).

Being a "girl" or a "boy" then, is not only being more competent than a "baby," but also being competently female or male, that is, learning to pro-duce behavioral displays of one's "essential" female or male identity. In this respect, the task of four- to five-year-old children is very similar to Agnes's:

> For example, the following interaction occurred on a preschool playground. A 55-month-old boy (D) was attempting to unfasten the clasp of a necklace when a preschool aide walked over to him.
>
> A: Do you want to put that on?
>
> D: No. It's for girls.
>
> A: You don't have to be a girl to wear things around your neck. Kings wear things around their necks. You could pretend you're a king.
>
> D: I'm not a king. I'm a boy. (Cahill 1986a, p. 176)

As Cahill notes of this example, although D may have been unclear as to the sex status of a king's identity, he was obviously aware that necklaces are used to announce the identity "girl." Having claimed the identity "boy" and having developed a behavioral commitment to it, he was leery of any display that might furnish grounds for questioning his claim.

In his way, new members of society come to be involved in a *self-regulating process* as they begin to monitor their own and others' conduct with regard to its gender implications. The "recruitment" process involves not only the appropriation of gender ideals (by the valuation of those ideals as proper ways of being and behaving) but also *gender identities* that are important to individuals and that they strive to maintain. Thus gender differences, or the sociocultural shaping of "essential female and male natures," achieve the sta-tus of objective facts. They are rendered normal, natural features of persons and provide the tacit rationale for differing fates of women and men within the social order.

Additional studies of children's play activities as routine occasions for the expression of gender-appropriate behavior can yield new insights into how our "essential natures" are constructed. In particular, the transition from what Cahill (1986a) terms "apprentice participation" in the sex-segregated worlds that are common among elementary schoolchildren to "bona fide participation" in the heterosocial world so frightening to adolescents is likely to be a keystone in our understanding of the recruitment process (Thorne 1986; Thorne and Luria 1986).

Gender and the *Division* of *Labor*

Whenever people face issues of *allocation*—who is to do what, get what, plan or execute action, direct or be directed, incumbency in significant social categories such as "female" and "male" seems to become pointedly relevant. How such issues are resolved conditions the exhibition, dramatization, or celebration of one's "essential nature" as a woman or man.

Berk (1985) offers elegant demonstration of this point in her investigation of the allocation of household labor and the attitudes of married couples toward the division of household tasks. Berk found little variation in either the actual distribution of tasks or perceptions of equity in regard to that distribution. Wives, even when employed outside the home, do the vast majority of household and child-care tasks. Moreover, both wives and husbands tend to perceive this as a "fair" arrangement. Noting the failure of conventional sociological and economic theories to explain this seeming contradiction, Berk contends that something more complex is involved than rational arrangements for the production of household goods and services:

> Hardly a question simply of who has more time, or whose time is worth more, who has more skill or more power, it is clear that a complicated relationship between the structure of work imperatives and the structure of normative expectations attached to work as *gendered* determines the ultimate allocation of members' time to work and home. (Berk 1985, pp. 195–96)

She notes, for example, that the most important factor influencing wives' contribution of labor is the total amount of work demanded or expected by the household; such demands had no bearing on husbands' contributions. Wives reported various rationales (their own and their husbands') that justified their level of contribution and, as a general matter, underscored the presumption that wives are essentially responsible for household production.

Berk (1985, p. 201) contends that it is difficult to see how people "could rationally establish the arrangements that they do solely for the production of household goods and services"—much less, how people could consider them "fair." She argues that our current arrangements for the domestic division of labor support *two* production processes: household goods and services (meals, clean children, and so on) and, at the same time, gender. As she puts it:

> Simultaneously, members "do" gender, as they "do" housework and child care, and what [has] been called the division of labor provides for the joint production of household labor and gender; it is the mechanism by which both the material and symbolic products of the household are realized. (1985, p. 201)

It is not simply that household labor is designated as "women's work," but that for a woman to engage in it and a man not to engage in it is to draw on and exhibit the "essential nature" of each. What produced and reproduced is not merely the activity and artifact of domestic life, but the material embodiment of wifely and husbandly roles, and derivatively, of womanly and manly conduct (see Beer 1983, pp. 70–89). What are also frequently produced and reproduced are the dominant and subordinate statuses of the sex categories.

How does gender get done in work settings outside the home, where dominance and subordination are themes of overarching importance? Hochschild's (1983) analysis of the work of flight attendants offers some promising insights. She found that the occupation of flight attendant consisted of something altogether different for women than for men:

> As the company's main shock absorbers against "mishandled" passengers, their own feelings are more frequently subjected to rough treatment. In addition, a day's exposure to people who resist authority in a woman is a different experience than it is for a man. . . . In this respect, it is a disadvantage to be a woman. And in this case, they are not simply women in the biological sense. They are also a highly visible distillation of middle-class American notions of femininity. They symbolize Woman. Insofar as the category "female" is mentally associated with having less status and authority, female flight attendants are more readily classified as "really" females than other females are. (Hochschild 1983, p. 175)

In performing what Hochschild terms the "emotional labor" necessary to maintain airline profits, women flight attendants simultaneously produce enactments of their "essential" femininity.

Sex and Sexuality

What is the relationship between doing gender and a culture's prescription of "obligatory heterosexuality" (Rubin 1975; Rich 1980)? As Frye (1983, p. 22) observes, the monitoring of sexual feelings in relation to other appropriately sexed persons requires the ready recognition of such persons "before one can allow one's heart to beat or one's blood to flow in erotic enjoyment of that person." The appearance of heterosexuality is produced through emphatic and unambiguous indicators of one's sex, layered on in ever more conclusive fashion (Frye 1983, p. 24). Thus, lesbians and gay men concerned with passing as heterosexuals can rely on these indicators for camouflage; in contrast, those who would avoid the assumption of heterosexuality may foster ambiguous indicators of their categorical status through their dress, behaviors, and style. But "ambiguous" sex indicators are sex indicators nonetheless. If one wishes to be recognized as a lesbian (or heterosexual woman), one must first establish a categorical status as female. Even as popular images portray lesbians as "females who are not feminine" (Frye 1983, p. 129), the accountability of persons for their "normal, natural sexedness" is preserved.

Nor is accountability threatened by the existence of "sex-change operations"—presumably, the most radical challenge to our cultural perspective on sex and gender. Although no one coerces transsexuals into hormone therapy, electrolysis, or surgery, the alternatives available to them are undeniably constrained:

> When the transsexual experts maintain that they use transsexual procedures only with people who ask for them, and who prove that they can "pass," they obscure the social reality. Given patriarchy's prescription that one must be *either* masculine or feminine, free choice is conditioned. (Raymond 1979, p. 135, italics added)

The physical reconstruction of sex criteria pays ultimate tribute to the "essentialness" of our sexual natures—as women *or* as men.

◉ Gender, Power, and Social Change

Let us return to the question: Can we avoid doing gender? Earlier, we proposed that insofar as sex category is used as a fundamental criterion for differentiation, doing gender is unavoidable. It is unavoidable because of the social consequences of sex-category membership: the allocation of power and resources not only in the domestic, economic, and political domains but also in the broad arena of interpersonal relations. In virtually any situation, one's sex category can be relevant, and one's performance as an incumbent of that category (i.e., gender) can be subjected to evaluation. Maintaining such pervasive and faithful assignment of lifetime status requires legitimation.

But doing gender also renders the social arrangements based on sex category accountable as normal and natural, that is, legitimate ways of organizing social life. Differences between women and men that are created by this process can then be portrayed as fundamental and enduring dispositions. In this light, the institutional arrangements of a society can be seen as responsive to the differences—the social order being merely an accommodation to the natural order. Thus if, in doing gender, men are also doing dominance and women are doing deference (cf. Goffman 1967, pp. 47–95), the resultant social order, which supposedly reflects "natural differences," is a powerful reinforcer and legitimator of hierarchical arrangements. Frye observes:

> For efficient subordination, what's wanted is that the structure not appear to be a cultural artifact kept in place by human decision or custom, but that it appear *natural*—that it appear to be quite a direct consequence of facts about the beast which are beyond the scope of human manipulation. . . . That we are trained to behave so differently as women and men, and to behave so differently toward women and men, itself contributes mightily to the appearance of extreme dimorphism, but also, the *ways* we act as women and men, and the *ways* we act toward women and men, mold our bodies and our minds to the shape of subordination and dominance. We do become what we practice being. (Frye 1983, p. 34)

If we do gender appropriately, we simultaneously sustain, reproduce, and render legitimate the institutional arrangements that are based on sex category. If we fail to do gender appropriately, we as individuals—not the institutional arrangements—may be called to account (for our character, motives, and predispositions).

Social movements such as feminism can provide the ideology and impetus to question existing arrangements, and the social support for individuals to explore alternatives to them. Legislative changes, such as that proposed by the Equal Rights Amendment, can also weaken the accountability of conduct to sex category, thereby affording the possibility of more widespread loosening of accountability in general. To be sure, equality under the law does not guarantee equality in other arenas. As Lorber (1986, p. 577) points out, assurance of "scrupulous equality of categories of people considered essentially different needs constant monitoring." What such proposed changes *can* do is provide the warrant for asking why, if we wish to treat women and men as equals, there needs to be two sex categories at all (see Lorber 1986, p. 577).

The sex category/gender relationship links the institutional and interactional levels, a coupling that legitimates social arrangements based on sex category and reproduces their asymmetry in face-to-face interaction. Doing gender furnishes the interactional scaffolding of social structure, along with a built-in mechanism of social control. In appreciating the institutional forces that maintain distinctions between women and men, we must not lose sight of the interactional validation of those distinctions that confers upon them their sense of "naturalness" and "rightness."

Social change, then, must be pursued both at the institutional and cultural level of sex category and at the interactional level of gender. Such a conclusion is hardly novel. Nevertheless, we suggest that it is important to recognize that the analytical distinction between institutional and interactional spheres does not pose an either/or choice when it comes to the question of effecting social change. Reconceptualizing gender not as a simple property of individuals but as an integral dynamic of social orders implies a new perspective on the entire network of gender relations:

> [T]he social subordination of women, and the cultural practices which help sustain it; the politics of sexual object-choice, and particularly the oppression of homosexual people; the sexual division of labor, the formation of character and motive, so far as they are organized as femininity and masculinity; the role of the body in social relations, as especially the politics of childbirth; and the nature of strategies of sexual liberation movements. (Connell 1985, p. 261)

Gender is a powerful ideological device, which produces, reproduces, and legitimates the choices and limits that are predicated on sex category. An understanding of how gender is produced in social situations will afford clarification of the interactional scaffolding of social structure and the social control processes that sustain it.

𝓔ndnotes

[1] This definition understates many complexities involved in the relationship between biology and culture (Jaggar 1983, pp. 106–13). However, our point is that the determination of an individual's sex classification is a *social* process through and through.

[2] This is not to say that gender is a singular "thing," omnipresent in the same form historically or in every situation. Because normative conceptions of appropriate attitudes and activities for sex categories can vary across cultures and historical

moments, the management of situated conduct in light of those expectations can take many different forms.

[3]Bernstein (1986) reports an unusual case of espionage in which a man passing as a woman convinced a lover that he/she had given birth to "their" child, who, the lover, thought, "looked like" him.

◉ ◉ ◉

Questions

1. What are the distinctions among sex, sex category, and gender that West and Zimmerman identify?

2. Formulate a description of your own "gender display." How does this influence other people's treatment of you?

3. Explain how people are held "accountable" to gender. What kinds of implications does this have for people who do not do gender properly?

4. While individuals do gender, West and Zimmerman suggest that gender is not just something individuals do. Explain what they mean.

5. How does the existence of transgendered individuals confirm the interactional quality of gender?

6. According to West and Zimmerman, why can't we "ever not do gender"?

◉ References

Beer, William R. 1983. *Househusbands: Men and Housework in American Families.* New York: Praeger.

Bem, Sandra L. 1983. "Gender Schema Theory and Its Implications for Child Development: Raising Gender-Aschematic Children in a Gender-Schematic Society." *Signs: Journal of Women in Culture and Society* 8:598–616.

Berger, Joseph, Bernard P. Cohen, and Morris Zelditch, Jr. 1972. "Status Characteristics and Social Interaction." *American Sociological Review* 37: 241–55.

Berger, Joseph, Thomas L. Conner, and M. Hamit Fisek, eds. 1974. *Expectation States Theory: A Theoretical Research Program.* Cambridge: Winthrop.

Berger, Joseph, M. Hamit Fisek, Robert Z. Norman, and Morris Zelditch, Jr. 1977. *Status Characteristics and Social Interaction: An Expectation States Approach.* New York: Elsevier.

Berk, Sarah F. 1985. *The Gender Factory: The Apportionment of Work in American Households.* New York: Plenum.

Bernstein, Richard. 1986. "France Jails 2 in Odd Case of Espionage." *New York Times* (May 11).

Blackwood, Evelyn. 1984. "Sexuality and Gender in Certain Native American Tribes: The Case of Cross-Gender Females." *Signs: Journal of Women in Culture and Society* 10:27–42.

Bourne, Patricia G., and Norma J. Wikler. 1978. "Commitment and the Cultural Mandate: Women in Medicine." *Social Problems* 25:430–40.

Cahill, Spencer E. 1982. "Becoming Boys and Girls." Ph.D. dissertation, Department of Sociology, University of California, Santa Barbara.

———1986a. "Childhood Socialization as Recruitment Process: Some Lessons from the Study of Gender Development." Pp. 163–86 in *Sociological Studies of Child Development,* edited by P. Adler and P. Adler. Greenwich, CT: JAI Press.

———1986b. "Language Practices and Self-Definition: The Case of Gender Identity Acquisition." *The Sociological Quarterly* 27:295–311.

Chodorow, Nancy. 1978. *The Reproduction of Mothering: Psychoanalysis and the Sociology of Gender.* Los Angeles: University of California Press.

Connell, R.W. 1983. *Which Way Is Up?* Sydney: Allen & Unwin.

———1985. "Theorizing Gender." *Sociology* 19:260–72.

Cucchiari, Salvatore. 1981. "The Gender Revolution and the Transition from Bisexual Horde to Patrilocal Band: The Origins of Gender Hierarchy." Pp. 31–79 in *Sexual Meanings: The Cultural Construction of Gender and Sexuality,* edited by S. B. Ortner and H. Whitehead. New York: Cambridge.

Firestone, Shulamith. 1970. *The Dialectic of Sex: The Case for Feminist Revolution.* New York: William Morrow.

Fishman, Pamela. 1978. "Interaction: The Work Women Do." *Social Problems* 25:397–406.

Frye, Marilyn. 1983. *The Politics of Reality: Essays in Feminist Theory.* Trumansburg, NY: The Crossing Press.

Garfinkel, Harold. 1967. *Studies in Ethnomethodology.* Englewood Cliffs, NJ: Prentice-Hall.

Gerson, Judith M., and Kathy Peiss. 1985. "Boundaries, Negotiation, Consciousness: Reconceptualizing Gender Relations." *Social Problems* 32:317–31.

Goffman, Erving. 1967. (1956). "The Nature of Deference and Demeanor." Pp. 47–95 in *Interaction Ritual*. New York: Anchor/Doubleday.

———1976. "Gender Display." *Studies in the Anthropology of Visual Communication* 3:69–77.

———1977. "The Arrangement Between the Sexes." *Theory and Society* 4:301–31.

Henley, Nancy M. 1985. "Psychology and Gender." *Signs: Journal of Women in Culture and Society* 11:101–119.

Heritage, John. 1984. *Garfinkel and Ethnomethodology*. Cambridge, England: Polity Press.

Hill, W. W. 1935. "The Status of the Hermaphrodite and Transvestite in Navaho Culture." *American Anthropologist* 37:273–79.

Hochschild, Arlie R. 1973. "A Review of Sex Roles Research." *American Journal of Sociology* 78:1011–29.

———1983. *The Managed Heart: Commercialization of Human Feeling*. Berkeley: University of California Press.

Hughes, Everett C. 1945. "Dilemmas and Contradictions of Status." *American Journal of Sociology* 50:353–59.

Humphreys, Paul, and Joseph Berger. 1981. "Theoretical Consequences of the Status Characteristics Formulation." *American Journal of Sociology* 86:953–83.

Jaggar, Alison M. 1983. *Feminist Politics and Human Nature*. Totowa, NJ: Rowman & Allanheld.

Kessler, S., D. J. Ashendon, R. W. Connell, and G. W. Dowsett. 1985. "Gender Relations in Secondary Schooling." *Sociology of Education* 58:34–48.

Kessler, Suzanne J., and Wendy McKenna. 1978. *Gender: An Ethnomethodological Approach*. New York: Wiley.

Kollock, Peter, Philip Blumstein, and Pepper Schwartz. 1985. "Sex and Power in Interaction." *American Sociological Review* 50:34–46.

Komarovsky, Mirra. 1946. "Cultural Contradictions and Sex Roles." *American Journal of Sociology* 52:184–89.

———1950. "Functional Analysis of Sex Roles." *American Sociological Review* 15:508–16.

Linton, Ralph. 1936. *The Study of Man*. New York: Appleton-Century.

Lopata, Helen Z., and Barrie Thorne. 1978. "On the Term 'Sex Roles.'" *Signs: Journal of Women in Culture and Society* 3:718–21.

Lorber, Judith. 1984. *Women Physicians: Careers, Status and Power*. New York: Tavistock.

———1986. "Dismantling Noah's Ark." *Sex Roles* 14:567–80.

Martin, M. Kay, and Barbara Voorheis. 1975. *Female of the Species*. New York: Columbia University Press.

Mead, Margaret. 1963. *Sex and Temperment*. New York: Dell.

———1968. *Male and Female*. New York: Dell.

Mithers, Carol L. 1982. "My Life as a Man." *The Village Voice* 27 (October 5):1ff.

Money, John. 1968. *Sex Errors of the Body*. Baltimore: John Hopkins.

———1974. "Prenatal Hormones and Postnatal Sexualization in Gender Identity Differentiation." Pp. 221–95 in *Nebraska Symposium on Motivation*, Vol. 21, edited by J. K. Cole and R. Dienstbier. Lincoln: University of Nebraska Press.

———and John G. Brennan. 1968. "Sexual Dimorphism in the Psychology of Female Transsexuals." *Journal of Nervous and Mental Disease* 147:487–99.

———and Anke, A. Erhardt. 1972. *Man and Woman/Boy and Girl*. Baltimore: John Hopkins.

———and Charles Ogunro. 1974. "Behavioral Sexology: Ten Cases of Genetic Male Intersexuality with Impaired Prenatal and Pubertal Androgenization." *Archives of Sexual Behavior* 3:181–206.

———and Patricia Tucker. 1975. *Sexual Signatures*. Boston: Little, Brown.

Morris, Jan. 1974. *Conundrum*. New York: Harcourt Brace Jovanovich.

Parsons, Talcott. 1951. *The Social System*. New York: Free Press.

———and Robert F. Bales. 1955. *Family, Socialization and Interaction Process*. New York: Free Press.

———Raymond, Janice G. 1979. *The Transsexual Empire*. Boston: Beacon.

Rich, Adrienne. 1980. "Compulsory Heterosexuality and Lesbian Existence." *Signs: Journal of Women in Culture and Society* 5:631–60.

Richards, Renee (with John Ames). 1983. *Second Serve: The Renee Richards Story*. New York: Stein and Day.

Rossi, Alice. 1984. "Gender and Parenthood." *American Sociological Review* 49:1–19.

Rubin, Gayle. 1975. "The Traffic in Women: Notes on the 'Political Economy' of Sex." Pp. 157–210 in *Toward an Anthropology of Women*, edited by R. Reiter. New York: Monthly Review Press.

Sacks, Harvey. 1972. "On the Analyzability of Stories by Children." Pp. 325–45 in *Directions in Sociolinguistics*, edited by J. J. Gumperz and D. Hymes. New York: Holt, Rinehart & Winston.

Schutz, Alfred. 1943. "The Problem of Rationality in the Social World." *Economics* 10:130–49.

Stacey, Judith, and Barrie Thorne. 1985. "The Missing Feminist Revolution in Sociology." *Social Problems* 32:301–16.

Thorne, Barrie. 1980. "Gender . . . How Is It Best Conceptualized?" Unpublished manuscript.

———1986. "Girls and Boys Together . . . But Mostly Apart: Gender Arrangements in Elementary Schools." Pp. 167–82 in *Relationships and Development,* edited by W. Hartup and Z. Rubin. Hillsdale, NJ: Lawrence Erlbaum.

———and Zella Luria. 1986. "Sexuality and Gender in Children's Daily Worlds." *Social Problems* 33:176–90.

Tresemer, David. 1975. "Assumptions Made About Gender Roles." Pp. 308–39 in *Another Voice: Feminist Perspectives on Social Life and Social Science,* edited by M. Millman and R. M. Kanter. New York: Anchor/ Doubleday.

West, Candace. 1984. "When the Doctor is a 'Lady': Power, Status and Gender in Physician-Patient Encounters." *Symbolic Interaction* 7:87–106.

———and Bonita Iritani. 1985. "Gender Politics in Mate Selection: The Male-Older Norm." Paper presented at the Annual Meeting of the American Sociological Association, August, Washington, DC.

———and Don H. Zimmerman. 1983. "Small Insults: A Study of Interruptions in Conversations Between Unacquainted Persons." Pp. 102–17 in *Language, Gender and Society,* edited by B. Thorne, C. Kramarae, and N. Henley. Rowley, MA: Newbury House.

Wieder, D. Lawrence. 1974. *Language and Social Reality: The Case of Telling the Convict Code.* The Hague: Mouton.

Williams, Walter L. 1986. *The Spirit and the Flesh: Sexual Diversity in American Indian Culture.* Boston: Beacon.

Wilson, Thomas P. 1970. "Conceptions of Interaction and Forms of Sociological Explanation." *American Sociological Review* 35:697–710.

Zimmerman, Don. H., and D. Lawrence Wieder. 1970. "Ethnomethodology and the Problem of Order: Comment on Denzin." Pp. 287–95 in *Understanding Everyday Life,* edited by J. Denzin. Chicago: Aldine.

What It Means to Be Gendered Me: Life on the Boundaries of a Dichotomous Gender System

Betsy Lucal

Have you ever been mistaken for a member of another gender? Most people go through their daily lives taking their gender for granted—that is, because they display their gender appropriately, it is never called into question. However, there are some people for whom proper gender categorization is at risk daily. Transgendered people, who live as a gender other than the one they were assigned at birth based on sex, risk being "read" as members of the wrong group. Other people have characteristics—hair styles, clothing choices, and such—that lead them to occasionally be taken for the wrong gender. What about the experiences of someone who is not transgendered but whose gender is regularly mistaken? The experiences of one such person are recounted and analyzed in this article.

I understood the concept of "doing gender" (West and Zimmerman 1987) long before I became a sociologist. I have been living with the consequences of inappropriate "gender display" (Goffman 1976; West and Zimmerman 1987) for as long as I can remember.

My daily experiences are a testament to the rigidity of gender in our society, to the real implications of "two and only two" when it comes to sex and gender categories (Garfinkel 1967; Kessler and McKenna 1978). Each day, I experience the consequences that our gender system has for my identity and interactions. I am a woman who has been called "Sir" so many times that I no longer even hesitate to assume that it is being directed at me. I am a woman whose use of public rest rooms regularly causes reactions ranging from confused stares to confrontations over what a man is doing in the

Reprinted from *Gender & Society* 13, no. 6 (December 1999), by permission of Sage Publications, Inc. Copyright © 1999 by Sociologists for Women in Society.

women's room. I regularly enact a variety of practices either to minimize the need for others to know my gender or to deal with their misattributions.

I am the embodiment of Lorber's (1994) ostensibly paradoxical assertion that the "gender bending" I engage in actually might serve to preserve and perpetuate gender categories. As a feminist who sees gender rebellion as a significant part of her contribution to the dismantling of sexism, I find this possibility disheartening.

In this article, I examine how my experiences both support and contradict Lorber's (1994) argument using my own experiences to illustrate and reflect on the social construction of gender. My analysis offers a discussion of the consequences of gender for people who do not follow the rules as well as an examination of the possible implications of the existence of people like me for the gender system itself. Ultimately, I show how life on the boundaries of gender affects me and how my life, and the lives of others who make similar decisions about their participation in the gender system, has the potential to subvert gender.

Because this article analyzes my experiences as a woman who often is mistaken for a man, my focus is on the social construction of gender for women. My assumption is that, given the gendered nature of the gendering process itself, men's experiences of this phenomenon might well be different from women's.

❧ The Social Construction of Gender

It is now widely accepted that gender is a social construction, that sex and gender are distinct, and that gender is something all of us "do." This conceptualization of gender can be traced to Garfinkel's (1967) ethnomethodological study of "Agnes."[1] In this analysis, Garfinkel examined the issues facing a male who wished to pass as, and eventually become, a woman. Unlike individuals who perform gender in culturally expected ways, Agnes could not take her gender for granted and always was in danger of failing to pass as a woman (Zimmerman 1992).

This approach was extended by Kessler and McKenna (1978) and codified in the classic "Doing Gender" by West and Zimmerman (1987). The social constructionist approach has been developed most notably by Lorber (1994, 1996). Similar theoretical strains have developed outside of sociology, such as work by Butler (1990) and Weston (1996). Taken as a whole, this work provides a number of insights into the social processes of gender, show-ing how gender(ing) is, in fact, a process.

We apply gender labels for a variety of reasons; for example, an individ-ual's gender cues our interactions with her or him. Successful social relations require all participants to present, monitor, and interpret gender displays (Martin 1998; West and Zimmerman 1987). We have, according to Lorber, "no social place for a person who is neither woman nor man" (1994, 96); that is, we do not know how to interact with such a person. There is, for example, no way of addressing such a person that does not rely on making an assump-tion about the person's gender ("Sir" or "Ma'am"). In this context, gender is "omnirelevant" (West and Zimmerman 1987). Also, given the sometimes fractious nature of interactions between men and women, it might be particu-larly important for women to know the gender of the strangers they encounter; do the women need to be wary, or can they relax (Devor 1989)?

According to Kessler and McKenna (1978), each time we encounter a new person, we make a gender attribution. In most cases, this is not difficult. We learn how to read people's genders by learning which traits culturally sig-nify each gender and by learning rules that enable us to classify individuals with a wide range of gender presentations into two and only two gender cate-gories. As Weston observed, "Gendered traits are called attributes for a reason: People attribute traits to others. No one possesses them. Traits are the product of evaluation" (1996, 21). The fact that most people use the same traits and rules in presenting genders makes it easier for us to attribute genders to them.

We also assume that we can place each individual into one of two mutu-ally exclusive categories in this binary system. As Bem (1993) notes, we have a polarized view of gender; there are two groups that are seen as polar oppo-sites. Although there is "no rule for deciding 'male' or 'female' that will always work" and no attributes "that always and without exception are true of only one gender" (Kessler and McKenna 1978, 158, 1), we operate under the assumption that there are such rules and attributes.

Kessler and McKenna's analysis revealed that the fundamental schema for gender attribution is to "See someone as female only when you cannot see [the person] as male" (1978, 158). Individuals basically are assumed to be male/men until proven otherwise, that is, until some obvious marker of con-ventional femininity is noted. In other words, the default reading of a non-feminine person is that she or he is male; people who do not deliberately mark themselves as feminine are taken to be men. Devor attributed this ten-dency to the operation of gender in a patriarchal context: "Women must mark themselves as 'other'," whereas on the other hand, "few cues [are required] to identify maleness" (1989, 152). As with language, masculine forms are taken as the generically human; femininity requires that something be added. Femininity "must constantly reassure its audience by a willing demonstration of difference" (Brownmiller 1984, 15).

Patriarchal constructs of gender also devalue the marked category. Devor (1989) found that the women she calls "gender blenders" assumed that femininity was less desirable than masculinity; their gender blending sometimes was a product of their shame about being women. This assumption affects not only our perceptions of other people but also individuals' senses of their own gendered selves.

Not only do we rely on our social skills in attributing genders to others, but we also use our skills to present our own genders to them. The roots of this understanding of how gender operates lie in Goffman's (1959) analysis of the "presentation of self in everyday life," elaborated later in his work on "gender display" (Goffman 1976). From this perspective, gender is a performance, "a stylized repetition of acts" (Butler 1990, 140, emphasis removed). Gender display refers to "conventionalized portrayals" of social correlates of gender (Goffman 1976). These displays are culturally established sets of behaviors, appearances, mannerisms, and other cues that we have learned to associate with members of a particular gender.

In determining the gender of each person we encounter and in presenting our genders to others, we rely extensively on these gender displays. Our bodies and their adornments provide us with "texts" for reading a person's gender (Bordo 1993). As Lorber noted, "Without the deliberate use of gendered clothing, hairstyles, jewelry, and cosmetics, women and men would look far more alike" (1994, 18–19). Myhre summarized the markers of femininity as "having longish hair; wearing makeup, skirts, jewelry, and high heels; walking with a wiggle; having little or no observable body hair; and being in general soft, rounded (but not too rounded), and sweet-smelling" (1995, 135). (Note that these descriptions comprise a Western conceptualization of gender.) Devor identified "mannerisms, language, facial expressions, dress, and a lack of feminine adornment" (1989, x) as factors that contribute to women being mistaken for men.

A person uses gender display to lead others to make attributions regarding her or his gender, regardless of whether the presented gender corresponds to the person's sex or gender self-identity. Because gender is a social construction, there may be differences among one's sex, gender self-identity (the gender the individual identifies as), presented identity (the gender the person is presenting), and perceived identity (the gender others attribute to the person).[2] For example, a person can be female without being socially identified as a woman, and a male person can appear socially as a woman. Using a feminine gender display, a man can present the identity of a woman and, if the display is successful, be perceived as a woman.

But these processes also mean that a person who fails to establish a gendered appearance that corresponds to the person's gender faces challenges to her or his identity and status. First, the gender nonconformist must find a way in which to construct an identity in a society that denies her or him any legitimacy (Bem 1993). A person is likely to want to define herself or himself as "normal" in the face of cultural evidence to the contrary. Second, the individual also must deal with other people's challenges to identity and status— deciding how to respond, what such reactions to their appearance mean, and so forth.

Because our appearances, mannerisms, and so forth constantly are being read as part of our gender display, we do gender whether we intend to or not. For example, a woman athlete, particularly one participating in a nonfeminine sport such as basketball, might deliberately keep her hair long to show that, despite actions that suggest otherwise, she is a "real" (i.e., feminine) woman. But we also do gender in less conscious ways such as when a man takes up more space when sitting than a woman does. In fact, in a society so clearly organized around gender, as ours is, there is no way in which to not do gender (Lorber 1994).

Given our cultural rules for identifying gender (i.e., that there are only two and that masculinity is assumed in the absence of evidence to the contrary), a person who does not do gender appropriately is placed not into a third category but rather into the one with which her or his gender display seems most closely to fit; that is, if a man appears to be a woman, then he will be categorized as "woman," not as something else. Even if a person does not want to do gender or would like to do a gender other than the two recognized by our society, other people will, in effect, do gender for that person by placing her or him in one and only one of the two available categories. We cannot escape doing gender or, more specifically, doing one of two genders. (There are exceptions in limited contexts such as people doing "drag" [Butler 1990; Lorber 1994].)

People who follow the norms of gender can take their genders for granted. Kessler and McKenna asserted, "Few people besides transsexuals think of their gender as anything other than 'naturally' obvious"; they believe that the risks of not being taken for the gender intended "are minimal for nontranssexuals" (1978, 126). However, such an assertion overlooks the experiences of people such as those women Devor (1989) calls "gender blenders" and those people Lorber (1994) refers to as "gender benders." As West and Zimmerman (1987) pointed out, we all are held accountable for, and might be called on to account for, our genders.

People who, for whatever reasons, do not adhere to the rules, risk gender misattribution and any interactional consequences that might result from this misidentification. What are the consequences of misattribution for social interaction? When must misattribution be minimized? What will one do to minimize such mistakes? In this article, I explore these and related questions using my biography.

For me, the social processes and structures of gender mean that, in the context of our culture, my appearance will be read as masculine. Given the common conflation of sex and gender, I will be assumed to be a male. Because of the two-and-only-two genders rule, I will be classified, perhaps more often than not, as a man—not as an atypical woman, not as a genderless person. I must be one gender or the other; I cannot be neither, nor can I be both. This norm has a variety of mundane and serious consequences for my everyday existence. Like Myhre (1995), I have found that the choice not to participate in femininity is not one made frivolously.

My experiences as a woman who does not do femininity illustrate a paradox of our two-and-only-two gender system. Lorber argued that "bending gender rules and passing between genders does not erode but rather preserves gender boundaries" (1994, 21). Although people who engage in these behaviors and appearances do "demonstrate the social constructedness of sex, sexuality, and gender" (Lorber 1994, 96), they do not actually disrupt gender. Devor made a similar point: "When gender blending females refused to mark themselves by publicly displaying sufficient femininity to be recognized as women, they were in no way challenging patriarchal gender assumptions" (1989, 142). As the following discussion shows, I have found that my own experiences both support and challenge this argument. Before detailing these experiences, I explain my use of my self as data.

❧ Myself as Data

This analysis is based on my experiences as a person whose appearance and gender/sex are not, in the eyes of many people, congruent. How did my experiences become my data? I began my research "unwittingly" (Krieger 1991).

This article is a product of "opportunistic research" in that I am using my "unique biography, life experiences, and/or situational familiarity to understand and explain social life" (Riemer 1988, 121; see also Riemer 1977). It is an analysis of "unplanned personal experience," that is, experiences that were not part of a research project but instead are part of my daily encounters (Reinharz 1992).

This work also is, at least to some extent, an example of Richardson's (1994) notion of writing as a method of inquiry. As a sociologist who specializes in gender, the more I learned, the more I realized that my life could serve as a case study. As I examined my experiences, I found out things—about my experiences and about theory—that I did not know when I started (Richardson 1994).

It also is useful, I think, to consider my analysis an application of Mills's (1959) "sociological imagination." Mills (1959) and Berger (1963) wrote about the importance of seeing the general in the particular. This means that general social patterns can be discerned in the behaviors of particular individuals. In this article, I am examining portions of my biography, situated in U.S. society during the 1990s, to understand the "personal troubles" my gender produces in the context of a two-and-only-two gender system. I am not attempting to generalize my experiences; rather, I am trying to use them to examine and reflect on the processes and structure of gender in our society.

Because my analysis is based on my memories and perceptions of events, it is limited by my ability to recall events and by my interpretation of those events. However, I am not claiming that my experiences provide the truth about gender and how it works. I am claiming that the biography of a person who lives on the margins of our gender system can provide theoretical insights into the processes and social structure of gender. Therefore, after describing my experiences, I examine how they illustrate and extend, as well as contradict, other work on the social construction of gender.

❧ Gendered Me

Each day, I negotiate the boundaries of gender. Each day, I face the possibility that someone will attribute the "wrong" gender to me based on my physical appearance.

I am six feet tall and large-boned. I have had short hair for most of my life. For the past several years, I have worn a crew cut or flat top. I do not shave or otherwise remove hair from my body (e.g., no eyebrow plucking). I do not wear dresses, skirts, high heels, or makeup. My only jewelry is a class ring, a "men's" watch (my wrists are too large for a "women's" watch), two small earrings (gold hoops, both in my left ear), and (occasionally) a necklace. I wear jeans or shorts, T-shirts, sweaters, polo/golf shirts, button-down collar shirts, and tennis shoes or boots. The jeans are "women's" (I do have hips) but do not look particularly "feminine." The rest of the outer garments are from men's departments. I prefer baggy clothes, so the fact that I have "womanly" breasts often is not obvious (I do not wear a bra). Sometimes, I wear a baseball cap or some other type of hat. I also am white and relatively young (30 years old).[3]

My gender display—what others interpret as my presented identity—regularly leads to the misattribution of my gender. An incongruity exists between my gender self-identity and the gender that others perceive. In my encounters with people I do not know, I sometimes conclude, based on our interactions, that they think I am a man. This does not mean that other people do not think I am a man, just that I have no way of knowing what they think without interacting with them.

ℒiving with ℐt

I have no illusions or delusions about my appearance. I know that my appearance is likely to be read as "masculine" (and male) and that how I see myself is socially irrelevant. Given our two-and-only-two gender structure, I must live with the consequences of my appearance. These consequences fall into two categories: issues of identity and issues of interaction.

My most common experience is being called "Sir" or being referred to by some other masculine linguistic marker (e.g., "he," "man"). This has happened for years, for as long as I can remember, when having encounters with people I do not know.[4] Once, in fact, the same worker at a fast-food restaurant called me "Ma'am" when she took my order and "Sir" when she gave it to me.

Using my credit cards sometimes is a challenge. Some clerks subtly indicate their disbelief, looking from the card to me and back at the card and checking my signature carefully. Others challenge my use of the card, asking whose it is or demanding identification. One cashier asked to see my driver's license and then asked me whether I was the son of the cardholder. Another clerk told me that my signature on the receipt "had better match" the one on the card. Presumably, this was her way of letting me know that she was not convinced it was my credit card.

My identity as a woman also is called into question when I try to use women-only spaces. Encounters in public rest rooms are an adventure. I have been told countless times that "This is the ladies' room." Other women say nothing to me, but their stares and conversations with others let me know what they think. I will hear them say, for example, "There was a man in there." I also get stares when I enter a locker room. However, it seems that women are less concerned about my presence there, perhaps because, given that it is a space for changing clothes, showering, and so forth, they will be able to make sure that I am really a woman. Dressing rooms in department stores also are problematic spaces. I remember shopping with my sister once and being offered a chair outside the room when I began to accompany her into the dressing room.

Women who believe that I am a man do not want me in women-only spaces. For example, one woman would not enter the rest room until I came out, and others have told me that I am in the wrong place. They also might not want to encounter me while they are alone. For example, seeing me walking at night when they are alone might be scary.[5]

I, on the other hand, am not afraid to walk alone, day or night. I do not worry that I will be subjected to the public harassment that many women endure (Gardner 1995). I am not a clear target for a potential rapist. I rely on the fact that a potential attacker would not want to attack a big man by mistake. This is not to say that men never are attacked, just that they are not viewed, and often do not view themselves, as being vulnerable to attack.

Being perceived as a man has made me privy to male-male interactional styles of which most women are not aware. I found out, quite by accident, that many men greet, or acknowledge, people (mostly other men) who make eye contact with them with a single nod. For example, I found that when I walked down the halls of my brother's all-male dormitory making eye contact, men nodded their greetings at me. Oddly enough, these same men did not greet my brother; I had to tell him about making eye contact and nodding as a greeting ritual. Apparently, in this case I was doing masculinity better than he was!

I also believe that I am treated differently, for example, in auto parts stores (staffed almost exclusively by men in most cases) because of the assumption that I am a man. Workers there assume that I know what I need and that my questions are legitimate requests for information. I suspect that I am treated more fairly than a feminine-appearing woman would be. I have not been able to test this proposition. However, Devor's participants did report "being treated more respectfully" (1989, 132) in such situations.

There is, however, a negative side to being assumed to be a man by other men. Once, a friend and I were driving in her car when a man failed to stop at an intersection and nearly crashed into us. As we drove away, I mouthed "stop sign" to him. When we both stopped our cars at the next intersection, he got out of his car and came up to the passenger side of the car, where I was sitting. He yelled obscenities at us and pounded and spit on the car window. Luckily, the windows were closed. I do not think he would have done that if he thought I was a woman. This was the first time I realized that one of the implications of being seen as a man was that I might be called on to defend myself from physical aggression from other men who felt challenged by me. This was a sobering and somewhat frightening thought.

Recently, I was verbally accosted by an older man who did not like where I had parked my car. As I walked down the street to work, he shouted that I should park at the university rather than on a side street nearby. I responded that it was a public street and that I could park there if I chose. He continued to yell, but the only thing I caught was the last part of what he said: "Your tires are going to get cut!" Based on my appearance that day—I was dressed casually and carrying a backpack, and I had my hat on backward—I believe he thought that I was a young male student rather than a female professor. I do not think he would have yelled at a person he thought to be a woman—and perhaps especially not a woman professor.

Given the presumption of heterosexuality that is part of our system of gender, my interactions with women who assume that I am a man also can be viewed from that perspective. For example, once my brother and I were shopping when we were "hit on" by two young women. The encounter ended before I realized what had happened. It was only when we walked away that I told him that I was pretty certain that they had thought both of us were men. A more common experience is realizing that when I am seen in public with one of my women friends, we are likely to be read as a heterosexual dyad. It is likely that if I were to walk through a shopping mall holding hands with a woman, no one would look twice, not because of their open-mindedness toward lesbian couples but rather because of their assumption that I was the male half of a straight couple. Recently, when walking through a mall with a friend and her infant, my observations of others' responses to us led me to believe that many of them assumed that we were a family on an outing, that is, that I was her partner and the father of the child.

Dealing with It

Although I now accept that being mistaken for a man will be a part of my life so long as I choose not to participate in femininity, there have been times when I consciously have tried to appear more feminine. I did this for a while when I was an undergraduate and again recently when I was on the academic job market. The first time, I let my hair grow nearly down to my shoulders and had it permed. I also grew long fingernails and wore nail polish. Much to my chagrin, even then one of my professors, who did not know my name, insistently referred to me in his kinship examples as "the son." Perhaps my first act on the way to my current stance was to point out to this man, politely and after class, that I was a woman.

More recently, I again let my hair grow out for several months, although I did not alter other aspects of my appearance. Once my hair was about two and a half inches long (from its original quarter inch), I realized, based on my encounters with strangers, that I had more or less passed back into the category of "woman." Then, when I returned to wearing a flat top, people again responded to me as if I were a man.

Because of my appearance, much of my negotiation of interactions with strangers involves attempts to anticipate their reactions to me. I need to assess whether they will be likely to assume that I am a man and whether that actually matters in the context of our encounters. Many times, my gender really is irrelevant, and it is just annoying to be misidentified. Other times, particularly when my appearance is coupled with something that identifies me by name (e.g., a check or credit card) without a photo, I might need to do something to ensure that my identity is not questioned. As a result of my experiences, I have developed some techniques to deal with gender misattribution.

In general, in unfamiliar public places, I avoid using the rest room because I know that it is a place where there is a high likelihood of misattribution and where misattribution is socially important. If I must use a public restroom, I try to make myself look as nonthreatening as possible. I do not wear a hat, and I try to rearrange my clothing to make my breasts more obvious. Here, I am trying to use my secondary sex characteristics to make my gender more obvious rather than the usual use of gender to make sex obvious. While in the rest room, I never make eye contact, and I get in and out as quickly as possible. Going in with a woman friend also is helpful; her presence legitimizes my own. People are less likely to think I am entering a space where I do not belong when I am with someone who looks like she does belong.[6]

To those women who verbally challenge my presence in the rest room, I reply, "I know," usually in an annoyed tone. When they stare or talk about me to the women they are with, I simply get out as quickly as possible. In general, I do not wait for someone I am with because there is too much chance of an unpleasant encounter.

I stopped trying on clothes before purchasing them a few years ago because my presence in the changing areas was met with stares and whispers. Exceptions are stores where the dressing rooms are completely private, where there are individual stalls rather than a room with stalls separated by curtains, or where business is slow and no one else is trying on clothes. If I am trying on a garment clearly intended for a woman, then I usually can do so without hassle. I guess the attendants assume that I must be a woman if I have, for example, a women's bathing suit in my hand. But usually, I think it is easier for me to try the clothes on at home and return them, if necessary, rather than risk creating a scene. Similarly, when I am with another woman who is trying on clothes, I just wait outside.

My strategy with credit cards and checks is to anticipate wariness on a clerk's part. When I sense that there is some doubt or when they challenge me, I say, "It's my card." I generally respond courteously to requests for photo ID, realizing that these might be routine checks because of concerns about increasingly widespread fraud. But for the clerk who asked for ID and still did not think it was my card, I had a stronger reaction. When she said that she was sorry for embarrassing me, I told her that I was not embarrassed but that she should be. I also am particularly careful to make sure that my signature is consistent with the back of the card. Faced with such situations, I feel somewhat nervous about signing my name—which, of course, makes me worry that my signature will look different from how it should.

Another strategy I have been experimenting with is wearing nail polish in the dark bright colors currently fashionable. I try to do this when I travel by plane. Given more stringent travel regulations, one always must present a photo ID. But my experiences have shown that my driver's license is not necessarily convincing. Nail polish might be. I also flash my polished nails when I enter airport rest rooms, hoping that they will provide a clue that I am indeed in the right place.

There are other cases in which the issues are less those of identity than of all the norms of interaction that, in our society, are gendered. My most common response to misattribution actually is to appear to ignore it, that is, to go on with the interaction as if nothing out of the ordinary has happened. Unless I feel that there is a good reason to establish my correct gender, I assume the identity others impose on me for the sake of smooth interaction. For example, if someone is selling me a movie ticket, then there is no reason to make sure that the person has accurately discerned my gender. Similarly, if it is clear that the person using "Sir" is talking to me, then I simply respond as appropriate. I accept the designation because it is irrelevant to the situation. It takes enough effort to be alert for misattributions and to decide which of them matter; responding to each one would take more energy than it is worth.

Sometimes, if our interaction involves conversation, my first verbal response is enough to let the other person know that I am actually a woman and not a man. My voice apparently is "feminine" enough to shift people's attributions to the other category. I know when this has happened by the apologies that usually accompany the mistake. I usually respond to the apologies by saying something like "No problem" and/or "It happens all the time." Sometimes, a misattributor will offer an account for the mistake, for example, saying that it was my hair or that they were not being very observant.

These experiences with gender and misattribution provide some theoretical insights into contemporary Western understandings of gender and into the social structure of gender in contemporary society. Although there are a number of ways in which my experiences confirm the work of others, there also are some ways in which my experiences suggest other interpretations and conclusions.

☻ What Does It Mean?

Gender is pervasive in our society. I cannot choose not to participate in it. Even if I try not to do gender, other people will do it for me. That is, given our two-and-only-two rule, they must attribute one of two genders to me. Still, although I cannot choose not to participate in gender, I can choose not to participate in femininity (as I have), at least with respect to physical appearance.

That is where the problems begin. Without the decorations of femininity, I do not look like a woman. That is, I do not look like what many people's commonsense understanding of gender tells them a woman looks like. How I see myself, even how I might wish others would see me, is socially irrelevant. It is the gender that I *appear* to be (my "perceived gender") that is most relevant to my social identity and interactions with others. The major consequence of this fact is that I must be continually aware of which gender I "give off" as well as which gender I "give" (Goffman 1959).

Because my gender self-identity is "not displayed obviously, immediately, and consistently" (Devor 1989, 58), I am somewhat of a failure in social terms with respect to gender. Causing people to be uncertain or wrong about one's gender is a violation of taken-for-granted rules that leads to embarrassment and discomfort; it means that something has gone wrong with the interaction (Garfinkel 1967; Kessler and McKenna 1978). This means that my nonresponse to misattribution is the more socially appropriate response; I am allowing others to maintain face (Goffman 1959, 1967). By not calling attention to their mistakes, I uphold their images of themselves as competent social actors. I also maintain my own image as competent by letting them assume that I am the gender I appear to them to be.

But I still have discreditable status; I carry a stigma (Goffman 1963). Because I have failed to participate appropriately in the creation of meaning with respect to gender (Devor 1989), I can be called on to account for my appearance. If discredited, I show myself to be an incompetent social actor. I am the one not following the rules, and I will pay the price for not providing people with the appropriate cues for placing me in the gender category to which I really belong.

I do think that it is, in many cases, safer to be read as a man than as some sort of deviant woman. "Man" is an acceptable category; it fits properly into people's gender worldview. Passing as a man often is the "path of least resistance" (Devor 1989; Johnson 1997). For example, in situations where gender does not matter, letting people take me as a man is easier than correcting them.

Conversely, as Butler noted, "We regularly punish those who fail to do their gender right" (1990, 140). Feinberg maintained, "Masculine girls and women face terrible condemnation and brutality—including sexual violence—for crossing the boundary of what is 'acceptable' female expression" (1996, 114). People are more likely to harass me when they perceive me to be a woman who looks like a man. For example, when a group of teenagers realized that I was not a man because one of their mothers identified me correctly, they began to make derogatory comments when I passed them. One asked, for example, "Does she have a penis?"

Because of the assumption that a "masculine" woman is a lesbian, there is the risk of homophobic reactions (Gardner 1995; Lucal 1997). Perhaps surprisingly, I find that I am much more likely to be taken for a man than for a lesbian, at least based on my interactions with people and their reactions to me. This might be because people are less likely to reveal that they have taken me for a lesbian because it is less relevant to an encounter or because they believe this would be unacceptable. But I think it is more likely a product of the strength of our two-and-only-two system. I give enough masculine cues that I am seen not as a deviant woman but rather as a man, at least in most cases. The problem seems not to be that people are uncertain about my gender, which might lead them to conclude that I was a lesbian once they realized I was a woman. Rather, I seem to fit easily into a gender category—just not the one with which I identify.

In fact, because men represent the dominant gender in our society, being mistaken for a man can protect me from other types of gendered harassment. Because men can move around in public spaces safely (at least relative to women), a "masculine" woman also can enjoy this freedom (Devor 1989).

On the other hand, my use of particular spaces—those designated as for women only—may be challenged. Feinberg provided an intriguing analysis of the public rest room experience. She characterized women's reactions to a masculine person in a public rest room as "an example of genderphobia" (1996, 117), viewing such women as policing gender boundaries rather than believing that there really is a man in the women's restroom. She argued that women who truly believed that there was a man in their midst would react differently. Although this is an interesting perspective on her experiences, my experiences do not lead to the same conclusion.[7] Enough people have said to me that "This is the ladies' room" or have said to their companions that "There was a man in there" that I take their reactions at face value.

Still, if the two-and-only-two gender system is to be maintained, participants must be involved in policing the categories and their attendant identities and spaces. Even if policing boundaries is not explicitly intended, boundary maintenance is the effect of such responses to people's gender displays.

Boundaries and margins are an important component of both my experiences of gender and our theoretical understanding of gendering processes. I am, in effect, both woman and not-woman. As a woman who often is a social man but who also is a woman living in a patriarchal society, I am in a unique position to see and act. I sometimes receive privileges usually limited to men, and I sometimes am oppressed by my status as a deviant woman. I am, in a sense, an outsider-within (Collins 1991). Positioned on the boundaries of gender categories, I have developed a consciousness that I hope will prove transformative (Anzaldua 1987).

In fact, one of the reasons why I decided to continue my nonparticipation in femininity was that my sociological training suggested that this could be one of my contributions to the eventual dismantling of patriarchal gender constructs. It would be my way of making the personal political. I accepted being taken for a man as the price I would pay to help subvert patriarchy. I believed that all of the inconveniences I was enduring meant that I actually was doing something to bring down the gender structures that entangled all of us.

Then, I read Lorber's (1994) *Paradoxes of Gender* and found out, much to my dismay, that I might not actually be challenging gender after all. Because of the way in which doing gender works in our two-and-only-two system, gender displays are simply read as evidence of one of the two categories. Therefore, gender bending, blending, and passing between the categories do not question the categories themselves. If one's social gender and personal (true) gender do not correspond, then this is irrelevant unless someone notices the lack of congruence.

This reality brings me to a paradox of my experiences. First, not only do others assume that I am one gender or the other, but I also insist that I *really am* a member of one of the two gender categories. That is, I am female; I self-identify as a woman. I do not claim to be some other gender or to have no gender at all. I simply place myself in the wrong category according to stereo-types and cultural standards; the gender I present, or that some people per-ceive me to be presenting, is inconsistent with the gender with which I identify myself as well as with the gender I could be "proven" to be. Socially, I display the wrong gender; personally, I identify as the proper gender.

Second, although I ultimately would like to see the destruction of our current gender structure, I am not to the point of personally abandoning gen-der. Right now, I do not want people to see me as genderless as much as I want them to see me as a woman. That is, I would like to expand the category of "woman" to include people like me. I, too, am deeply embedded in our gender system, even though I do not play by many of its rules. For me, as for most people in our society, gender is a substantial part of my personal iden-tity (Howard and Hollander 1997). Socially, the problem is that I do not present a gender display that is consistently read as feminine. In fact, I con-sciously do not participate in the trappings of femininity. However, I do iden-tify myself as a woman, not as a man or as someone outside of the two-and-only-two categories.

Yet, I do believe, as Lorber (1994) does, that the purpose of gender, as it currently is constructed, is to oppress women. Lorber analyzed gender as a "process of creating distinguishable social statuses for the assignment of rights and responsibilities" that ends up putting women in a devalued and oppressed position (1994, 32). As Martin put it, "Bodies that clearly delineate gender status facilitate the maintenance of the gender hierarchy" (1998, 495).

For society, gender means difference (Lorber 1994). The erosion of the boundaries would problematize that structure. Therefore, for gender to operate as it currently does, the category "woman" *cannot* be expanded to include people like me. The maintenance of the gender structure is dependent on the creation of a few categories that are mutually exclusive, the members of which are as different as possible (Lorber 1994). It is the clarity of the boundaries between the categories that allows gender to be used to assign rights and responsibilities as well as resources and rewards.

It is that part of gender—what it is used for—that is most problematic. Indeed, is it not *patriarchal*—or, even more specifically, *heteropatriarchal*—constructions of gender that are actually the problem? It is not the differences between men and women, or the categories themselves, so much as the meanings ascribed to the categories and, even more important, the hierarchical nature of gender under patriarchy that is the problem (Johnson 1997). Therefore, I am rebelling not against my femaleness or even my womanhood; instead, I am protesting contemporary constructions of femininity and, at least indirectly, masculinity under patriarchy. We do not, in fact, know what gender would look like if it were not constructed around heterosexuality in the context of patriarchy.

Although it is possible that the end of patriarchy would mean the end of gender, it is at least conceivable that something like what we now call gender could exist in a postpatriarchal future. The two-and-only-two categorization might well disappear, there being no hierarchy for it to justify. But I do not think that we should make the assumption that gender and patriarchy are synonymous.

Theoretically, this analysis points to some similarities and differences between the work of Lorber (1994) and the works of Butler (1990), Goffman (1976, 1977), and West and Zimmerman (1987). Lorber (1994) conceptualized gender as social structure, whereas the others focused more on the interactive and processual nature of gender. Butler (1990) and Goffman (1976, 1977) view gender as a performance, and West and Zimmerman (1987) examined it as something all of us do. One result of this difference in approach is that in Lorber's (1994) work, gender comes across as something that we are caught in—something that, despite any attempts to the contrary, we cannot break out of. This conclusion is particularly apparent in Lorber's argument that gender rebellion, in the context of our two-and-only-two system, ends up supporting what it purports to subvert. Yet, my own experiences suggest an alternative possibility that is more in line with the view of gender offered by West and Zimmerman (1987): If gender is a product of interaction, and if it is produced in a particular context, then it can be changed if we change our performances. However, the effects of a performance linger, and gender ends up being institutionalized. It is institutionalized, in our society, in a way that per-petuates inequality, as Lorber's (1994) work shows. So, it seems that a combi-nation of these two approaches is needed.

In fact, Lorber's (1994) work seems to suggest that effective gender rebel-lion requires a more blatant approach—bearded men in dresses, perhaps, or more active responses to misattribution. For example, if I corrected every per-son who called me "Sir," and if I insisted on my right to be addressed appro-priately and granted access to women-only spaces, then perhaps I could start to break down gender norms. If I asserted my right to use public facilities without being harassed, and if I challenged each person who gave me "the look," then perhaps I would be contributing to the demise of gender as we know it. It seems that the key would be to provide visible evidence of the non-mutual exclusivity of the categories. Would *this* break down the patriarchal components of gender? Perhaps it would, but it also would be exhausting.

Perhaps there is another possibility. In a recent book, *The Gender Knot*, Johnson (1997) argued that when it comes to gender and patriarchy, most of us follow the paths of least resistance; we "go along to get along," allowing our actions to be shaped by the gender system. Collectively, our actions help patriarchy maintain and perpetuate a system of oppression and privilege. Thus, by withdrawing our support from this system by choosing paths of greater resistance, we can start to chip away at it. Many people participate in gender because they cannot imagine any alternatives. In my classroom, and in my interactions and encounters with strangers, my presence can make it difficult for people not to see that there *are* other paths. In other words, fol-lowing from West and Zimmerman (1987), I can subvert gender by doing it differently.

For example, I think it is true that my existence does not have an effect on strangers who assume that I am a man and never learn otherwise. For them, I do uphold the two-and-only-two system. But there are other cases in which my existence can have an effect. For example, when people initially take me for a man but then find out that I actually am a woman, at least for that moment, the naturalness of gender may be called into question. In these cases, my presence can provoke a "category crisis" (Garber 1992, 16) because it challenges the sex/gender binary system.

The subversive potential of my gender might be strongest in my class-rooms. When I teach about the sociology of gender, my students can see me as the embodiment of the social construction of gender. Not all of my stu-dents have transformative experiences as a result of taking a course with me; there is the chance that some of them see me as a "freak" or as an exception.

Still, after listening to stories about my experiences with gender and reading literature on the subject, many students begin to see how and why gender is a social product. I can disentangle sex, gender, and sexuality in the contemporary United States for them. Students can begin to see the connection between biographical experiences and the structure of society. As one of my students noted, I clearly live the material I am teaching. If that helps me to get my point across, then perhaps I am subverting the binary gender system after all. Although my gendered presence and my way of doing gender might make others—and sometimes even me—uncomfortable, no one ever said that dismantling patriarchy was going to be easy.

Endnotes

[1]Ethnomethodology has been described as "the study of commonsense practical reasoning"(Collins 1988, 274). It examines how people make sense of their everyday experiences. Ethnomethodology is particularly useful in studying gender because it helps to uncover the assumptions on which our understandings of sex and gender are based.

[2]I thank an anonymous reviewer for suggesting that I use these distinctions among the parts of a person's gender.

[3]I obviously have left much out by not examining my gendered experiences in the context of race, age, class, sexuality, region, and so forth. Such a project clearly is more complex. As Weston pointed out, gender presentations are complicated by other statuses of their presenters: "What it takes to kick a person over into another gendered category can differ with race, class, religion, and time" (1996, 168). Furthermore, I am well aware that my whiteness allows me to assume that my experiences are simply a product of gender (see, e g., hooks 1981; Lucal 1996; Spelman 1988; West and Fenstermaker 1995). For now, suffice it to say that it is my privileged position on some of these axes and my more disadvantaged position on others that combine to delineate my overall experience.

[4]In fact, such experiences are not always limited to encounters with strangers. My grandmother, who does not see me often, twice has mistaken me for either my brother-in-law or some unknown man.

[5]My experiences in rest rooms and other public spaces might be very different if I were, say, African American rather than white. Given the stereotypes of African American men, I think that white women would react very differently to encountering me (see, e.g., Staples [1986] 1993).

[6]I also have noticed that there are certain types of rest rooms in which I will not be verbally challenged; the higher the social status of the place, the less likely I will

25

be harassed. For example, when I go to the theater, I might get stared at, but my presence never has been challenged.

[7]An anonymous reviewer offered one possible explanation for this. Women see women's rest rooms as their space; they feel safe, and even empowered, there. Instead of fearing men in such space, they might instead pose a threat to any man who might intrude. Their invulnerability in this situation is, of course, not physically based but rather socially constructed. I thank the reviewer for this suggestion.

❧ ❧ ❧

Questions

1. What does the "gender attribution" process involve? How does it show the interactional character of gender?

2. What do Lucal's experiences tell us about the consequences of failing to display one's gender "properly"?

3. Explain how Lucal reacts to and deals with being mistaken for a man.

4. How can gender-bending or blending actually have conservative consequences for the gender order? In other words, how can it help to uphold existing gender categories?

5. Compare and contrast the implications of mistaking a woman for a man versus mistaking a man for a woman. Would the mistaken person react similarly? Would you, as the person who has mistaken them for the wrong gender, react similarly?

6. Is it possible to have gender differences without gender inequality? Defend your position.

❧ References

Anzaldua, G. 1987. *Borderlands/La Frontera.* San Francisco: Aunt Lute Books.

Bem, S. L. 1993. *The lenses of gender.* New Haven, CT: Yale University Press.

Berger, P. 1963. *Invitation to sociology.* New York: Anchor.

Bordo, S. 1993. *Unbearable weight*. Berkeley: University of California Press.

Brownmiller, C. 1984. *Femininity*. New York: Fawcett.

Butler, J. 1990. *Gender trouble*. New York: Routledge.

Collins, P. H. 1991. *Black feminist thought*. New York: Routledge.

Collins, R. 1988. *Theoretical sociology*. San Diego: Harcourt Brace Jovanovich.

Devor, H. 1989. *Gender blending: Confronting the limits of duality*. Bloomington: Indiana University Press.

Feinberg, L. 1996. *Transgender warriors*. Boston: Beacon.

Garber, M. 1992. *Vested interests: Cross-dressing and cultural anxiety*. New York: HarperPerennial.

Gardner, C. B. 1995. *Passing by: Gender and public harassment*. Berkeley: University of California.

Garfinkel, H. 1967. *Studies in ethnomethodology*. Englewood Cliffs, NJ: Prentice Hall.

Goffman, E. 1959. *The presentation of self in everyday life*. Garden City, NY: Doubleday.

———. 1963. *Stigma*. Englewood Cliffs, NJ: Prentice Hall.

———. 1967. *Interaction ritual*. New York: Anchor/Doubleday.

———. 1976. Gender display. *Studies in the Anthropology of Visual Communication* 3: 69–77.

———. 1977. The arrangement between the sexes. *Theory and Society* 4: 301–31.

hooks. b. 1981. *Ain't I a woman: Black women and feminism*. Boston: South End Press.

Howard, J. A., and J. Hollander. 1997. *Gendered situations, gendered selves*. Thousand Oaks, CA: Sage.

Kessler, S. J., and W. McKenna. 1978. *Gender: An ethnomethodological approach*. New York: John Wiley.

Krieger, S. 1991. *Social science and the self*. New Brunswick, NJ: Rutgers University Press.

Johnson. A. G. 1997. *The gender knot: Unraveling our patriarchal legacy*. Philadelphia: Temple University Press.

Lorber, J. 1994. *Paradoxes of gender*. New Haven, CT: Yale University Press.

———. 1996. Beyond the binaries: Depolarizing the categories of sex, sexuality, and gender. *Sociological Inquiry* 66: 143–59.

Lucal, B. 1996. Oppression and privilege: Toward a relational conceptualization of race. *Teaching Sociology* 24: 245–55.

————. 1997. "Hey, this is the ladies' room!": Gender misattribution and public harassment. *Perspectives on Social Problems* 9: 43–57.

Martin, K. A. 1998. Becoming a gendered body: Practices of preschools. *American Sociological Review* 63: 494–511.

Mills, C. W. 1959. *The sociological imagination.* London: Oxford University Press.

Myhre, J.R.M. 1995. One bad hair day too many, or the hairstory of an androgynous young feminist. In *Listen up: Voices from the next feminist generation,* edited by B. Findlen. Seattle, WA: Seal Press.

Reinharz, S. 1992. *Feminist methods in social research.* New York: Oxford University Press.

Richardson, L. 1994. Writing: A method of inquiry. In *Handbook of Qualitative Research,* edited by N. K. Denzin and Y. S. Lincoln. Thousand Oaks, CA: Sage.

Riemer, J. W. 1977. Varieties of opportunistic research. *Urban Life* 5: 467–77.

————. 1988. Work and self. In *Personal sociology,* edited by P. C. Higgins and J. M. Johnson. New York: Praeger.

Spelman, E. V. 1988. *Inessential woman: Problems of exclusion in feminist thought.* Boston: Beacon.

Staples, B. 1993. Just walk on by. In *Experiencing race, class, and gender in the United States,* edited by V. Cyrus. Mountain View, CA: Mayfield. (Originally published 1986)

West, C., and S. Fenstermaker. 1995. Doing difference. *Gender & Society* 9: 8–37.

West, C., and D. H. Zimmerman. 1987. Doing gender. *Gender & Society* 1: 125–51.

Weston, K. 1996. *Render me, gender me.* New York: Columbia University Press.

Zimmerman, D. H. 1992. They were all doing gender, but they weren't all passing: Comment on Rogers. *Gender & Society* 6: 192–98.

The Five Sexes: Why Male and Female Are Not Enough

ANNE FAUSTO-STERLING
Brown University

How many sexes are there? For most Westerners, the answer is simple. There are two—male and female. However, Anne Fausto-Sterling argues that the Western notion of two sexes is false. Because of natural variations in human physiology, she contends that we should talk about five sexes (female, male, the true hermaphrodite, the male pseudohermaphrodite, and the female pseudohermaphrodite). In this article she explains her thinking and describes how those who are intersexual have been treated historically.

In 1843 Levi Suydam, a twenty-three-year-old resident of Salisbury, Connecticut, asked the town board of selectmen to validate his right to vote as a Whig in a hotly contested local election. The request raised a flurry of objections from the opposition party, for reasons that must be rare in the annals of American democracy: it was said that Suydam was more female than male and thus (some eighty years before suffrage was extended to women) could not be allowed to cast a ballot. To settle the dispute a physician, one William James Barry, was brought in to examine Suydam. And, presumably upon encountering a phallus, the good doctor declared the prospective

"The Five Sexes: Why Male and Female Are Not Enough," by Anne Fausto-Sterling, reprinted from *The Sciences*, March/April 1993, pp. 20–25.

voter male. With Suydam safely in their column the Whigs won the election by a majority of one.

Barry's diagnosis, however, turned out to be somewhat premature. Within a few days he discovered that, phallus notwithstanding, Suydam menstruated regularly and had a vaginal opening. Both his/her physique and his/her mental predispositions were more complex than was first suspected. S/he had narrow shoulders and broad hips and felt occasional sexual yearnings for women. Suydam's "feminine propensities, such as a fondness for gay colors, for pieces of calico, comparing and placing them together, and an aversion for bodily labor, and an inability to perform the same, were remarked by many," Barry later wrote. It is not clear whether Suydam lost or retained the vote, or whether the election results were reversed.

Western culture is deeply committed to the idea that there are only two sexes. Even language refuses other possibilities; thus to write about Levi Suydam I have had to invent conventions—*s/he* and *his/her*—to denote someone who is clearly neither male nor female or who is perhaps both sexes at once. Legally, too, every adult is either man or woman, and the difference, of course, is not trivial. For Suydam it meant the franchise: today it means being available for, or exempt from, draft registration, as well as being subject, in various ways, to a number of laws governing marriage, the family and human intimacy. In many parts of the United States, for instance, two people legally registered as men cannot have sexual relations without violating anti-sodomy statutes.

But if the state and the legal system have an interest in maintaining a two-party sexual system, they are in defiance of nature. For biologically speaking, there are many gradations running from female to male; and depending on how one calls the shots, one can argue that along that spectrum lie at least five sexes—and perhaps even more.

For some time medical investigators have recognized the concept of the intersexual body. But the standard medical literature uses the term *intersex* as a catch-all for three major subgroups with some mixture of male and female characteristics: the so-called true hermaphrodites, whom I call herms, who possess one testis and one ovary (the sperm- and egg-producing vessels, or gonads); the male pseudoher-maphrodites (the "merms"), who have testes and some aspects of the female genitalia but no ovaries; and the female pseudohermaphro-dites (the "ferms"), who have ovaries and some aspects of the male genitalia but lack testes. Each of those categories is in itself complex; the percentage of male and female characteristics, for instance, can vary enormously among members of the same subgroup. Moreover, the inner lives of the people in each subgroup—their special needs and their problems, attractions and repulsions—have gone unex-plored by science. But on the basis of what is known about them I suggest that the three intersexes, herm, merm and ferm, deserve to be considered additional sexes each in its own right. Indeed, I would argue further that sex is a vast, infinitely malleable continuum that defies the constraints of even five categories.

Not surprisingly, it is extremely difficult to estimate the frequen-cy of intersexuality, much less the frequency of each of the three addi-tional sexes: it is not the sort of information one volunteers on a job application. The psychologist John Money of Johns Hopkins University, a specialist in the study of congenital sexual-organ defects, suggests intersexuals may constitute as many as 4% of births. As I point out to my students at Brown University, in a student body of about 6,000 that fraction, if correct, implies there may be as many as 240 intersexuals on campus—surely enough to form a minority cau-cus of some kind.

In reality though, few such students would make it as far as Brown in sexually diverse form. Recent advances in physiology and surgical technology now enable physicians to catch most intersexuals at the moment of birth. Almost at once such infants are entered into a program of hormonal and surgical management so that they can slip quietly into society as "normal" heterosexual males or females. I emphasize that the motive is in no way conspiratorial. The aims of the policy are genuinely humanitarian, reflecting the wish that people be able to "fit in" both physically and psychologically. In the medical community, however, the assumptions behind the wish—that there be only two sexes, that heterosexuality alone is normal, that there is one true model of psychological health—have gone virtually unexamined.

The word *hermaphrodite* comes from the Greek names Hermes, variously known as the messenger of the gods, the patron of music, the controller of dreams or the protector of livestock, and Aphrodite, the goddess of sexual love and beauty. According to Greek mythology, those two gods parented Hermaphroditus, who at age 15 became half male and half female when his body fused with the body of a nymph he fell in love with. In some true hermaphrodites the testis and the ovary grow separately but bilaterally; in others they grow together within the same organ, forming an ovo-testis. Not infrequently, at least one of the gonads functions quite well, producing either sperm cells or eggs, as well as functional levels of the sex hormones—androgens or estrogens. Although in theory it might be possible for a true hermaphrodite to become both father and mother to a child, in practice the appropriate ducts and tubes are not configured so that egg and sperm can meet.

In contrast with the true hermaphrodites, the pseudo-hermaphrodites posses two gonads of the same kind along with the usual male (XY) or female (XX) chromosomes. Thus merms have testes and XY chromosomes, yet they also have a vagina and a clitoris, and at puberty they often develop breasts. They do not menstruate, however. Ferms have ovaries, two X chromosome and sometimes a uterus, but they also have at least partly masculine external genitalia. Without medical intervention they can develop beards, deep voices and adult-size penises.

No classification scheme could more than suggest the variety of sexual anatomy encountered in clinical practice. In 1969, for example, two French investigators, Paul Guintet of the Endocrine Clinic in Lyons and Jacques Decourt of the Endocrine Clinic in Paris, described 98 cases of true hermaphroditism—again, signifying people with both ovarian and testicular tissue—solely according to the appearance of the external genitalia and the accompanying ducts. In some cases the people exhibited strongly feminine development. They had separate opening for the vagina and the urethra, a cleft vulva defined by both the large and small labia, or vaginal lips, and at puberty they developed breasts and usually began to menstruate. It was the oversize and sexually alert clitoris, which threatened sometimes at puberty to grow into a penis, that usually impelled them to seek medical attention. Members of another group also had breasts and a feminine body type, and they menstruated. But their labia were at least partly fused, forming an incomplete scrotum. The phallus (here an embryological term for a structure that during usual development goes on to form either a clitoris or a penis) was between 1.5 and 2.8 inches long: nevertheless, they urinated through a urethra that opened into or near the vagina.

By far the most frequent form of true hermaphrodite encountered by Guinet and Decourt—55%—have a more masculine physique. In such people the urethra runs either through or near the phallus, which looks more like a penis than a clitoris. Any menstrual blood exits periodically during urination. But in spite of the relatively male appearance of the genitalia, breasts appear at puberty. It is possible that a sample larger than 98 so-called true hermaphrodites would yield even more contrasts and subtleties. Suffice it to say that the varieties are so diverse that it is possible to know which parts are present and what is attached to what only after exploratory surgery.

The embryological origins of human hermaphrodites clearly fit what is known about male and female sexual development. The embryonic gonad generally chooses early in development to follow either a male or a female sexual pathway; for the ovo-testis, however, that choice is fudged. Similarly, the embryonic phallus most often ends up as a clitoris or a penis, but the existence of intermediate states comes as no surprise to the embryologist. There are also urogenital swellings in the embryo that usually either stay open and become the vaginal labia or fuse and become a scrotum. In some hermaphrodites, though, the choice of opening or closing is ambivalent. Finally, all mammalian embryos have structures that can become the female uterus and the fallopian tubes, as well as structures that can become part of the male sperm-transport system. Typically either the male or the female set of those primordial genital organs degenerates, and the remaining structures achieve their sex-appropriate future. In hermaphrodites both sets of organs develop to varying degrees.

Intersexuality itself is old news. Hermaphrodites, for instance, are often featured in stories about human origins. Early biblical scholars believed Adam began life as a hermaphrodite and later divided into two people—a male and a female—after falling from grace. According to Plato there once were three sexes—male, female and hermaphrodite—but the third sex was lost with time.

Both the Talmud and the Tosefta, the Jewish books of law, list extensive regulations for people of mixed sex. The Tosefta expressly forbids hermaphrodites to inherit their fathers' estates (like daughters), to seclude themselves with women (like sons) or to shave (like men). When hermaphrodites menstruate they must be isolated from men (like women); they are disqualified from serving as witnesses or as priests (like women), but the laws of pederasty apply to them.

In Europe a pattern emerged by the end of the Middle Ages that, in a sense, has lasted to the present day: hermaphrodites were compelled to choose an established gender role and stick with it. The penalty for transgression was often death. Thus in the 1600s a Scottish hermaphrodite living as a woman was buried alive after impregnating his/her master's daughter.

For question of inheritance, legitimacy, paternity, succession to title and eligibility for certain professions to be determined, modern Anglo-Saxon legal systems require that newborns be registered as either male or female. In the U.S. today sex determination is governed by state laws. Illinois permits adults to change the sex recorded on their birth certificate should a physician attest to having performed the appropriate surgery. The New York Academy of Medicine, on the other hand, has taken an opposite view. In spite of surgical alterations of the external genitalia, the academy argued in 1966, the chromosomal sex remains the same. By that measure, a person's wish to conceal his or her original sex cannot outweigh the public interest in protection against fraud.

During this century the medical community has completed what the legal world began—the complete erasure of any form of embodied sex that does not conform to a male-female, heterosexual pattern. Ironically, a more sophisticated knowledge of the complexity of sexual systems has led to the repression of such intricacy.

In 1937 the urologist Hugh H. Young of Johns Hopkins University published a volume titled *Genital Abnormalities, Hermaphroditism and Related Adrenal Diseases*. The book is remarkable for its erudition, scientific insight and open-mindedness. In it Young drew together a wealth of carefully documented case histories to demonstrate and study the medical treatment of such "accidents of birth." Young did not pass judgment on the people he studied, nor did he attempt to coerce into treatment those intersexuals who rejected that option. And he showed unusual even-handedness in referring to those people who had sexual experiences as both men and women as "practicing hermaphrodites."

One of Young's more interesting cases was a hermaphrodite named Emma who had grown up as a female. Emma had both a penis-size clitoris and a vagina, which made it possible for him/her to have "normal" heterosexual sex with both men and women. As a teenager Emma had had sex with a number of girls to whom s/he was deeply attracted; but at the age of 19 s/he had married a man. Unfortunately, he had given Emma little sexual pleasure (though *he* had had no complaints), and so throughout that marriage and subsequent ones Emma had kept girlfriends on the side. With some frequency s/he had pleasurable sex with them. Young describes his subject as appearing "to be quite content and even happy." In conversation Emma occasional told him of his/her wish to be a man, a circumstance Young said would be relatively easy to bring about. But Emma's reply strikes a heroic blow for self-interest:

> Would you have to remove the vagina? I don't know about that because that's my meal ticket. If you did that, I would have to quit my husband and go to work, so I think I'll keep

it and stay as I am. My husband supports me well, and even though I don't have any sexual pleasure with him, I do have lots with my girlfriends.

Yet even as Young was illuminating intersexuality with the light of scientific reason, he was beginning its suppression. For his book is also an extended treatise on the most modern surgical and hormonal methods of changing intersexuals into either males or females. Young may have differed from his successors in being less judgmental and controlling of the patients and their families, but he nonetheless supplied the foundation on which current intervention practices were built.

By 1969, when the English physicians Christopher J. Dewhurst and Ronald R. Gordon wrote *The Intersexual Disorders,* medical and surgical approaches to intersexuality had neared a state of rigid uniformity. It is hardly surprising that such a hardening of opinion took place in the era of the feminine mystique—of the post-Second World War flight to the suburbs and the strict divisions of family roles according to sex. That the medical consensus was not quite universal (or perhaps that it seemed poised to break apart again) can be gleaned from the near-hysterical tone of Dewhurst and Gordon's book, which contrasts markedly with the calm reason of Young's founding work. Consider their opening description of an intersexual newborn:

> One can only attempt to imagine the anguish of the parents. That a newborn should have a deformity . . . [affecting] so fundamental an issue as the very sex of the child . . . is a tragic event which immediately conjures up visions of a hopeless psychological misfit doomed to live always as a sexual freak in loneliness and frustration.

Dewhurst and Gordon warned that such a miserable fate would, indeed, be a baby's lot should the case be improperly managed; "but fortunately," they wrote, "with correct management the outlook is infinitely better than the poor parents—emotionally stunned by the event—or indeed anyone without special knowledge could ever imagine."

Scientific dogma has held fast to the assumption that without medical care hermaphrodites are doomed to a life of misery. Yet there are few empirical studies to back up that assumption, and some of the same research gathered to build a case for medical treatment contradicts it. Francies Benton, another of Young's practicing hermaphrodites, "had not worried over his condition, did not wish to be changed, and was enjoying life." The same could be said of Emma, the opportunistic hausfrau. Even Dewhurst and Gordon, adamant about the psychological importance of treating intersexuals at the infant stage, acknowledged great success in "changing the sex" of older patients. They reported on 20 cases of children reclassified into a different sex after the supposedly critical age of 18 months. They asserted that all the reclassifications were "successful," and they wondered then whether reregistration could be "recommended more readily than [had] been suggested so far."

The treatment of intersexuality in this century provides a clear example of what the French historian Michel Foucault has called biopower. The knowledge developed in biochemistry, embryology, endocrinology, psychology and surgery has enabled physicians to control the very sex of the human body. The multiple contradictions in that kind of power call for some scrutiny. On the one hand, the medical "management" of intersexuality certainly developed as part of an attempt to free people from perceived psychological pain (though whether the pain was the patient's, the parents' or the physician's is unclear). And if one accepts the assumption that in a sex-divided culture people can realize their greatest potential for happiness and productivity only if they are sure they belong to one of only two acknowledged sexes, modern medicine has been extremely successful.

On the other hand, the same medical accomplishments can be read not as progress but as a mode of discipline. Hermaphrodites have unruly bodies. They do not fall naturally into a binary classification; only a surgical shoehorn can put them there. But why should we care if a "woman," defined as one who has breasts, a vagina, a uterus and ovaries and who menstruates, also has a clitoris large enough to penetrate the vagina of another woman? Why should we care if there are people whose biological equipment enables them to have sex "naturally" with both men and woman? The answers seem to lie in a cultural need to maintain clear distinctions between the sexes. Society mandates the control of intersexual bodies because they blur and bridge the great divide. Inasmuch as hermaphrodites literally embody both sexes, they challenge traditional beliefs about sexual differences: they posses the irritating ability to live sometimes as one sex and sometimes the other, and they raise the specter of homosexuality.

But what if things were altogether different? Imagine a world in which the same knowledge that has enabled medicine to intervene in the management of intersexual patients has been placed at the service of multiple sexualities. Imagine that the sexes have multiplied beyond currently imaginable limits. It would have to be a world of shared powers. Patient and physician, parent and child, male and female, heterosexual and homosexual—all those oppositions and others would have to be dissolved as sources of division. A new ethic of medical treatment would arise, one that would permit ambiguity in culture that had overcome sexual division. The central mission of medical treatment would be to preserve life. Thus hermaphrodites would be concerned primarily not about whether they can conform to society but about whether they might develop potential life-threatening conditions—hernias, gonadal tumors, salt imbalance caused by adrenal malfunction—that sometimes accompany hermaphroditic development. In my ideal world medical intervention for intersexuals would take place only rarely before the age of reason; subsequent treatment would be a cooperative venture between physician, patient and other advisers trained in issues of gender multiplicity.

I do not pretend that the transition to my utopia would be smooth. Sex, even the supposedly "normal," heterosexual kind, continues to cause untold anxieties in Western society. And certainly a culture that has yet to come to grips—religiously and, in some states, legally—with the ancient and relatively uncomplicated reality of homosexual love will not readily embrace intersexuality. No doubt the most troublesome arena by far would be the rearing of children. Parents, at least since the Victorian era, have fretted, sometimes to the point of outright denial, over the fact that their children are sexual beings.

All that and more amply explains why intersexual children are generally squeezed into one of the two prevailing sexual categories. But what would be the psychological consequences of taking the alternative road—raising children as unabashed intersexuals? On the surface that tack seems fraught with peril. What, for example, would happen to the intersexual child amid the unrelenting cruelty of the school yard? When the time came to shower in gym class, what horrors and humiliations would await the intersexual as his/her anatomy was displayed in all its nontraditional glory? In whose gym class would s/he register to begin with? What bathroom would s/he use? And how on earth would Mom and Dad help shepherd him/her through the mine field of puberty?

In the past 30 years those questions have been ignored, as the scientific community has, with remarkable unanimity, avoided contemplating the alternative route of unimpeded intersexuality. But modern investigators tend to overlook a substantial body of case histories, most of them compiled between 1930 and 1960, before surgical intervention became rampant. Almost without exception, those reports describe children who grew up knowing they were intersexual (though they did not advertise it) and adjusted to their unusual status. Some of the studies are richly detailed—described at the level of gym-class showering (which most intersexuals avoided without incident); in any event, there is not a psychotic or a suicide in the lot.

Still, the nuances of socialization among intersexuals cry out for more sophisticated analysis. Clearly, before my vision of sexual multiplicity can be realized, the first openly intersexual children and their parents will have to be brave pioneers who will bear the brunt of society's growing pains. But in the long view—though it could take generations to achieve—the prize might be a society in which sexuality is something to be celebrated for its subtleties and not something to be feared or ridiculed.

Questions

1. What is intersexuality?

2. Despite the natural variation in human physiology, why are people so insistent that there are only two sexes?

3. Why is Fausto-Sterling pessimistic about the acceptance of intersexuality?

4. How might your life be different if you were a merm, ferm, or herm who had avoided surgical and hormonal intervention?

5. Suppose that you and your partner gave birth to an intersexed baby. How would you respond to those who advocated sex reassignment surgery and hormone therapy for your child?

The M / F Boxes

E. J. GRAFF

Are you male or female? That's an easy question for most people to answer, but not so easy for some. Approximately one in two thousand infants each year are born with ambiguous genitals. Physicians often surgically reassign the infants to one sex or the other so that they conform to social expectations. In this article, E. J. Graff explores implications of the dualistic notion that people and their anatomy should be decidedly male or female. Graff also exposes the obstacles and dangers that people who do not conform to this notion face, and explains how transgender activists may help us rethink our basic assumptions about sex.

A 15-year-old girl is incarcerated in a Chicago mental hospital in 1981 and kept there for three years because she won't wear a dress. A Winn-Dixie truck driver is fired from a job he held for twenty years when his boss learns that he wears women's clothes at home. A small-time hustler in Falls City, Nebraska, is raped and then murdered when he's discovered to be physically female. A woman bleeds to death after a Washington, DC, hit-and-run accident when, after finding male genitals under her clothes, paramedics stand by laughing.

M or F? For most of us that's a simple question, decided while we were in utero. Checking off that box—at the doctor's, on the census, on a driver's license—takes scarcely a thought. But there's an emerging movement of increasingly vocal people whose bodies or behavior unsettle that clear division. They're calling themselves "transgendered": It's a spongy neologism that, at its broadest, absorbs everyone from medically reassigned transsexuals to cross-dressing men to women so masculine that security guards are called to eject them from women's restrooms. Fellow travelers include intersexuals (once called hermaphrodites), whose bodies are both/and rather than either/or. The slash between M/F cuts painfully through these lives.

And so they've started to organize. Brought together by the Internet, inspired by the successes of the gay rights movement, and with national sympathy gained from the movie *Boys Don't Cry*, intersex and transgender activists are starting to get a hearing in organizations ranging from college campuses to city councils, from lesbian and gay rights groups to pediatric conferences. And, like the feminist and gay rights movements before them, the new sex-and-gender activists may force us to rethink, in life and in law, how we define and interpret the basics of sex.

A first clue to how zealously the M/F border is guarded—to how sex is literally constructed—comes at birth. One in 2,000 infants is born with genitalia ambiguous enough to make doctors hem and haw when parents ask the first question: boy or girl? Since the late 1950s/early 1960s, standard medical procedure has been to lie and obfuscate. Rather than explain that the child is "a mixture of male and female," writes Anne Fausto-Sterling, author of *Sexing the Body,* medical manuals advise physicians to reassign the child surgically to one sex or another, telling parents only that "the gonads were incompletely developed . . . and therefore required removal." A large clitoris may be cut down; a micro-penis may be removed and a vagina built; a testis or testes are sliced out—sometimes over the parents' explicit objections.

Now some of those children have come of age and are telling their stories: severe depression, sexual numbness and a long-time despair at having been folded, spindled and mutilated. The leader of this nascent movement is Cheryl Chase, who in 1993 organized the Intersex Society of North America. ISNA opposes reassignment surgery on intersex infants and advocates raising intersex children as social males or females, educating them about their bodies and letting them choose at puberty whether they'd like surgical assistance or a shift in social sex. ISNA's cause was helped when Johns Hopkins sex researcher and PhD John Money, who wrote the intersex silence-and-reassignment protocol, was profoundly discredited. After a child he called "John" was accidentally castrated soon after birth, Money advised his parents to have him undergo surgery to construct a vagina, raise him as "Joan" and give him female hormones at puberty. Money reported this involuntary sex reassignment as fully successful. But in 1997, both a medical journal report and a *Rolling Stone* article revealed that the reassignment had been a disaster. Despite the insistence of parents, doctors, psychologists and teachers, "Joan" had always insisted that she was "just a boy with long hair in girl's clothes." In adolescence, John took back his manhood.

How did John "know" he was male—and by extension, how do any of us decide we're girls or boys? One theory is that, in utero, John had undergone the androgen bath that turns an undifferentiated fetus—which otherwise becomes female—male, giving him a male identity and masculine behavior. In the other rare cases where XY infants lose penises and are raised as girls, some insist on being boys—but others happily identify as (masculine, lesbian) women, which suggests that things aren't quite so simple. Scientists recognize that our brains and nervous systems are somewhat plastic, developing in response to environmental stimuli. Sexuality—all of it, from identity to presentation to sexual orientation—is no exception; it develops as a biological interaction between inborn capacities and outside influences. As a result, most of us have a narrow range in which we feel "natural" as we gender ourselves daily through clothes, stance, stride, tone. For most, that gendered behavior is consonant with biological sex: Girls present as female, if not feminine, and fall in love with boys; boys present as male or masculine and fall in love with girls. But those in whom gendered behavior is vice versa—feminine boys, highly masculine girls—get treated as unnatural, even though their gendering is just as biological as the rest of ours. What happens to these transgendered folks can be so brutal that the pediatric surgeons who cut off infant clitorises or penises look like merely the advance guard of the M/F border patrol.

Take, for instance, Daphne Scholinski, so masculine that at age 6, strangers chastised her when she tried to use women's restrooms. In her dry, pitiless memoir *The Last Time I Wore a Dress,* Scholinski tells the story of being committed to a mental hospital at 15 for some very real problems, including severe neglect, her father's violence and her own delinquency. The hospital ignored her shocking childhood and instead "treated" her masculinity. Scholinski got demerits if she didn't wear makeup. She was put on a boys' ward, where she was twice raped, to encourage her to be more feminine. Her confinement was so disturbing that she still gets posttraumatic stress flashbacks, including nightmares so terrifying that she wakes up and vomits. And so Scholinski is starting an organization dedicated to reforming the diagnosis of childhood GID, or gender identity disorder, under which she was treated.

Or consider the treatment of Darlene Jespersen and Peter Oiler. After working for Harrah's Reno casino for eighteen years, in the summer of 2000, Jespersen was fired from her bartending job when Harrah's launched a new policy requiring all its female employees to wear foundation, powder, eyeliner, lipstick and so on. "I tried it," says Jespersen in a plaintive voice, "but I felt so naked." The obverse happened to Peter Oiler, a weathered, middle-aged man with large aviator glasses, a pleasant drawl and a bit of an overbite. After twenty years of being rotated through progressively more responsible jobs in Winn-Dixie's shipping yards, in 1999 Oiler was driving a fifty-foot truck delivering grocery supplies throughout southeastern Louisiana—until Winn-Dixie learned that he called himself "transgendered." Oiler tried to explain that he simply wore women's clothes on the weekends: He wasn't going to become a woman; he didn't want to wear makeup and heels on company time. In January 2000 Oiler was fired.

Jespersen and Oiler are stunned. Jespersen is suing Harrah's. Says Oiler, "I was raised to believe that if you do an honest day's work, you'll get an honest day's pay." The ACLU Lesbian and Gay Rights Project has taken up his case, in part because of the sheer injustice—and in part to get courts to treat discrimination against people who violate sex stereotypes as illegal sex discrimination. If a woman can wear a dress, or if a man can refuse makeup, why not vice versa? In doing so, the ACLU, like the three national lesbian and gay legal organizations, would be building on the 1989 Supreme Court decision *Price Waterhouse v. Ann Hopkins*. Price Waterhouse had told Hopkins that she wasn't going to make partner because she was too masculine—and, in actual written memos, advised her to wear jewelry and makeup, to go to charm school, to be less aggressive. The Supreme Court declared such stereotyping to be sex discrimination.

Will judges see Peter Oiler's dismissal as illegal sex stereotyping? There have been some recent hints that they might. In Massachusetts, for instance, the US Court of Appeals for the First Circuit said Lucas Rosa could sue a bank that instructed feminine Rosa, who had shown up to apply for a loan wearing a dress, to go home and come back in men's clothes; a female, after all, would have been considered for the loan. Another Massachusetts judge said that a male student could come to school in a dress, since female students could. A Washington transsexual prisoner raped by a prison guard, and two New York municipal employees harassed for being gay, were allowed to sue when judges ruled they'd been attacked for violating stereotyped expectations of their sex.

Our society has learned to see why women would want masculine privileges like playing soccer and serving on the Supreme Court, but there's been no matching force expanding the world for males. Boys and men still patrol each other's masculinity with a *Glengarry Glen Ross* level of ridicule and violence that can seem, to women, nearly surreal. Those males who violate the M-box's limits on behavior are quite literally risking their lives.

Which means that, if you're a performing drag queen, a cross-dressing straight man like Peter Oiler, or a transsexual who still has some male ID, do not under any circumstances get stopped by a cop. In New York City, says Pauline Park, a co-founder of NYAGRA (New York Association for Gender

Rights Advocacy), even if the police don't actually beat you, "you could be arrested and detained for days or weeks. They don't let people out until they plead guilty to prostitution. They put them in the men's cell, where they're often assaulted and sometimes raped, as a tactic to get people to plead guilty."

And don't turn to emergency medical personnel. In August 1995 Tyra Hunter's car crashed in Washington, DC. When firefighting paramedics cut away her dress and found male genitals, they laughed and mocked her. She bled to death in the hospital. In August 2000 a jury awarded Hunter's mother $1.75 million in a wrongful-death action. Hunter's experience, unfortunately, is not unusual. Once a month, someone transgendered is murdered, and those are just the documented cases. Transgender activists are beginning to mark November 28, the anniversary of another such death, as a Day of Remembrance, with candlelight vigils and a determination to slow the steady drumbeat of murder.

"We're despised. We're pariahs in this society," says Miranda Stevens-Miller, chair of the transgender rights organization It's Time, Illinois, about transsexuals and otherwise transgendered people. Many transsexuals are fired once they begin to transition. Others lose custody and visitation rights, houses, leases. Many are shut out of office and other public restrooms for years—an indignity that cuts to the very core of being human, since every living body needs to pee. And so the most urgent transgender organizing is happening locally, in organizations such as TGNet Arizona, NYAGRA and It's Time, Oregon. They're teaching Trans 101 to local employers, doctors, city councils, lesbian and gay organizations, judges, families, landlords, friends. They're attempting to collect statistics on firings, beatings, murders, bathroom harassment, police abuse. Often these groups are driven by the energy and determination of one or two people who spend their own time and pennies writing and photocopying leaflets, giving workshops for corporate and college groups, and lobbying city councils and lesbian and gay organizations for inclusion in hate-crimes and antidiscrimination laws. Lately, they're having remarkable success at adding "gender identity and expression" to the protected categories in local and state employment nondiscrimination and hate-crimes laws; they've won in locales ranging from Portland, Oregon, to DeKalb, Illinois, to the state of Rhode Island.

Nationally, trans groups are still in the skirmishing phase faced by any new movement, with the inevitable splits over strategy and personality. The group with the most name recognition, GenderPAC, angers some transgender activists by avoiding the "T" word in its advocacy, saying that it aims at gender freedom for everyone; it acts on behalf of such people as Darlene Jespersen and Peter Oiler, or boys called "faggot" for not being noticeably masculine. Currently the most significant transgender organizations nationally are IFGE (International Foundation for Gender Education), GEA (Gender Education and Advocacy) and the Working Group on Trans Equality, a loose network of grassroots trans activists aiming at a coordinated national presence. Perhaps the biggest success so far is that all the major lesbian and gay organizations and many smaller ones have added transgendered folks to their mission statements as folks who are equally, if differently, queer.

Or is it so different? All of us deviate from what's expected from our sex. While the relationship between transgender activists and lesbian and gay groups has at times been contentious, some lesbian and gay activists, notably Chai Feldblum, Georgetown law professor, are starting to urge that we all organize around our common deviance from sex stereotypes. The differences between homosexual, transgender and transsexual experiences are not that great: All are natural variations on the brain's gendered development that have cropped up throughout human history, from Tiresias to Radclyffe Hall, from Billy Tipton to Quentin Crisp. For the most part, the mainstream sees us on one sliding scale of queerness. And occasionally our struggles and goals intersect quite neatly. For instance, homos can't always tell whether we're harassed at work because someone figures out that we date others of the same sex, or simply because we're too butch or too fey.

And none of us can rely on having our marriages recognized by the institutions around us when we need them—because marriage is one of the last laws on the books that discriminate based on sex. Recently, Joe Gardiner asked a Kansas court to invalidate his dead father's marriage to transwoman (born male, medically and legally reassigned as female) J'Noel Gardiner, saying J'Noel was "really" a man—and therefore could not have legally married a man. The lower court agreed with the son that XY = man, which meant the son would inherit his father's fat estate. But the Kansas appeals judge remanded the case back down for a new trial. Sex, the appeals court declared, isn't decided simply by a chromosome test. Rather, sex is a complex constellation of characteristics that includes not only chromosomes but also "gonadal sex, internal morphologic sex, external morphologic sex, hormonal sex, phenotypic sex, assigned sex and gender of rearing, and sexual identity." The court approvingly quoted Johns Hopkins researcher and medical doctor William Reiner, who wrote, "The organ that appears to be critical to psychosexual development and adaptation is not the external genitalia, but the brain."

☻ ☻ ☻

Questions

1. Are the terms "transgendered" and "intersexual" interchangeable? Explain.

2. What is the ISNA? What are its goals? Visit and explore the ISNA website at http://www.isna.org. What did you learn about the organization that you didn't learn from this article?

3. What forms of discrimination do transgendered people in our society face? Do you think that activism is likely to change this? Why, or why not?

4. What are the three most important things you learned from this article? Why are they important, not only for you but also for others, to understand?

5. Have you ever seen someone whose sex you could not determine from their appearance? How did that make you feel, and why? Did this article give you any insight into your reactions?

To Be Poor and Transgender

Kai Wright

*Transgender people—people who live in a gender different from the sex cat-
egory they were assigned at birth—face multiple barriers in a society such
as ours that assumes sex and gender are congruent. To be poor and transgender, as Kai Wright explains in this article, complicates life even more. Basic
human needs like economic security and healthcare can be difficult to obtain
because of people's assumptions about those who transgress gender norms in
this fundamental way. "Transgender" is a term that can apply to a variety of
people: Some transgender individuals have had sex-reassignment surgery
(SRS); others rely on social cues to live their lives in the gender with which
they identify. Because SRS is often considered elective surgery, it is beyond
the economic means of many people.*

*S*harmus has been a sex worker for about five years. She started after
breaking up with a boyfriend who was supporting her while she was
out of work. It was quick money, and, as with many of her transgender
friends, she didn't believe there were many other jobs out there for her.

"You have your good nights, and your bad nights," says Sharmus, thirty-
five. "There are no fringe benefits. Summer time is the best time; the winter is
hard," she explains, casually ticking off the pros and cons of being a prostitute. "It's just hard getting a job. Nobody really wants to hire you, and when
they do hire you they give you a hard time."

Sex work was not in her plans back when she transitioned from male to
female at age twenty-one. "Sometimes I regret it," she sighs. "My lifetime goal
was to be a schoolteacher."

Her uncertainty is to be expected. Our culture depicts people whose discomfort with gender norms goes beyond being tomboys or feminine men as
mere curiosity items for trash TV ("Your woman is really a man!" episodes of
Jerry Springer). This collective ignorance leaves people like Sharmus without
much guidance. Many go through puberty and into adulthood without

Reprinted by permission from the *Progressive*, October 2001.

meeting people like themselves. The resulting high rates of depression, drug use, violence, and suicidal thoughts are unsurprising.

"One of the greatest agonies one can experience is gender dysphoria," says transgender activist Jessica Xavier. "When your anatomy doesn't match who you are inside, it's the worst feeling in the world."

Sharmus and Xavier are part of a group whose existence challenges normative gender. They include drag performers, heterosexual cross-dressers, and people from all walks of life who live permanently in a gender other than that assigned at birth. They range from individuals who have had thousands of dollars worth of reconstructive surgery to people who simply style themselves in a way that feels comfortable.

Around the nation, a growing cadre of activists is working to build bridges between all of these populations and to encourage the formation of an umbrella community called "transgender." What the members of this latest American identity group share is a far more practical understanding of gender politics than that of the ethereal, academic world to which it is often relegated. From employment to health services, transgender folks, particularly those in low-income environments, face enormous barriers when navigating even the most basic aspects of life—all because of their gender transgressions.

"We continue to be one of the most stigmatized populations on the planet," says Xavier, the former director of a national coalition of transgender political groups called It's Time!—America. Xavier recently cajoled the local health department into financing a survey of around 250 transgender people in D.C. Forty percent of respondents had not finished high school, and another 40 percent were unemployed. Almost half had no health insurance and reported not seeing a physician regularly. A quarter reported being HIV-positive, and another 35 percent reported having seriously considered suicide.

Xavier's was the latest in a series of such studies done in cities where relatively emboldened trans activists have pushed local officials to begin considering public policy solutions to their health care concerns. Across the board, they have found largely the same thing: higher rates of just about every indicator of social and economic distress. "And all because of the stigma," Xavier concludes.

One problem that stands out, Xavier and others say, is the need for accessible counseling and medical supervision for those who are in the process of gender transitioning. Most medical professionals require certain steps, outlined in a set of protocols dubbed the "Benjamin Standards of Care." First, a therapist must diagnose you with "Gender Identity Disorder," which the American Psychiatric Association established in 1979. In adults, the diagnosis essentially confirms that your "gender dysphoria" is profound enough that the drastic step of making physiological alterations to God's plan is an acceptable treatment.

The diagnosis clears you for reconstructive surgery and hormone therapy. Hormone use for gender transitioning is strictly off-label, but select doctors will nevertheless prescribe a particular hormone and simply file paperwork for one of its approved usages. While there is disagreement within the trans community about how this process should be altered, most unite around frustration with the gatekeeping nature of it all—the notion that one must first ask permission, then be declared insane, before being allowed to violate our gender rules.

For Angela (a pseudonym), this means choosing between the career she's spent ten years building and her recent decision to live as a male. Angela, twenty-eight, gained security clearance while serving in the Marines. Despite having climbed to officer rank, she fled the forces when it became clear they were going to throw her out for being a lesbian.

As a civilian, her clearance allowed her to land a well-paying job at an aerospace engineering firm. The position has afforded her partner of four years a comfortable life, and even occasionally helps support her partner's budding acting career. But all of that will be jeopardized once a gender-identity-disorder diagnosis is placed in Angela's medical records. Technically, it's a mental health problem, and that would likely prompt the revocation of her clearance when it next comes up for review. So Angela and her partner are again searching for new ways she can use her skills.

Middle class professionals like Angela have options. The barriers to a legal and safe gender transition are surmountable, if profound. But for people like Sharmus, the whole discussion is absurd.

Sharmus has never had "body work" done, but she's taken some hormones in the past. In her world, spending thousands of dollars on therapy, surgery, and hormone treatments is impossible, but a hyper-feminine appearance is still highly valued—not only for personal aesthetics, but also for professional development. So a thriving black market has developed. In D.C., for $200 to $300, you can have silicone injected into your chest to create breasts. Thirty bucks will get you around 100 hormone pills, though injections are usually cheaper.

"When I was taking the hormone shots, my girlfriend was shooting me," Sharmus explains. "You get a knot in the breasts first, then your skin gets soft. After about two months, my breasts started forming."

With hormones, often someone who has taken them before supplies and mentors a curious friend. Similar arrangements develop with silicone, but just as often there's a dealer in town who also injects clients. The silicone is not encased, as it would be with an implant, but rather injected with large syringes directly into varying body parts. In some cases, the materials injected are not even silicone, but substitutes made from more readily available things such as dishwashing liquid or floor wax. Similarly, some men wanting estrogen will simply take birth-control pills. Testosterone is harder to improvise, but even the real thing can irreparably damage internal organs when taken improperly. All of this can result in fatalities.

"I have known several people that passed," Sharmus sighs. She steers clear of silicone and stopped taking unsupervised hormones. A couple of years ago, she started working with an organization called Helping Individual Prostitutes Survive, or HIPS. She conducts outreach for HIPS, offering information on how to protect against HIV and other sexually transmitted diseases, and encouraging colleagues to leave the silicone alone.

Omar Reyes, whose drag persona is former Miss Gay America, works for La Clinica del Pueblo, a D.C. clinic serving the city's ballooning Latino community. Reyes uses his male birth name and male pronouns but considers himself transgender because of his drag work and his discomfort with male gender "norms." In his monthly transgender support group and in conversations with other dragas he meets at his weekly show, Reyes harps on the malas noticias about silicone. But he recognizes why it's attractive: It's cheap, and it's fast.

"They put silicone in their face and their bodies and, in just a very short period, they can look like a woman," he says. This is particularly important for drag performers and sex workers, whose income may depend on how exaggeratedly feminine they look. "We have to deal with the fact that they want to look like a woman, and this is the short-term way to do it."

Reyes and Xavier want to see someone in D.C. start a low-cost clinic devoted to counseling and treatment for people who are transitioning. Gay health centers in Boston, Los Angeles, New York City, San Francisco, and Seattle all such clinics already and are developing their own sets of protocols for how the process should work. Earlier this year, San Francisco became the first jurisdiction in the United States to include sex reassignment surgery and related treatments in its health plan for civil servants. This is the kind of thing Xavier says we need to see more of.

But even if the services were there, getting people into them would take work. Most transgender people tell horrifying stories of the treatment they have experienced in health care settings. In one of the most high-profile cases nationally, a trans woman named Tyra Hunter died in 1995 when D.C. paramedics refused to treat her wounds from a car accident. After removing her clothes at the scene of the accident and discovering her male genitals, a para-medic allegedly ceased treating Hunter and began shouting taunts. She died at the hospital later. Following a lengthy court battle, Hunter's family won a suit against the city.

There are many less prominent examples. From the hospital nurse who gawks when helping a trans woman into her dressing gown to the gynecologist who responds with disbelief when a trans man comes in for a checkup, the small indignities act as perhaps the greatest barriers to health care.

"They feel like when you go for services, people are going to give attitude," Reyes says. "Therefore, you find that they don't even think about going for help when they really need it."

Tanika Walker, who goes by Lucky, is your standard eighteen-year-old hard ass: short-sighted, stubborn-headed, determined to be the roughest guy in the room. Born and raised in rough-and-tumble southeast Washington, D.C., Lucky has a mop of dreadlocks, light mustache, tattoos, and brands—including the name of a deceased sibling spelled out in cigarette burns. These all send one message: I'm the wrong dude to mess with.

Like Angela, Lucky is in the process of transitioning genders to become a young man. It's an emotional journey she began when she was fourteen years old. Along the way, she's been yanked out of school and tossed out of her home. She's also been involved in a lot of disastrous relationships marred by violence, often her own.

"I know that I'm homosexual, that I'm a lesbian," Lucky says, groping to explain her feelings. "But at the same time, it's like, I look so much like a boy. I act so much like a boy. I want to be a boy."

So far, however, Lucky's transition is primarily stylistic. She still uses her birth name and answers to female pronouns, but she describes her gender as "not anything." She uses only the men's bathroom because she's had too many fights with women who thought she was a Peeping Tom in the ladies' room. And she'd much rather her friends call her "dawg" than "girlfriend." Among African American lesbians, Lucky fits into a category of women often dubbed "doms," short for dominant.

"I never had chests," Lucky brags. "Never. Around the time you're supposed to start getting chests, I didn't get any. So I was like, am I made to be like this? I was the little girl all of the other little girls couldn't play with cause I was too boyish."

The dyke jokes started early, sometime in middle school. She settled on a violent response to the taunting just as early. Her fighting became routine enough that by sophomore year the school suggested counseling for her "identity crisis." She balked and, instead, came out to her mom, who promptly threw her out of the house. "I was like, how am I having an identity crisis? I know what I am," Lucky remembers. "My mom said I had to go."

Lucky enrolled herself in the Job Corps and by the time she was seventeen had her GED. She came back to D.C., moved in with her godsister, and began dating a thirty-two-year-old woman.

But the relationship quickly turned violent, and the godsister put Lucky out as well. She turned to one of her brothers and started dating someone her own age. But it was a stormy relationship, and Lucky battered her partner. After one of their more brutal fights, the young woman called the police and Lucky wound up in jail for a month for aggravated assault. That was this April. In May, she started dating another young woman, and she believes this relationship will work out. She's also started hanging out at the Sexual Minority Youth Assistance League (SMYAL).

One urgent lesson she's trying to learn is that violence isn't her only option when conflict arises. But she dismisses the severity of her problem. "I would be, like, 'Go away and leave me alone,'" she says, describing how the fights started. "And she would just keep hitting me in the arm or something. But it didn't really affect me; it would just be real irritating. She used to do stupid stuff like that to aggravate me. So I just hit her. And when I hit her, I blacked her eye out or something."

She sums up her life in a gigantic understatement, saying, "It's just some things I've been through that a normal eighteen-year-old female wouldn't have been through."

Twenty-year-old Vassar College senior Kiana Moore began transitioning at seventeen. She is articulate and engaging, has never been in trouble, and is studying to become a clinical psychologist. As the only transgender person on her campus, she comes out to the entire first-year class every term during one of the school's diversity programs. She spent this summer interning at SMYAL, counseling Lucky and fifteen to twenty other mainly black transgender youth. What these young folks, need, she says, are more role models.

"I am here at SMYAL working as an intern, but where else can you go around this country and see a trans intern? Where can you see a trans person who's in college?" Moore asks. "And so you don't really have anyone to connect to or know about. So if they are at high risk [for social problems], that's why. Because there's nothing there for them at all."

Moore has what Xavier calls "passing privilege." She's a beautiful and confident black woman most people would never assume is transgender. That's something usually achieved only by those with significant resources.

And once trans people have found they can pass—usually middle class whites living in the suburbs—they don't want to ruin it by becoming an activist or a role model.

"You lose something if you help, because then you put yourself in the spotlight. And if you are a pretty, passable female, you don't want to do that," Moore explains. "We don't want to be advocates, because then we're Kiana the transsexual instead of Kiana the new neighbor."

And thus the activists trying to build a transgender community and social movement face much the same battle gay activists confronted for years: Those with the resources to help have too much to lose.

But Moore sees promise in the youth she spent the summer with. "Every time I talk to them I always give them a big hug before, during, and after the session, because that's the only way I can say I'm here and I think you're stronger than me," she says. "They deal with their problems, and they come in here, and they smile, every day. And they take care of each other."

☻ ☻ ☻

Questions

1. Explain why transgender people tend to have high rates of "just about every indicator of social and economic distress."

2. In what ways do physicians serve as "gatekeepers" for transgender people who want to transition? How has this contributed to the development of a black market?

3. List some reasons that job prospects are often limited for transgender people. How does social class play a role here?

4. Why do transgender people have such traumatic experiences when they seek healthcare?

5. What is "passing privilege"?

6. Is it surprising that people who have successfully transitioned are reluctant to become transgender activists or role models? Explain.

Disposable People

BOB MOSER

The violence directed toward transgendered people has escalated from taunts and harassment, to beatings and murder. Indeed, the murder rate for transgendered people may be rising faster than all other hate killings. But why? This article offers some answers to that question. It might also cause you to think about why we respond with violence toward those who do not fit our cultural norms of gender and sex.

In a city with no shortage of desolate neighborhoods, you'd be hard-pressed to find a bleaker spot than the corner of 50th and C streets. On one side there's a decaying school, its playground barren as a prison yard. Extending up a couple of blocks is a string of deserted apartment buildings with boards and burned-out holes where windows used to be. Just across the way, folks still live in a set of matching brick buildings. It's a tough place to grow up, especially when you're different. Especially when you're convinced that you're a girl with a boy's anatomy. Especially when the other kids taunt you and throw bricks at you and you have to quit school because you can't stand it anymore. Especially when you're determined to live openly as a transgendered woman, considered by many the lowest of the low.

Stephanie Thomas could have told you all about it. Until last Aug. 12.

Around 11:30 p.m. the night of the 11th, 19-year-old Thomas and her best pal, 18-year-old Ukea Davis, reportedly told friends they were going to a nearby gas station for cigarettes. Nobody can say for sure where they actually went. But just about everybody in the city knows that a little after 3 a.m., the friends were sitting in Thomas' Camry at a stop sign on the corner of 50th and C. Almost home. Then a car came up beside them, and the two were pelted with fire from a semiautomatic weapon. According to an eyewitness report, another car approached after the shooting. A man got out to see what had happened. Davis was already dead. When the man nudged Thomas' shoulder to see if she was still alive, she moaned in confirmation. But her helper fled as the first car returned. The gunman got out and fired more shots, making sure Thomas was dead. By the time rescue workers reached the bloody car, she was. Like her friend's, Thomas' body had been pumped full of bullets—at least 10 apiece.

A block up 50th, Thomas' mother, Queen Washington, got the news at 5:30 a.m. She'd been well aware that it was dangerous to be transgender in D.C.—or anywhere else in America, for that matter. But she hadn't seen this coming.

"If he'd known somebody was after him, I'd have known," says Washington, a feisty administrative assistant at the federal Bureau of Land Management who never got used to calling Stephanie "she." "We were tight. He'd come by just that afternoon with his girlfriends, before he went to get his nails done. We kept it real, him and I. He knew I'd always protect him as much as I could."

Washington knew early on that protecting her youngest kid, whose name was Wilbur when she adopted him at three months, wouldn't be easy. "He was a beautiful child, always very dainty, always very feminine. In first grade, a teacher—a teacher, mind you!—called him gay. I had to immediately go up to the school and get her straight. He came home that day and my neighbor told him gay meant happy. We looked it up in the dictionary. 'See?' I said. 'It's true!'"

It would have been tough enough to grow up gay on 50th Street, even when you could run home to the lavishly decorated apartment where Washington has lived for 35 years. But Wilbur wasn't gay. By the time he was 8 or 9, his mother "knew for sure that he wanted to be a girl." At 14, he began to live that way, borrowing the name Stephanie from a cousin he admired. He joined a local support group called SMYAL (Sexual Minority Youth Assistance League), where he met Davis. The two became inseparable friends, helping each other "transition" into living as females. Washington, who has stubbornly refused to abandon her neighborhood because "kids here need someone to love them, need to see people who are trying to be about something with their lives," became a kind of surrogate mom to Davis, whose own folks were not so accepting. But it wasn't easy for her, either.

"It's hard for a mother," Washington says, thumbing through a scrapbook she's assembled in memory of her son-turned-daughter. The pictures show Wilbur on the beach during family vacations; Wilbur clowning with his cousins; Wilbur in his early teens, grim-faced and downcast. "That's the last picture of him as a boy," his mother says, "before he became who he was." By contrast, she flips to a photo of Stephanie at 18, bear-hugging her mom. "Look at that smile!" she says. "He was a happy person—after he came out. You see? He didn't have those sad eyes no more."

The only thing that would have been worse than the brutal murders, Washington says, would have been never seeing that smile. "At least he had a chance to be who he was," she says. "I told him, God don't make no mistakes. I know you didn't make yourself. Who would make up a life like this? Who would be something the world hates?"

❧ Vigils and Violence

Even in a city with the nation's highest murder rate, the execution-style slayings of two transgendered teenagers was bound to cause a stir. Mayor Anthony Williams spoke at an emotional vigil for Davis and Thomas. D.C.'s congressional delegate, Eleanor Holmes Norton, forcefully urged police to investigate the double homicide as a hate crime. The best friends' joint funeral was packed. *The Washington Post* devoted a 3,500-word feature to the two lost lives. Local transgender activists redoubled their efforts to forestall another tragedy. Police vowed to do the same.

This Aug. 12, on the first anniversary of their deaths, there was another vigil for Davis and Thomas. By now the sadness had hardened into bitterness—over the lack of an arrest in the case, over police officials' reluctance to classify the murder as a hate crime, and over the continued violence that had claimed another transgendered victim, Kim Mimi Young, in April. The mayor came again, along with the chief of police. Frustrations were vented. Promises were made.

And then all hell broke loose.

Early on the morning of Aug. 16, four days after the vigil, one of the District's best-known transgender nightclub performers, 25-year-old Latina immigrant Bella Evangelista, was shot and killed by a man who had paid her for sex. Police arrested 22-year-old Antoine D. Jacobs as he pedaled away from the scene on a bicycle, charging him with first-degree murder and later with a hate crime.

Four nights later, shortly after a vigil was held for Evangelista, police found the dead body of Emonie Kiera Spaulding. The 25-year-old transgendered woman had been brutally beaten, shot, and dumped nude in a stand of scraggly, trash-strewn woods bordering Malcolm X Avenue. Her clothes were found a day later in a nearby dumpster. Another 22-year-old, Antwan D. Lewis, was arrested a few days later and charged with second-degree murder—but not, so far, with a hate crime.

The same night Spaulding's body was found, another transgendered woman, Dee Andre, survived a shooting near the U.S. Capitol. Alarmed transgender activists convened a series of community meetings, hoping to calm nerves and band together against the violence. Instead, the meetings only added to the sense that D.C.'s transgender community was in a state of emergency: "We heard of at least 14 other assaults happening that same week," says Jessica Xavier, a local activist and volunteer coordinator.

If this wave of crimes could somehow be tied together—if there were a serial perpetrator, or some kind of "trigger" event—the city's transgender population might be resting a little easier. But the assaults and murders appeared to be isolated cases of hatred. And though the sequence of events was extraordinary, the violence was not.

In 2000, Xavier had conducted the first study of transgendered people in the District. At the time, the results had seemed plenty disturbing. Of the 4,000 transgendered residents Xavier identified, a whopping 17% said they had been assaulted with a weapon because of their gender identity. Four years later, the violence appeared to be spiraling out of control even more—despite the fact that D.C.'s Metropolitan Police in 2000 had launched an innovative Gay and Lesbian Liaison Unit (GLLU) designed to tamp down the violence.

"We're scared," says Mara Kiesling, executive director of the Washington-based National Center for Transgender Equality. "This spree of violence made us feel more vulnerable than we deserve to feel. I'm sure it's increased the hopelessness for a lot of people. When you start hearing about 18 events in a week, you don't know what to do."

But if they aren't sure what to do, folks in Washington's transgender community certainly know what to think. "What we're seeing is a war against transgendered women," says Xavier. "And it's not only here—it's happening everywhere in this country."

❧ 21 Months, 27 Murders

With its abundance of support groups and readily available hormone and steroid treatments, Washington has long been a destination of choice for transgendered people on the East Coast. Now, with the past year's spree of killings and the constant drumbeat of assaults that has accompanied it, the city has also become a microcosm of what life—and death—is often like for transgendered people in cities across the U.S. While the past year's murders and assaults are "unrelated" in the law-enforcement sense of the term, most of the incidents do have at least one thing in common: "transphobia," which Jessica Xavier calls "the most powerful hatred on the planet."

"We are regarded by most as disposable people," she says.

Though the government compiles no statistics on anti-transgender hate crimes or murders, the unofficial numbers appear to back up her assertion. While the FBI reported a total of 11 U.S. murders motivated by racial, religious, or sexual-orientation bias in 2002, the *Intelligence Report* has documented 14 murders of transgendered people in the U.S. in that one year. By the end of September 2003, according to news and police reports, at least 13 more transgendered people had been slain.

In some cases, the details remain too murky to say for certain whether these murders were hate-motivated. But all 27 have at least one of the telltale signs of a hate crime—especially the sort of extreme brutality, or "overkill," that was all too evident in the bullet-torn bodies of Stephanie Thomas and Ukea Davis.

"The overkill is certainly an indicator that hate was present," says Jack Levin, a criminologist at Northeastern University who has written several books about hate crimes and murder. "When you see excessively brutal crimes, and you know the victim is gay or black or Latino or transgender, you have to suspect that hate was a motive. There's a sense of outrage in these crimes that someone different is breathing or existing."

One reason it's so tough to prove that anti-transgender murders are hate crimes is that so few are ever solved. Of the 27 murders in 2002 and the first nine months of 2003, arrests had been made in only 7—fewer than one-third—at press time. The general "clearance rate" for murders is almost twice as high, around 60%. "The police are very slow in solving murders committed against marginalized Americans, whether they're black, Latino, gay, prostitutes or transgender," Levin says. "When more than one of those characteristics is present in a victim"—usually the case in anti-transgender murders—"they *really* don't act quickly. They're much more likely to form a task force and offer a reward when the victim is a straight, middle-class college student."

When it comes to hate crimes that stop short of murder—assaults, harassment—it's virtually impossible to gauge the extent of the problem. The reason is simple: the victims of anti-transgender hate crimes almost never report them. One national group that keeps statistics on anti-transgender hate crimes, the National Coalition of Anti-Violence Programs, reports a consistent rise of reported incidents since 1999. In 2002, the NCAVP found that an average of 20 transgendered people were victimized by a hate crime every month. Some find that number far too conservative. "I get 10 to 15 calls about assaults every month just here in D.C.," says Earline Budd, who runs a grassroots group called Transgender Health Empowerment.

❀ Out and At-Risk

What has made transgendered people such popular targets? "It's partly because we're coming out into the daylight," says Toni Collins, who works with Earline Budd at Transgender Health Empowerment.

Jack Levin, the criminologist, agrees. "There are more transgendered people who are coming out, willing to expose themselves to the possibility of victimization," he says. "It reminds me of the period beginning in the '80s when gay and lesbian Americans began to come out in larger numbers. They exposed themselves to the risk of being victims of homophobic offenders. The same thing is happening with transgendered people now. They are encountering much the same violence, for much the same reasons."

In the case of transgendered victims, the violence often has a pattern. "So many of these crimes are discovery crimes: 'We thought you were X, but you were actually Y, so we killed you,'" says Lisa Mottet of the National Gay and Lesbian Task Force's Transgender Civil Rights Project. In the notorious cases of Gwen Araujo, the 17-year-old beaten and strangled last year in California, and Brandon Teena, whose brutal murder inspired the movie *Boys Don't Cry,* the "discovery" was made by friends. More often, it's a sex partner. "For someone who is confused about his sexual identity, or kind of shaky in the sex department," Levin says, "it may seem like a personal attack on his virility, on his sense of machismo, to find himself with a transgendered woman."

Budd, like many transgender activists, believes the "discovery crime" motivation is often bogus. Most transgendered people are up front with potential sex partners about their identities and anatomies, she says—and even in cases where they're not, "how can you say that's an excuse for killing somebody or beating them up?"

Bella Evangelista's murderer, Antoine Jacobs, is reportedly considering a "panic defense" when he goes to court. According to Sgt. Brett Parson, head of Washington's GLLU police unit, Jacobs told police he and Evangelista "were engaging in sex for hire, he liked it, the act was completed, they parted ways, and some of his friends said, 'Hey, man, that's a dude,' and he returned and shot her." Budd suspects that Jacobs simply got embarrassed when his friends found out he'd been with Evangelista, who was well known as a transgendered woman in the neighborhood where Jacobs lived. "This was all to show off for the guys," she says. "He came back and confronted her, and when she turned around to walk away, he pulled out a gun and shot her and just continued to shoot her. In the back. And that's a panic defense? Come on now."

Beyond fear and machismo, activists point to two bigger factors that help stoke the violence. One is the dearth of antidiscrimination and hate-crime laws that mention gender identity (as opposed to sexual orientation, a category that does not apply to transgendered people). Though four states and nine municipalities have added transgendered people to their statutes so far in 2003, only 24% of the U.S. population is currently covered.

Then there's the forgotten factor. "Look at the victims," says Mottet. "Because they are transgendered, they *have* to be in places that are extremely dangerous to begin with. Even if they're assaulted or killed for reasons other than hate, they still wouldn't have been targeted if they weren't transgendered, because they'd be able to stay in school, have family support, and hold down jobs. Society pushes people into the streets in order to survive, and they're not allowed to survive there. That's a societal hate crime."

Media accounts of murders like Bella Evangelista's or Emonie Spaulding's often link the crimes to street prostitution. That infuriates transgender activists, who say it's a form of blaming the victim. "The implication is that it's your fault for being beaten or killed," says Jessica Xavier. "But a lack of privilege means you *don't* have a choice." Or as Mottet puts it, "Sure, they have a choice: They can freeze and starve, or they can try to make a living."

"The classic profile," says Mara Kiesling, "is a 13-year-old who's thrown out of the house when she decides to transition. She's kicked out of school for wearing girls' clothes. She can't get a job because her ID says 'Andre' but she looks like a girl. What's going to happen? Most likely, she'll end up in a situation that makes her especially vulnerable—living in shelters and low-income neighborhoods, doing sex work as a matter of survival."

☺ On the Streets

Earline Budd and Toni Collins can tell you all about matters of transgender survival. The co-founders of D.C.'s Transgender Health Empowerment both landed on the streets in their teens. Both ultimately struggled their way to better lives, partly because they got their diplomas. But with their activism, they maintain a tight bond with the "girls" in the streets today. Collins, a tall elegant woman who's about to mark her 20th anniversary as an information-systems manager for a D.C. firm, recently spoke to transgendered teenagers in SMYAL, the support group Stephanie Thomas and Ukea Davis belonged to. "Out of the 20 in the group, all between 15 and 18 years old, only two were currently in school. One had a job. That left 17 of those 20 with no intention of going back to school. They dropped out because they were harassed."

Sooner or later, most of these teens will wind up on 5th and K. This triangle-shaped, open-air downtown corner, a few blocks from the city's silvery new convention center, has in recent years become Washington's best-known transgender "stroll"—a place to advertise their wares for potential clients. "A lot of the girls who frequent 5th and K are homeless," says Budd. "That's one of the reasons they prostitute—along with substance abuse. But it's always a matter of survival. The fact that they're estranged from their families is the starting point."

Prostitution is dangerous enough when you're several blocks down K Street, in the separate area where straight hookers find clients. But 5th and K tends to attract the sketchiest kinds of customers. "The straight female prostitutes are turning dates for $100 a whop," says Collins. "Guys know they can go over to 5th and K and get a transgender to give them what they want for little if anything. These girls are desperate, and they don't have pimps to keep them from getting beaten and make sure they get paid OK— or even get paid at all. Sometimes they'll give you $20, get what they want, then beat you and take the $20 back."

Budd and Collins have no end of horror stories from their time on the streets. Budd has especially vivid memories of a gang in the 1980s whose idea of fun was "to catch you, beat you, snatch your wig and knock you out." Now, she says, it's even worse. "5th and K is just rampant for assaults. I think guys feel like, 'Man, I'm going to go out and beat me up a faggot tonight, one of them ones dressed in women's clothes.'" As in most major urban areas, such hate criminals know exactly where to find their victims.

Budd believes the Washington police's GLLU, recently given an award by Transgender Health Empowerment, may have begun to make a dent in the violence. "They make a lot of drive-throughs in that area, and it's probably decreased the amount of crimes that happen right there." But not necessarily the crimes that happen when "girls" are picked up and driven away.

Even with the GLLU putting a kinder face on the police force, activists and cops agree that almost none of the violence that happens to transgendered women on the stroll—or elsewhere—is ever reported. Why? The main reason is that Washington—like San Francisco, Houston, Philadelphia, New York and every other big city with a large transgender population—has a history of police abuse that everybody in its transgender community can recite, chapter and verse.

"Cops?" Collins says. "You don't even want to get me started on that."

❧ 'Her Life Didn't Count'

Washington's seminal bad-cop moment happened almost exactly seven years before the double murders of Stephanie Thomas and Ukea Davis—on the very same street corner where the teenagers met their deaths.

On the morning of Aug. 7, 1995, a car accident left 24-year-old passenger Tyra Hunter bleeding profusely on the corner of 50th and C. Hunter, who had been on her way to work as a hairdresser, was pulled out of the car by bystanders before firefighters and Emergency Medical Service workers arrived at the scene. Eyewitness Catherine Poole told investigators that Hunter was conscious and "starting to complain of pain" when the rescuers arrived.

"[T]he ambulance person that was treating [Hunter] said to her that 'Everything is going to be all right, honey,'" Poole continued. "At that point, she started to urinate on herself. The ambulance person started to cut the pants legs on the jeans. . . . [H]e started cutting up the leg and suddenly stopped, and jumped back when he found out that she was a man and said, 'This bitch ain't no girl . . . it's a nigger, he's got a dick.'" Two other witnesses corroborated the slur, and backed Poole's assertion that the emergency service workers and firefighters stopped treating Hunter for upwards of five minutes while "laughing and telling jokes" about her.

Two hours later, Hunter died of blunt trauma at D.C. General Hospital—after also being denied treatment by a doctor. No firefighters, emergency or hospital personnel were disciplined, and the city refused to take responsibility for the death, saying that Hunter was too seriously injured to survive. But when Hunter's mother sued the city, a jury found that Hunter's civil rights had been violated at the accident scene, and that her death had likely been caused by medical negligence. (Experts testified that with proper treatment, she had an 86% chance of surviving.) After the jury awarded Margie Hunter $2.9 million in damages, the city further alienated its transgendered residents by appealing the decision—ultimately agreeing to a $1.75 million settlement.

The message of Hunter's mistreatment was clear, wrote local activist Richard Rosendall: "She was transgender, and her life didn't count."

Transgender activists say law enforcement personnel have been sending that message for years. When she was a youngster on the streets, says Toni Collins, "You'd be surprised how many policemen I had sex with. They'd say, 'You do it with me, or I'm going to arrest you for prostitution.' Then they'd tell me to go home and I better not tell anybody."

She did as ordered. "Who would you tell?" she asks.

Sgt. Brett Parson, the GLLU chief, acknowledges the "violent history" between transgendered people and law enforcement. But he doesn't agree that police are more biased against sexual and gender minorities than the average population. Nor does Gary Shapiro, a hate crime expert with New York's Nassau County Police Department. "More and more, every day, there's pressure on officers to be knowledgeable and sensitive—to racial differences, language differences, sexual differences," Shapiro says. Still, he acknowledges that the transgender community's perception of cops as enemies is "understandable. Especially in that area, we've still got a long way to go."

Parson knows it's a long haul. His unit has won the trust of Washington's transgender activists, but it's a tougher challenge on 5th and K. "I talked to a transgender girl last night and she says, 'By the way, where were you last week when I got beat up?' I said, 'I don't know—but why didn't you call me?' She said, 'Why would I call you guys? You're not going to do anything.' I haven't gotten through to her yet that we *will* do something. Then a lot of times when someone gets killed, we'll find out they've been assaulted a lot."

It's always possible that the killers were among those who'd been committing assaults. But as long as the assaults go unreported—as long as transgendered women feel like they can't trust the cops—there's no way of knowing whether lives like Emonie Spaulding's or Bella Evangelista's might have been spared.

◉ Dreams and Nightmares

These days, most people understand that hate crimes are message crimes. Most people know that when a transgendered person is victimized, it doesn't just affect her friends and family—it terrifies a whole community of people who can't help feeling they might be next. But most people, luckily, don't know what it feels like to be on the receiving end of such a message.

Ruby Bracamonte is not so lucky. On a bright cold day in early November, she sits wrapped up in a baby-blue sweatshirt, recalling in a whispery voice how she heard the news that one of her closest friends, Bella Evangelista, had been murdered. In a grim bit of irony, Bracamonte was with her Latina transgender support group at a local community center on Aug. 16. The group was busy with an ongoing project: documenting, in words and images, the lives of transgendered Latinas in the U.S.

"The next thing we know, a police officer walks in. He's like, 'I'm sorry, but we have this body we found and we need somebody to recognize it.'

There was silence. He passed around a picture of what had happened to her. And that's how we found out. That picture is still in my head."

Before Evangelista's killing, transgendered Latinas in Washington had hoped that they might evade the worst of the violence, since the previous murder victims had all been African American. "For a lot of years, a lot of us have been very open," Bracamonte says. "It seemed OK. We have been mostly accepted in Hispanic neighborhoods. We may be called names, but we don't get killed. That's what we thought. Boy, have we learned."

Bracamonte, who in the early 1990s began transitioning into living as a woman with a group of friends that included Evangelista, has learned more than most. For years, Bracamonte, who has a steady job and a nice apartment, had been keeping her door open to down-and-out transgendered friends. When her friend was killed, her private activism went public, as she became the media's favorite spokesperson for Washington's transgendered Latinas. The notoriety transformed her cell phone into an unofficial hotline.

"In the last two weeks, I've gotten four calls. One girl called because her roommate had been gone for 10 days. We still don't know what happened. People just disappear. Then last weekend, my roommate called—her teeth had been knocked out. Another friend of mine left school and went to a party. When she was on her way home, another attack. Another friend of mine was in Adams-Morgan, a very nice neighborhood, and got jumped while waiting in line for a restaurant. They kicked the hell out of him, sent him to the hospital. Why?"

Sometimes, Bracamonte can't help feeling like she's found too many friends. "Last week, I broke. It becomes very painful. When you see it every day, when you see it all the time, you think, 'What do I do? What do I do?'"

To fend off that feeling of helplessness, Bracamonte is making plans. Somehow, someway, she's determined to open a house for her homeless sisters, complete with a thrift store and a restaurant where they can earn their keep. "They can come and work and pay for their own little room. They can have a shower. That's my dream."

But lately it's mostly been nightmares.

"This is a human rights issue," Bracamonte says. "This is an issue that is affecting humans. It doesn't matter how people feel about others; they are human beings. But many of our young people are not being treated like humans.

"It doesn't just take place here," she says, her voice so soft it's hard to make out over the insistent chirping of her phone. "It's everywhere. It's the whole nation. But nobody wants to hear it."

Bracamonte has been fighting off tears, but she loses the battle when she thinks about what today's voicemail messages might say. "What happened to Bella, it's going to happen again," she says. "I guess I need to just face it."

Questions

1. What does it mean to be transgender?

2. Why is Washington, D.C. a destination of choice for transgendered people on the East Coast?

3. Explain why it is difficult to prove that anti-transgender murders are hate crimes.

4. What has made transgendered people such targets of crime?

5. Come up with at least three ideas about how to stem the violence that is directed toward transgendered people. What is the likelihood that these ideas could be implemented in your community?

Fearful Others: Transsexual Discourses and the Construction of Female-Bodied Transpeople

JASON CROMWELL

Jason Cromwell's Transmen and FTMs: Identities, Bodies, Genders, and Sexualities *is one of the few books that focuses on the experiences of female-bodied transpeople—that is, individuals who were assigned to the female sex category at birth but who live their social lives as another gender. In this excerpt, Cromwell examines the distance between medical and psychological discourse, which has often ignored female-bodied transpeople, and the experiences of those people. While we as a society are just beginning to deal publicly with individuals who want to change their sex/gender, people who would prefer not to be categorized according to the existing dichotomous possibilities are defined as a threat. Transmen and FTMs (as well as transwomen and MTFs) force us to reconsider our assumption that genitals and gender are synonymous.*

To date the literature reflects the male-female discrepancy in the sex ratio of this population and consequently a much greater body of information is available on male-to-female transsexuals.

—Bolin 1988:3[1]

(I will consider female-to-male transsexuals in another paper).

—Stone 1991:284

Transvestism in women . . . is so rare it is almost nonexistent.

—Stoller 1982:99

[F]emale-to-male transsexuals . . . are a relatively homogenous group.

—Steiner, ed. 1985:3

*T*hese comments are only a few examples of the marginal treatment of female-to-male transsexuals and female transvestites.[2] Perhaps, at least in the vast literature concerning transsexuals, transvestites, and gender diversity in general, Raymond is correct in her estimation that FTMs/transmen are "tokens" designed to validate transsexualism as a human phenomenon (1994 [1979]:xxi). Often women, children, racial and ethnic minorities, gender, and sexual minorities are constructed as others by those in power. Individuals become a group or a class of people, as in all women are . . . , children are . . . , and certain races are . . .

Like the epigraphs for this chapter, such statements deny the lived experiences of individuals as a result of discourses that construct them. Transvestism and transsexualism are constructed from a male perspective and are most often about male gender diversity. Analogous to early sexologists' construction of female sexuality in general and lesbianism in particular, female gender diversity has been viewed from a male perspective. But as women, whether feminists or not, have illustrated, the constructed discourses create a paradox "of a being that is at once captive and absent in discourse, constantly spoken of but itself inaudible or inexpressible, displayed as spectacle and still unrepresented or unrepresentable, invisible yet constituted as the object and the guarantee of vision; a being whose existence and specificity are simultaneously asserted and denied, negated and controlled" (De Lauretis 1990:115). Although De Lauretis addresses the "nonbeing of woman," her statement applies to the paradox of female gender diversity.

❧ *Incoherent Subjects*

Dichotomizing pathologizes (and pathology dichotomizes).

—Blacking 1977:14

Smith-Rosenberg comprehends that "the fearful project onto the bodies of those they have named social misfits their own desire for social control" (1989:103). Thus, in the early nineteenth century a female individual who cross-dressed to reject the traditional female role would be constructed by sexologists as an "unstable, incoherent subject, the embodiment of disorder, the fearful Other" (110). That early studies focused on behaviors and physical appearances (113) is germane to transsexual discourses.

Although Smith-Rosenberg's discussion is limited to a specific historical period in Western culture, many still fear those who do not conform to the sex and gender order. Fearful others are feared precisely because observers do not have control over the signs of sex and gender. Without being aware of it, observers can be "fooled" by outward signs. Although some individuals are comfortable with ambiguity and even play with it, nonconformity (being a fearful other) frequently has its costs. One is ridicule. Another, extreme and brutal, is violence or even murder, as in the case of Brandon Teena (née Teena Brandon), who was viciously raped by the two men who eventually murdered him and two of his friends (Konigsberg 1995; Minkowitz 1994; "Woman Who Cross-Dressed Found Dead" 1994).

Although an individual may perceive of himself as a man, observers may perceive of him as a lesbian; social identity and personal identity may not match. Some men and women fear lesbians because they are a threat to both the heterosexual order and gender norms. Most people link behavior with sexual identity. Social norms insist that men are males who have masculine behaviors and a sexual preference for women and women are females who have feminine behaviors and a sexual preference for men (Irvine 1990:231).

Gay men, lesbians, transvestites, transsexuals, and others who live in "gender borderlands" challenge the traditional concepts of man, woman, masculinity, and femininity. In doing so, they become fearful others.[3] Because they challenge traditional concepts, often attempts are made to eliminate them through internalized fear of "being different, being other, and therefore lesser, therefore sub-human, in-human, non-human" (Anzaldúa 1987:18).

One way in which to brand a category of people as less than human is to label those who compose it as failures. FTMs and transmen are often represented in the media as well as in transsexual discourses as "failed heterosexuals" (Cahn 1993:343) or as failed butch lesbians (Person and Ovesey 1974:6; Stoller 1973:387; Stoller 1985:15). They are also portrayed as failed women who because of these presumably failed statuses are "want-to-be men." They are branded as failed heterosexuals because in social presentation, dress, talk, and behavior in what is constructed as the purview of men they are supposedly uninterested in and not attracted to nontransgendered males (that is, they are failed women). They are branded failed butch lesbians because they take on too much masculinity. In doing that they threaten the femaleness of lesbian identities. On both heterosexual and lesbian fronts, female-bodied men violate "gender as well as sexual codes" (Cahn 1993:350). By asserting their masculine identities and refusing to accept the inherent femaleness of their bodies as equal to femininity, they become lesbians by heterosexual (gender and sexual) codes and men by lesbian gender codes.

Like gay men and lesbians, transpeople, regardless of their particular identities, who do not affirm the primary categories of gender are feared and consequently ignored, disavowed, discounted, discredited, and frequently accused of not being a true person. In order to be treated as real they must be cured and thus reaffirm the primary sex and gender categories. When the mind does not agree with the primacy of the body, a discourse must be constructed for the "wrong body."

❧ The Construction of the Wrong Body

> What gives psychiatry the right to define transsexuality, to set the diagnostic criteria to which transsexuals must respond.
>
> —Namaste 1994:12

In the late 1890s homosexuals were in the wrong body—at least their souls were confined in the wrong body: *Anima muliebris viruli corpore inclusa* [a feminine soul confined by a masculine body] (Ulrichs 1975 [1898], cited in Kennedy 1981:106). Men in female bodies. Women in male bodies. In the early 1950s transsexuals became trapped in the wrong bodies.[4] As sexologists (in particular Krafft-Ebing, de Savitsch, and Gutheil) delineated differences among categories of homosexuals, it became clear that some individuals were insistent about being women in male bodies and men in female bodies (cf. Heidenreich 1997:268–74; see also Rosario 1994).

One of the paradoxes of transsexual discourse is the notion of having a wrong body. Despite Money's claim that the concept of being trapped in the wrong body was "adopted by transsexuals as their own" (1990:xiv), the idea has been imposed upon transpeople by those who control access to medical technologies and have controlled discourses about transpeople. Some individuals may believe or may come to believe that they are in the wrong body or at least use language that imparts the same meaning. As one transsexual told me in a personal communication, "When a man *is a man in every way* [except] the lower part of his body, *he is trapped,* and I mean *trapped,* in a woman's body" (emphasis in the original). For many transsexuals, once the wrong body has been surgically altered they no longer consider themselves to be transsexual.

> About the question of whether or not I consider myself a transsexual. I don't but . . . that is what I would be classified as by a health professional. (Paul T.)

> I was a transsexual. Now I'm just a man. (James E.)

Their wrong body (a biophysical entity of sex), now "corrected," becomes a gendered body of woman or man. Such individuals are insisting on the right to declare a gender, thus overruling and subverting society's biological designation of sex.

In the preceding paragraphs I emphasized two phrases: wrong body and surgically altered. My intent is twofold: to problematize the definition that has come to embody the transsexual syndrome (i.e., the "wrong body," Stone 1991:297) and to problematize the concept of surgical correction.

For whom is the body wrong and for whom is the surgery corrective?[5] As Stone notes, "In pursuit of differential diagnosis a question sometimes asked of a prospective transsexual is 'Suppose that you could be a man [or woman] in every way except for your genitals; would you be content?' There are several possible answers, but only one is clinically correct" (297). The correct answer, of course, is "No, I would not be content." To answer yes or maybe is to be rendered a diagnosis—at best of nontranssexual, at worst of pathology. Shapiro comments that "transsexuals' fixation on having the right genitals is *clearly less pathological* than if they were to insist that they are *women with penises* or *men with vaginas*" (260, emphasis added).[6]

To conceive of oneself as either a woman with a penis or a man with a vagina is considered pathological because "under the binary phallocratic founding myth by which Western bodies and subjects are authorized, only one body per gendered subject is 'right.' All other bodies are wrong" (Stone 1991:297). According to the imposed order one can only be one or the other, not both and certainly not neither, regardless of choice. Yet the order does not prevent individuals from challenging, and thus subverting, it. Jack Watson observes, "If I didn't have the label transsexual I'd probably think of myself as a man with a female body. I belong to neither sex, yet I'm both: I have a beard and a deep voice, I've had a mastectomy but I still have a vagina. I don't have a problem with that, neither does my wife, but society does."

The phrase *wrong body* inadequately describes the feeling that one's body is not a part of one's self. The body's experience is incongruent with the mind's. The insider within the body does not recognize the outside of the body as belonging. Attempts to describe this phenomenon, because of the limitations of language, seemingly lead back to the concept of wrong body. "Wrong body" connotes surface understanding rather than depth of feeling. Using a language that cannot accurately hear or adequately interpret the individual experience of transness results in the discourse of the wrong body.

In part, the answer to the question of for whom the body is wrong and for whom the surgery is corrective is embedded in the sex and gender ideology of what constitutes femaleness and maleness (or woman and man) within Western societies. Furthermore, the concept of wrong body may be appropriate for male-to-female transsexuals if for no other reason than the fact that hormones do not greatly modify male physiology, which is not the case for female-bodied transpeople. Many transmen and FTMs, however, do not identify with this terminology. Many are dissatisfied with having breasts and menstruating, neither of which accounts for the entire body.

The majority of FTMs and transmen do not have gender dysphoria; it is the rare FTM or transman who does not know from an early age what his gender identity is. What many experience, however, is body-part dysphoria, which focuses on elements such as breasts and menstruation that are quintessentially female. Those who do talk about having breasts do so with feelings that range from revulsion and denial to matter-of-fact acceptance. Yet I have never met an FTM or transman who did not want chest surgery. Because breasts are the primary sign of female woman and, by implication, femininity, to reject them acknowledges that fact (Money and Brennan 1968:496). If breasts were defined as male, transmen and FTMs would not be dysphoric about them or have them removed. Because breasts are a sign of femininity, however, chest reconstructions are requested.

Breasts are hated more than genitals, which the majority of people in one's life do not see. Props fill in for male genitalia. Ironically, transmen and FTMs are accused of imitating men when in fact they are improvising and using the available language to communicate personal identities on a social level. More ironically, they are accused of doing so unconsciously. They intentionally communicate the signs of masculinity and maleness, however, because those signs demonstrate their personal social identity. They reject the fact that having breasts and female genitals mandates being women and feminine. They also reject that female equals woman equals feminine. Instead, they are masculine, which equals men, which equals male (at the social level) in spite of having the signs (female genitals, breasts, and menstruation) that dictate being female. Many transmen see their bodies as containers but feel they are not confined to their bodies in expressing their beings.

❧ What Is a Transsexual?

What gives critics . . . the right to represent transgender, with virtually no understanding of transgender specificity?

—Namaste 1994:12

Many seem unable to grasp the concept that transpeople have not identified with their bodies or have done so only superficially. It seems unfathomable to them that an individual can be born with one body and identify as a person who has a different body; that is, a person born with a female body can identify as a man or vice versa. "Sure I was born female," Dave agrees. "But I don't know what it is to be a woman, or for that matter, what it is to be a girl. While it's true I was raised female, I don't know what it *is* to be female. I practiced and put on a face that the world saw as being female. But locked inside was a child (I say child, because there is no concrete image of either a boy or a girl), who knew that irrespective of how I was treated I was *not* what everyone thought" (emphasis in the original).

It is also difficult for many to understand that individuals can identify as men with vaginas or women with penises: "I consider myself a *man* (social gender)," Charles says, "who happens to be *female* (biological sex)" (emphasis in the original).[7]

Garber asks, "But what *is* a transsexual? Is he or she a member of one sex 'trapped' in the other's body? Or someone who has taken hormones and undergone other somatic changes to more closely resemble the gender into which he (or she) was not born? More pertinent to this inquiry, does a transsexual *change subjects*? Or just bodies—or body parts?" (1989:151, emphasis in the original). These are biological-determinist questions that equate gender with genitals. In particular they are essentialist in that they express "a belief in the real, true essence of things, the invariable and fixed properties which define the 'whatness' of a given entity" (Fuss 1989:xi).

Although Garber argues that transvestites and transsexuals essentialize their genitalia (1989:143), she essentializes their entire being and imposes the belief that men are born with male bodies and women are born with female bodies. Underlying Garber's question of whether transsexuals change is a mistaken belief that they identify as either a man or a woman in the first place. "I've been accused of 'betraying womanhood,'" relates Sean. "How can I betray something I've never identified with?"

For most female-bodied transpeople there is no shift from conceiving of oneself as female to as a man or to a variation on the theme. What needs to be understood is that the individual may have never identified as a woman but rather may have always identified as a man or as something else. In spite of messages from family, peers, and society in general, and in spite of biological evidence (in particular, genitalia) to the contrary, most female-bodied transpeople have always had the self-concept of being male and/or man, although the degree varies. The self-image (and belief) of many is that they are boys who will grow up to be men. As I have written elsewhere, "When I was young I did not think of my body and my mind as belonging to two very different people. My name, if shortened (which I preferred) could be androgynous. It was easy to believe that I was as I saw myself. But when I reached puberty the girl-turning-woman caught up with my image of the boy-turning-man" (Taylor and Taylor 1983:13).[8]

What shifts once transition is initiated is social identity, that is, how others perceive these individuals. In spite of transsexual discourses to the contrary, surgery is not the ultimate destination for many. Some elect not to have it for reasons of health or finance or even because the results are viewed as less than adequate if not outright horrific. They choose to live instead as men with vaginas. "I am able to pass as a male 98 percent of the time just as I am," David Hughes told me. "I am 6 foot, 150 pounds, have a deep baritone voice, look and pass as male. With all of this in my favor, I see no reason at this time to invest money and health issues into hormones and surgery. If I could change my name legally, it would probably be all that I would need to live out my life as male. Perhaps if treatment were safer and cheaper, I would invest in transition as an option."

☻ The Construction of Female-to-Male Transsexualism

> Discourse becomes oppressive when it requires that the speaking subject, in order to speak, participate in the very terms of that oppression.
>
> —Butler 1990:16

The discourses that have constructed transvestism and transsexualism have two elements: a disproportion of male-to-female transsexuals to female-to-male transsexuals and a nonexistence of female transvestites. The answer to how these discourses have become "truths" is rooted in the definitions of transvestism and transsexualism as well as a sex and gender ideology whose mechanisms attempt to "cure" male-bodied transpeople and ignore those who are female-bodied.

> The essential features of the disorder [transsexualism] are stated to be a persistent sense of discomfort and inappropriateness about one's anatomic sex and a persistent wish to be rid of one's genitals and to live as a member of the other sex ([American Psychiatric Association] 1980, pp. 261–62).

> The preceding definition is all one really needs to approach the literature on female-to-male transsexuals, who are a relatively homogeneous group. Male gender patients, on the other hand, present with a wide range of clinical signs and symptoms, and it is mainly in regard to gender-disturbed males that authors vary in their terminology. (Steiner, Blanchard, and Zucker, 1985:3)

It is because FTMs and transmen are treated by medico-psychological practitioners as a homogeneous group that there appears to be disproportion in numbers. By assuming that transmen and FTMs are homogeneous, clinics are able to ignore and disregard the wide range of signs that individuals may exhibit. Yet that is not the only reason there appears to be a prevalence of MTFs/transwomen over FTMs/transmen. Other contributing influences are the focus of most researchers on the so-called sexual dysfunction of men; transmen's and FTMs' ability to pass more easily; their awareness of the reality of the quality of genital surgeries and frequent rejection of them; and the fact that transmen and FTMs have primarily sought care from private physicians and therapists.[9]

Furthermore, while many clinics insisted on phalloplasty as a necessary part of the "rehabilitative" process (Dushoff 1973:203), other clinics have excluded FTMs and transmen "categorically because of the greater complexity in surgical technique" (Ehrhardt, Grisanti, and McCauley 1979). It is the clinics and hospitals affiliated with universities that have kept close account of the numbers. If fewer transmen and FTMs go to these types of centers, then many are left uncounted. Therefore, several factors go into the counting, including who goes to the research facilities and/or clinics; whether phalloplasty is required or even available; what transmen and FTMs expect, especially regarding surgical outcomes; and what clinicians expect concerning who qualifies as an FTM/transman.[10]

In what ways are transmen and FTMs constructed to be a homogeneous group? Although Steiner does not clearly define what is meant by a "homogeneous group," a careful reading of the medico-psychological literature points to three stereotypes concerning female-bodied transpeople, specifically FTMs/transmen: androgyny, particularly in behavior; heterosexual object choices; and an obsession with having penises.[11] Minh-ha asserts that "the stereotype is not a simplification because it is a false representation of a given reality. It is a simplification because it is an arrested, fixated form of representation" (1991:163). Therefore, although some female-bodied transpeople may have fit into these stereotypes, others have been required to conform to the arrested and fixated ideas put forth by medico-psychological practitioners.

𝒯he 𝒜ndrogyny 𝒮tereotype

FTMs/transmen are more androgynous than other groups of men. They are also more flexible in their behaviors and comfortable expressing a range of behaviors (Fleming, MacGowan, and Salt 1984:52). Transmen/FTMs "do not adhere strongly to stereotypically masculine roles [nor do they] reject stereotypically feminine characteristics. . . . [they] incorporate aspects of their former roles into their new roles and do not totally reject them" (Fleming, MacGowan, and Salt 1984:56). "I feel all men and women (whether genetic or transsexual) have elements or aspects of both, male and female," Dave says. "I have feminine aspects which do NOT embarrass me at all!" Although some FTMs are flexible and have a large repertoire of behaviors, others strongly adhere to masculine stereotypes. "I have known since age fourteen that I was masculine except biological[ly]," recalls Jack Hyde. "For almost fifteen years I have dressed masculine and lived masculine. I look very masculine. Some people probably consider me very macho, you know, a tough guy. They're right. I certainly dress the part, and most of the time I act it."

Transmen and FTMs do not always rigidly adhere to stereotypes. Consequently, they challenge the prevailing paradigm by bringing into question what it means to be a man or masculine. Many are more fluid in their identifications with the signs or props of masculinity and maleness. All men, transgendered or not, use props and display signs of their maleness. Whether wearing business suits and power ties, more casual attire, or more casual clothing still, working-class, redneck, cowboys, and even drunks on the street signal their masculinity. Many social behaviors indicate how they do so. Are they macho or do they exhibit new age sensitivity? Does the person consider himself to be a virile womanizer, a liberated man, Mr. Nice Guy, an average Joe, a red-blooded Marlboro Man, or a man among men. The difference is that transmen and FTMs have additional props and most are more consciously aware of the constructedness of masculinity and manhood. Using props, however, often brands individuals as "fake" men, as does being flexible and comfortable in expressing a wide range of masculine behaviors.

The Heterosexuality Stereotype

FTMs and transmen "form stable and enduring intimate sexual relationships with biological women. These female-to-male transsexuals and their partners considered their relationships heterosexual" (Fleming, MacGowan, and Costos 1985:47–48). From childhood, transmen and FTMs are purportedly attracted only to "feminine females" (Benjamin 1964:467; Stoller 1972:48, 1975:224). But not all FTMs and transmen agree, even when married to or partnered with women. "I'd have to say my sexuality shifts—mostly I identify as bisexual—sometimes I think of myself as a gay married man—but I never think of myself as straight," observes Jack Watson.

Repeatedly the medico-psychological literature, and consequently the majority of practitioners, has insisted that transmen and FTMs are attracted only to feminine women and are "repelled by the idea of sexual relations with males" (Stoller 1973:386). But some individuals contradict the heterosexual stereotype. "What I really want is a sexual relationship with a gay man, as a gay man. One clinic told me that I could not possibly live as a gay man since gay men were primarily interested in large penises and were not sexually aroused when shown photos of female-to-male surgeries" (Sullivan 1989:69–70).

While the biases of medico-psychological practitioners toward heterosexuality is being challenged by transsexuals and some practitioners, homophobia still prevails (Bockting 1987; Coleman and Bockting 1988; Pauly n.d.). It is of note that transsexual discourses have stated that FTMs and transmen "deny that they are homosexual and avoid homosexual women, except occasionally as nonsexual acquaintances" (Stoller 1982:48). Yet some FTMs do live as lesbians before living as men (chapter 3). "I can't remember *ever* being happy about being female," a correspondent told me in a personal communication. "I can't remember being happy but for two years that I was involved in a homosexual relationship. That happiness was not in the sexual aspect, but of being the 'man' and of being with people who accepted me as I was. I *don't* consider myself gay. I only consider myself 'straight' with a woman's body structure." Steiner, too, states that "all transsexual biological females are homosexual in erotic object choice" (1985:353). In less confusing words, the erotic choices of all transmen and FTMs are said to be women.

That position has long existed within medico-psychological discourses and is part of practitioners' "incorrigible beliefs" (Devor 1989:2). De Savitsch has acknowledged that both males and females "desire to change sex," but for females the primary motivation to do so is "homosexual libido" (1958:86). Benjamin reports that transmen's and FTMs' "love objects" are feminine women and that they "deny being homosexual" (1965:467). Early in his career Stoller stated, "Female [-to-male] transsexualism strikes me as a form of homosexuality more than a distinct condition" (1973:387). Similarly, Pauly has observed that "by definition, all female [-to-male] transsexuals are homosexual, in that these biological females who psychologically reject their femaleness and assume a masculine role are interested in and at one point become involved with females as sexual partners" (1974a:502). Devor (1997) likewise insists that FTMs and transmen, regardless of personal and social identities, have homosexual relationships with women.

Equating FTMs' and transmen's relationships with women as homosexual is a biological-determinist argument. If an individual does not self-identify as a man and chooses women as sexual partners, then she would indeed have a homosexual erotic choice. When an individual self-identifies as a man, however, and chooses women as sexual partners, then his erotic choice is heterosexual. The insistence that transmen and FTMs are homosexual because they are attracted to women is a component of the body-equals-sex-equals-gender formula and demonstrates the inflexibility of that rigid equation.

Nonetheless, it is a compelling formula. Pauly, for example, also states that the "failure to discriminate between gender and the sexual aspects of this condition is a source of great confusion" (1974a:502). "In distinguishing these two conditions," he adds, "the lesbian would *never* request that her breasts or genitalia be removed surgically, any more than the heterosexual individual would permit this. Obviously, one is not going to sacrifice organs which are a source of pleasure and stimulation" (504).[12]

How then can transmen and FTMs "by definition" be homosexual? Pauly fails to realize just how enmeshed he is and does not discriminate between lesbians and FTMs/transmen or between gender identity and sexual identity when he discusses the sexual identity of FTMs/transmen. Thus, he (along with Steiner, Stoller, Money, Devor, and others) views FTMs/transmen relationships with females as homosexual instead of heterosexual.

Elsewhere, however, Pauly has concluded that "the statement that all female-to-male transsexuals are homosexuals in their sexual preference can no longer be made" (1998:243). He refers to FTMs and transmen who have relationships with women as "heterogenderal" and those who have relationships with men as "homogenderal" (244), terms similar to what Devor refers to as "gendered sexuality," that is, the "interactions of sex and gender with sexuality" (1977:xxv–xxvi). She uses the terms *bisexual, homosexual,* and *heterosexual* "when considering persons' bodies" and *bi, gay, lesbian,* and *straight* "when considering their genders" (xxvi), a schema that makes it "possible to speak with accuracy and without contradiction about a cross-living transsexual man who is sexually attracted to female women as both homosexual and straight." Such a plan, however, does not take into consideration how a person feels and self-identifies, thus it neither speaks with accuracy nor ends confusion. The arguments are further examples of essentializing the body and imposing a worldview on others.

It would be much less confusing and far more respectful if the "experts" would listen to transpeople and attempt to move beyond the reification of bodies in order to understand their perspective. They are not "cross-living" but rather living. Those who have relationships with and are attracted to women are heterosexually identified; those who have a "homosexual preference" (Pauly 1974a:501) are attracted to and have sexual relationships with men. Some who have relationships with and are attracted to both men and women are bisexually identified. That simple scheme is based on identities rather than bodies. In the long run, sexual orientation matters only to those who are in relationships, regardless of whether the individuals identify as gay, lesbian, bi, straight, homosexual, heterosexual, or bisexual.

The Obsession with Having Penises Stereotype

According to transsexual discourses, FTMs and transmen are obsessed with ridding themselves of breasts and internal female organs and "with the idea of having a penis" (Lothstein 1983:13; cf. Steiner 1985:353). Numerous studies have documented that almost all transmen and FTMs elect to have chest reconstruction and that the majority have hysterectomies (Fleming, Costos, and MacGowan 1984:585; Fleming, MacGowan, and Costos 1985:49). Although they wish to be rid of their breasts, it is the rare individual who becomes obsessed with doing so. Likewise, the primary motivation for removing internal female organs (after testosterone has caused menses to cease) is to prevent potential disease. The majority of transmen and FTMs ignore their breasts until they are able to obtain chest surgery, and they deal with menses matter-of-factly before experiencing the effects of testosterone.

The "absence of the penis [is] loathsome" and the "ultimate goal is the attainment of a functional penis" (Krueger 1983:77; Pauly 1974b:521). As I was informed in a personal communication, "I am content with my choice to change and if I had to do it all again—I certainly would. But I don't feel whole because of my lack of 'genitals' and don't feel comfortable even thinking of initiating sex with someone." Yet Alex W. observed, "When you ask me, if I am a transsexual I have to pause—because although I take hormones, have had a mastectomy and a hysterectomy—I don't intend to have any more surgery. I'm comfortable and happy where I am. I present as a man in my life but I have no problem with having a vagina."

Only a few clinicians have recognized that all FTMs and transmen are not obsessed with attaining a penis. As early as 1964, for example, Benjamin realized that phalloplasty was "too complicated an undertaking and [FTMs and transmen] rarely insist upon it" (467). Stoller, too, noted, "Most do not insist on an *artificial* penis—*but only* because they are told by the urologists that it is not possible to make a *real-appearing* penis that can be urinated through or has erectile capacity" (1973:387, emphases added). Surgery is a possibility for some but by no means a necessity or obsession. "I'm living full-time as a man now," David Hughes has said. "I feel comfortable at the stage I'm at. Depending on finances, priorities, and the degree of medical risk I'm willing to take once, and if, I can afford these further procedures [hysterectomy and genital surgery] I will decide whether or not to have them done; they are not necessary at this point, as I see it."

❧ *C*hallenging *S*urgical *N*ecessity

> Transsexuals are not wholly male or female either before or after transition.
>
> —Green 1994b:6

One challenge to transsexual discourses is the necessity of genital surgeries. One contributing factor of this challenge is that no significant changes have been made or accomplished in the quality, functionality, or aesthetics of genital surgeries since the 1960s, despite surgeons' claims to the contrary. Some FTMs/transmen call the results of phalloplastic surgeries "frankendicks," a term that conjures up an image of foreign parts attached to one's body, with resultant scarring and ugliness. Many feel that the term is an apt descriptor for the results of most phalloplasties.[13]

At one time, surgeons, even in the early 1990s, considered phalloplasty to be the only procedure adequate to meet the needs of FTMs and transmen. For example, Noe and Birdsell stated, "Hypertrophy [enlargement] of the clitoris by means of hormonal therapy has not been accepted as an adequate substitute for a penis" (1975:153), and a prominent genital surgeon declared during a 1991 conference that he did not do "clitoral free-ups [metoidioplasties] because, what's the point? It certainly doesn't provide an adequate penis."[14] Of course, "adequate" is, in this formulation, related to the ability to penetrate one's partner during intercourse, an activity for which most surgeons would consider metoidioplasties inadequate.

The surgeon has since changed his mind and now performs metoidioplasties because FTMs/transmen continue to request them over phalloplasties. But who should determine what is adequate, FTMs/transmen or their surgeons? In the surgeon's case the answer was the clients, even though metoidioplasties are still not adequate in his personal opinion.[15] Transmen and FTMs who are considering genital surgeries, for the most part, do choose metoidioplasty. For many, the surgery is more than adequate; for many others, genital surgery is unnecessary because their genitalia are already fully functional.

At least some FTMs and transmen dislike their genitalia and neither look at them nor touch them except as necessary for hygiene. A few hate them. The majority have felt hate for their genitals at some point in life. Many, however, have come to terms with having female genitalia. Some few have even come to the point of loving them.

It is a very rare transman or FTM who has never wished he could have a large erection or that he did not have to use props (e.g., dildoes and urinary devices). But those desires are not obsessive and no different than those other people hold deeply. Every FTM/transman measures the costs of genital surgery. Some go into phalloplastic surgery knowing the risks on a realistic basis. Too many, however, have gone into it with an attitude that they are "the exception" and nothing will go wrong (Kincaid 1995:8–11; Thompson 1995). It is likely that many who do elect phalloplasty regret having done so and may not be willing to admit their mistake, although that is only conjecture because no FTMs/transmen who were several years postphalloplasty agreed to talk with me. A rare few would do it again at all costs and risks, even after experiencing a failed phalloplasty (Kincaid 1995:11).

Some few FTMs/transmen feel they will never become "real" men unless they have phalloplastic surgery (Anonymous 1995:7; Thompson 1995). It is they who have given medico-psychological practitioners the impression that all FTMs/transmen are obsessed with having penises, which is not the case at all. As Kory states, "No one thinks to ask 'why' someone is having surgery. But everyone questions 'why' I chose not to have it. I chose not to have surgery because of the costs both physically and financially. Mostly physically, though. What it does to your body, the scars, the lack of feeling, the lack of function. I think even if surgery could make my body over and it would feel and function as a male's body does, I wouldn't do it. I would lose what I've become, I would be someone different than I am and I like who I am."

It is this sense of being proud of what one has done in life and of having proven wrong the idea that men cannot be men without male genitalia (as well as the less than normal results of phalloplasties) that has led many transmen and FTMs to reject phalloplasty and, if opting for genital surgery, choose metoidioplasty instead.

◎ Arousing the Dreadful

Like everyone else, FTMs and transmen are heterogeneous. Yet they are ignored or discounted because many do not conform to clinicians' homogeneous concept of what they should be. Garber (1989:146–47) lists a number of reasons for this: (1) gender identity clinics were set up to service males; (2) the majority of applicants are male; (3) most researchers are male, with their male bias intact; (4) social pressures ease transmen and FTMs' ability to live as men without surgery (it is considered natural or normal for women to want to be or live as men); and (5) a traditional latitude exists for men who express dysfunction. There are also deeper reasons, which Lothstein has posed as a series of questions:

> Why is there so much resistance to learning about female [-to-male] transsexualism? Is there something inherent in the female [-to-male] transsexual's quest that silences our curiosity? Does the female [-to-male] transsexual's psyche arouse something dreadful within each of us that says "hands off"? Have male researchers ignored the topic because they view a woman's desire to become a man as natural, and therefore a trivial phenomenon to investigate? Or have male researchers ignored this aspect of female sexuality, just as they have ignored other problems of female sexuality, because of their homocentrism? (1983:14)

The answer to Lothstein's last two questions is an empathic yes—and quite similar to Garber's reasons—because of male researchers' homocentrism. First, because the desire to become men is viewed as natural, female-to-male transsexualism is trivialized.[16] The degree to which FTMs and transmen can physically become men is limited. Second, because researchers have focused on males, females have been neglected in all research areas. It should come as no surprise that transmen and FTMs are neglected also.

The more telling questions are Lothstein's first three. There is resistance to learning about FTMs and transmen because their quest arouses something dreadful in male researchers' psyches. Garber pinpoints the dreadful when she states, "What lies behind some of the resistance to or neglect of the female-to-male transsexuals is, I think, a sneaking feeling that it should not be so easy to 'construct' a 'man'—which is to say, a male body" (1989:147). The body part is, in fact, easy; hormones will provide all of the secondary sex characteristics. But the "ultimate/absolute insignia of maleness, the penis" (142) is supposedly not so easy to construct. Dan C. observed, "Throughout his slide presentation every time he [the surgeon] said 'penis' he changed it to 'phallus' immediately. It was clear to me that he doesn't make penises he makes phalluses. I wouldn't let him touch me. And it's not just his attitude. Did you see the scars that he leaves?"

Although often conflated, the terms *phallus* and *penis* are used distinctly here. The phallus is a symbol of maleness, in particular male power; the penis is a physical part of the male anatomy. This distinction is reflected in the language most surgeons use, which indicates that they believe themselves to be creating a phallus rather than a penis, hence they use the terms *phalloplasty* and *neophallus* in their discourses (Steiner, ed. 1985:339) and at conferences.[17] That is, surgery can only construct a poor facsimile of a penis but never a real one. David Gilbert, a surgeon, has stated, "It's never a God-given penis, but a phallus" (cited in Denny and Schaffer 1992:27). In other words, only real men can possess real penises. "In sex reassignment surgery there remains an implicit privileging of the phallus, a sense that a 'real one' can't be made, but only born. The (predominantly male) surgeons who do such reconstructive surgery have made individual advances in technique, but the culture does not yet strongly support the construction of 'real men' by this route" (Garber 1989:149).[18]

A phallus is a symbol that represents social power. As such, it "is not the equivalent of the penis" (Vance 1980:130; Grosz 1993:105). I do not believe that surgeons think of phallus as a symbol of social power but rather as not equivalent to a penis—as a "pretended or fantasmatic unity" (Reich 1992:116).

Nevertheless, it is common knowledge among transmen and FTMs that surgeons do not create real penises. "I've said for years," Dan C. told me, "that surgeons can't and won't construct a 'real penis' simply because to do so would be a threat to their definition of what it is to be male. If female bodies can have penises made then what does being a man mean? What we need is an FTM to become a surgeon. Then the surgery will improve because he won't be threatened."

One reason that many transpeople do not have surgery is resistance to a system that dictates that one has to be either a man (with a penis) or a woman (with a vagina). "I've chosen not to have genital surgery," Paul T. says. "On the one hand, the cost is too much for the end result. On the other hand, I see not having a penis as a subversion of the notion that in order to be a man I must have one. I get great pleasure out of knowing other people assume I have one when I don't." There is also resistance to stereotypes of maleness and femaleness as well as to heterosexuality, a requirement to qualify for the surgery. "I live very successfully as a man," Paul T. comments. "Surgery just isn't a priority right now. I don't think it ever will be. But not having surgery doesn't keep me from being sexual. I enjoy sex with gay men as well as lesbians, anyone who identifies themselves as queer. I'm a queer bi-gendered person."

More and more, transsexuals do not invest in their genitalia as signifiers of womanliness or manliness. Perhaps an alternate explanation is that many individuals now recognize that genitals do not signify gender. "What most men don't realize is that having a penis isn't what makes them a man" suggests David S. Through networking and the sharing of discourses many transpeople are resisting the imposed order that dictates the necessity of being either a man or a woman. Those who choose not to give into that order find that their self-definition does not have to include society's "ultimate insignias" (e.g., Bornstein 1994). Of course, Stoller and others would argue that they are not real or true transsexuals. Many individuals, however, do not care how the dominant discourses attempt to construct them and the validity of their lives.

❧ The Construction of Female Transvestism

The authority of authoritative discourses is never absolute, always problematic.

—DiGiacomo 1992:113

Although discourses attempt to homogenize the existence of FTMs and trans-men, they also deny the existence of female transvestites. Dekker and van de Pol state that female transvestism has not existed since the end of the nine-teenth century (1989:102–3). To explain that statement, they offer the closing gap between men and women and the cultural tolerance of women wearing men's clothing. It is not clear whether their analysis is limited to their geo-graphic area. If that is not the case, however, their analysis is grossly inaccu-rate.[19] In England and the United Sates at least, the tradition has not ended but rather has been made invisible. In part, that is because sexologists have limited the definition of transvestism. A transvestite is a heterosexual male who dresses as a woman and is erotically aroused by doing so (Stoller 1975:143).

> I do not remember ever wanting to wear "girls" clothes. But my mother was in control and I had to wear what she bought. As I got older, I had more choice—or really more power to make decisions about what I would wear. I gradually added more and more men's clothes to my wardrobe. At the age of thirty, I remember taking my dresses, shoes, purses, etc. and depositing them in a dumpster. I wore women's slacks and very tailored blouses to work. Finally, at the age of about thirty-three or thirty-four, I began wearing men's clothes 100 percent of the time. I did not meet another woman like myself until just a few months ago. (personal communication)

Because Stoller considers transvestism in females to be extremely rare, he argues that an absence of eroticism in female individuals who dress as men is because they are really transsexuals (Stoller 1968:195, cited in Garber 1989:143–44).[20] Many female transvestites neither dress for erotic purposes nor consider themselves to be men or identify themselves as such (cf. Devor 1989:chs. 4, 6). "I daily wear men's clothing, but I only dress fully to pass less than once a month," says Jay P.

Although behavior is only a small part of some female transvestites' lives, for others it is significant. "When I tell people I feel more comfortable in men's clothing, I don't mean physical comfort (anyone who has ever properly worn a men's tie, knows it is not physically comfortable). When I wear men's clothing I feel a deep sense of satisfaction. I feel very right, emotionally. I feel free. I like what I see when I look at myself in the mirror" (Bernstein 1991:5). Stoller's definition excludes females, but it also excludes males (both heterosexual and homosexual) who cross-dress for reasons other than eroticism. Given those limitations, there are very few male transvestites. That fact leaves the majority of men who cross-dress with no definition or label for their behavior.

In the lay vocabulary, the term *transvestism* most often means the simple act of cross-dressing; hence, laymen sometimes refer to cross-dressing homosexual males as transvestites. Nowadays, few sexologists use the term *transvestism* to mean simply cross-dressing. Sexologists, oddly enough, have never gotten around to inventing a dignified label for cross-dressing non-transsexual homosexuals, and so are sometimes reduced to referring, in their scholarly works, to "drag queens." (Steiner 1985:5, emphasis in the original)[21]

Equating the term *transvestite* with cross-dressing is helpful, but it still focuses on males to the exclusion of females. The danger of limited definitions is that they can create confusion for women who dress as men (and vice versa). Following an appearance on the *Geraldo Show* in September 1989, for example, I received the following communication:

Recently, I saw a talk show where they were talking about having changed their sex. This isn't what I want but I don't know where else to turn. I feel so confused. When I get home from work I like to change into men's clothes. Sometimes its just jeans and t-shirt. But other times I wear jockey shorts, t-shirt, suit and tie, everything else men wear. I bind my breasts and stuff rolled up socks in my shorts. When I feel like I really look like a man I go out. I don't try to pick up anybody, male or female. I just like to go out that way. Is something wrong with me? Am I sick? Am I a transsexual?

I replied that her behavior did not mean she was a transsexual but rather that she was a cross-dresser. "I can't tell you how relieved I was to read your letter," she replied. "I've heard about and read about men who wore women's clothes but I've never heard of women wearing men's clothes." The writer is just one of many who have been confused by the lack of a definition for their behavior or confused by ambiguous or restrictive definitions.

Another danger of limited definitions of transvestism is found in Garber (1989; see also Garber 1992), who cites Stoller as a recognized authority on transvestite and transsexual issues. In using such an authority Garber and others are doing just what feminists protested about during the beginning of the women's movement: Men are speaking for women's experiences and claiming to know what women were or should be. Until Bolin (1988), Newton (1972), and Stone (1991) there was no academic writing about the experiences of transvestites and transsexuals other than that by "authorities" such as Stoller and Lothstein.[22]

Garber sees "these apparently marginal and aberrant cases, that of the transvestite and the transsexual" as viable for both defining and problematizing the concept of "male subjectivity" (1989:143), but I disagree. Although male transvestites do retain a male identity, I suspect that most male-to-female transsexuals do not. Furthermore, although male transvestites retain a male identity, it is not, as Stoller purports, an eroticized identity focused on the retention of penises. Based on my research, it seems that Stoller's so-called mechanisms of transvestism are phallocratic posturings of eroticism that may reflect the experiences of a few male transvestites. They are by no means the experience of the majority, nor are they the experiences of female transvestites. Furthermore, transmen and FTMs have their own ways of defining male subjectivity and what it means to be female-bodied men.

◉ Dangerous Actors

Meaning and experience cannot be read literally and directly out of discourse.

—DiGiacomo 1992:113

In order to understand the fear invoked by the existence of fearful others, we must ask, as Smith-Rosenberg suggests (taking Mary Douglas's lead), "Who is the dangerous actor? Who is endangered? What is the dangerous act?" (1989:105). For this discussion, the dangerous actors are female-bodied trans-people (as well as all male-bodied transpeople) who do not become one or the other but instead choose a middle ground. The endangered are men in partic-ular, but it seems that some women feel endangered also, especially those who invest in the maintenance of sex and gender structures (biological determin-ists). The dangerous act is that of living as the other gender with little or no surgical intervention. That action may be seen as endangering because observers have no control over how the sexed body is signified as a gendered being. They can be seemingly tricked by outward signs of gender. Pagliassotti states that fear clearly: "Although genitalia may be hidden beneath clothing, they are the 'true' signifiers of sex, which can be uncovered by inspection, whereas the clothes in contrast, may be 'false' signifiers of sex" (1993:480). Thus the dangerous actor is capable of revealing the arbitrary relationship between the signifier and the signified and reconstructing the notion of sex and gender as bodies that are naturally gendered and sexed (cf. Butler 1990:123). The dangerous act is especially dangerous to discourses (both transsexual and mainstream) that maintain the status quo of sex and gender differences. To live as men (or women) with partial or entirely female (or male) bodies may mean that ultimately there is no, or little, difference. The act is also dangerous because it resists and subverts dominant ideologies. The individual has "declared . . . *self* hood and [a] *will*fulness against the determination of biology" (Smith-Rosenberg 1989:105, emphasis in the original).

Critics view transsexuals and transvestites as representatives of "a challenge to traditional notions of maleness and femaleness" (Irvine 1990:270) as well as making "the reference ('man' or 'woman') knowable" (Garber 1989:156). Although both views may be a possibility, they remain an improbability. On the one side, biological determinists—and on the other side, perpetuators of a mental illness model (also biological determinists)—are really the same. Both seek to cure and would rather eradicate than accept (cf. Irvine 1990:257).

What both sides need to understand is that although a wrong body discourse may lead to a cure for some, it also constructs gender diversity as pathology and not everyone wants to be cured. For many, "There is something about being both male and female, about having an entry into both worlds. Contrary to some psychiatric tenets, half and halfs are not suffering from a confusion of sexual identity, or even from a confusion of gender. What we are suffering from is an absolute despot duality that says we are able to be only one or the other. It claims that human nature is limited and cannot evolve into something better. But I, like other queer people, am two in one body, both male and female" (Anzaldúa 1987:19).

For individuals who conceive of themselves as men with vaginas or as female-bodied men, or even as transsexuals or transgendered, it is normalcy not pathology that leads them to reject the surgeon's knife. The same holds true for individuals who have sex reassignment surgery.

In order to move beyond the dominant discourses we must ask why critics keep turning to "medical discourses for specificity and distinction, [only] to find, instead a blurring of categories and boundaries?" (Garber 1989:152). Perhaps it is because they have neglected to consult the individuals about whom the discourses are ostensibly written. But the discourses are not really about transsexuals and transvestites. They are about the beliefs of doctors, clinicians, and society concerning what it is to be male or female, transvestite and/or transsexual, neither/nor as well as both/and.

*E*ndnotes

[1]Although this quotation does not in itself marginalize FTMs and transmen, I use it as an example of the paucity of literature on the topic. As I will argue later on in this

chapter, it is because there is so little data on FTMs/transmen that the dominant discourses are capable of marginalizing them.

[2]A version of this chapter appears in Denny (1998). At the time the article was published I had not received permission to quote people by name. Many are now out as transpeople, and their names, initials, or chosen pseudonyms are used in place of the age and occupation designations previously used.

[3]Irvine (1990:270) makes a similar argument but without the additional conceptualization of fearful other. The concept of gender borderlands is taken from Anzaldúa.

[4]See Chauncey (1989) for an excellent discussion of the history of homosexuality and Rosario (1994) for a cogent explication of the confusion in the early literature between homosexuality and what came to be labeled as transsexuality.

[5]There are significant differences between male-to-female transsexuals and female-bodied transpeople regarding the "corrective" benefits of surgical sex reassignment. There is, in fact, a significant difference in attitude toward transsexualism as a disorder. For example, following a transgender speakout in Seattle on April 29, 1992, where a male-to-female transsexual repeatedly used the term *affliction* to describe her transsexualism, one FTM/transman consultant said, "I resent people using words like 'afflicted.' I'm not afflicted." Also see chapters 9 and 10 of this volume.

[6]In a juxtaposition, Shapiro (1991), a transsexual discourse, follows Stone (1991), a transdiscourse. Many consider Stone to be the founder of trans theory because she was the first out transperson to publish at the academic level and in doing so to challenge transsexual discourses.

[7]Rather than "men with vaginas" some practitioners use the term *penisless men* (e.g., Steiner, ed. 1985:356). In a Freudian sense (men have penises, women do not) that seems like an underhanded way of labeling female-bodied transpeople who do not have surgery as females rather than men.

[8]John Taylor is a pseudonym I used in 1983 before coming out as a transperson. The original article was written for a journal published by Quakers. At the time I felt it was imperative to protect my identity because I was uncertain about how my spiritual community would respond to the fact that I am trans. I am fortunate, however, in that the community has never shunned me but rather welcomed me.

[9]These latter two considerations may, in themselves, be artifacts of FTMs and transmen being male-identified as well as being unwilling to jump through hoops for results that will be less than satisfactory.

[10]My appreciation to Jacob Hale for our discussions concerning the discrepancies in numbers.

[11]Steiner's claim of homogeneity for FTMs/transmen is curious in that her edited collection contains few references to FTMs and only one small section takes up FTMs as subjects separate from MTFs/transwomen.

[12]Pauly presumes that all women derive pleasure and stimulation from their breasts. He is unaware that a few lesbians have their breasts removed because they do not like them.

[13]This is in no way intended to denigrate those who choose phalloplastic surgeries but rather an explanation of why a number of individuals elect not to have particular procedures.

[14]One example of how, even within the transcommunity, FTMs and transmen are invisible is demonstrated by an experience I had at this conference. After settling into my room, I went to register for the meeting and was asked, "Is it under Jason or your 'femme' name?" "I don't have a femme name," I replied. "I gave it up years ago." The registrar's mouth dropped open when I told her I was an FTM.

[15]This surgeon is not alone in his attitude. Surgeons who perform genital surgeries are invested in creating penises for penetration. Gail Lebovic, Dr. Donald Laub's associate, has stated, "I don't really understand why they have this surgery [metoidioplasty]. I mean, if you're going to have a penis. . . ." (cited in Bloom 1994:44). Laub stated this attitude more overtly: "Men want penises. But the metoidioplasty mimics nature, and that's appealing. . . . Sexual and urinary functioning is intact and they can go on having sex however they have it. Like lesbians do." Some FTMs and transmen have interpreted that statement as implying—at least to many surgeons—that those who do not have phalloplasty are really lesbians.

[16]Both Garber (1989) and Irvine (1990) discuss this point.

[17]One surgical technique that male-to-female transsexuals have is referred to as penile inversion. If the attitude was the same, then it would be "phallo-inversion."

[18]I know of only one female surgeon, Gail Lebovic, who performs genital surgery in the United States. There are, however, a number of female surgeons who do chest reconstructions and hysterectomies.

[19]As opposed to Dekker and van de Pol, the San Francisco Lesbian and Gay History Project states that "the tradition of passing women, begun in the nineteenth century, lives on today, a small but important part of lesbian and women's history" (1989:194).

[20]When Stoller (1965:194) discusses an individual who expresses a disinterest in having a penis or the surgery to create one, he places all masculine referents in quotation marks, signifying that the individual's identity as a man is invalid. "He" is really a "she." This devaluing of and judgment upon the individual's self-identity is both phallocentric and Freudian; the absence of a penis or the absence of a desire for one equals female.

[21]How ironic that the word *queens* is considered undignified for scholarly works—and how revealing it is that Steiner bemoans that no sexologist has invented a label more suitable to medico-psychological practitioners' tastes.

[22]It is significant that Bolin's *In Search of Eve* (1988) is regarded by many MTFs/transwomen as an accurate and honest interpretation of their lives and the process they must undergo with respect to medico-psychological practitioners. Even more significant, and likely because it is so highly regarded, the book is virtually ignored by the medico-psychological establishment. I have seen only one book review concerning her work in any of their publications, and that review denigrated the value of Bolin's work because data had been collected on only 16 individuals versus the 150 in the reviewer's study. It was also denounced because of its criticism of the controlling nature of medico-psychological practitioners and its social cultural perspective "rather than a psychological or empirical research standpoint" (Mate-Kole 1992:209–10). The same reviewer also felt the book would be of great "assistance to the student or avid reader in sociology/anthropology than to the clinicians or psychology/psychiatry student."

As Denny (1993a:169–70) pointed out in a letter of response (which the journal initially rejected), the reviewer had put things "precisely backwards: It is the clinician who has the most to gain by reading" Bolin's book. The fact that a clinician has seen 150 clients does not invalidate Bolin's study when one considers the amount of time spent with individuals in each study. The reviewer also fails to recognize the artificial environment in which patients are seen and "the imbalance of power between clinicians and patients."

A point can be made concerning the control of discourses and how they are validated and made legitimate. I am aware of only one review of Bolin's book, and it appeared in 1992—four years after publication. By way of contrast, the work of Lothstein, a psychoanalyst who is considered an authority, was reviewed in 1984—a year after publication.

❧ ❧ ❧

Questions

1. What is "body-part dysphoria"? Which body parts are likely to be especially problematic for female-bodied transpeople?

2. List and explain the three stereotypes of FTMs found in the medical and psychological literature.

3. Why would people in our society be uncomfortable with the idea that, "genitals do not signify gender"?

4. Though more people may accept the idea of gender/sex reassignment, the idea that someone does not want to be identified as a member of either of these two groups is baffling. Provide a sociological explanation for this concept.

5. What are the flaws of the "wrong body" discourse about transgendered people?

6. Explain why, in the context of our society, many people—including physicians—assume that the most important thing to a transman or FTM is getting a penis.

Gender, Class, and Terrorism

Michael Kimmel

What is the link between Timothy McVeigh, Mohammed Atta, and Adolf Hitler? By moving beyond religion, culture, and hatred of the United States, Kimmel argues that the link between these young men is emasculation. What motivated their hatred and killing of others is their masculinity, masculine entitlement, and thwarted ambitions. He provides a profile of all three with a focus on two social contexts where men are most emasculated.

The events of September 11 have sent scholars and pundits alike scrambling to make sense of those seemingly senseless acts. While most analyses have focused on the political economy of globalization or the perversion of Islamic teachings by Al Qaeda, several commentators have raised gender issues.

Some have reminded us that in our haste to lionize the heroes of the World Trade Center collapse, we ignored the many women firefighters, police officers, and rescue workers who also risked their lives. We've been asked to remember the Taliban's vicious policies toward women; indeed, even Laura Bush seems to be championing women's emancipation.

A few have asked us to consider the other side of the gender coin: men. Some have rehearsed the rather tired old formulae about masculine blood-lust or the drive for domination and conquest, with no reference to the magnificent humanity displayed by so many on September 11. In an article in Slate, the Rutgers anthropologist Lionel Tiger trotted out his old male-bonding thesis but offered no understanding of why Al Qaeda might appeal to some men and not others. Only the journalist Barbara Ehrenreich suggests that there may be a link between the misogyny of the Taliban and the masculinity of the terrorists.

As for myself, I've been thinking lately about a letter to the editor of a small, upstate-New York newspaper, written in 1992 by an American GI after his return from service in the gulf war. He complained that the legacy of

Reprinted from the *Chronicle of Higher Education* 48, no. 22 (February 8, 2002), by permission of the author.

the American middle class had been stolen by an indifferent government. The American dream, he wrote, has all but disappeared; instead, most people are struggling just to buy next week's groceries.

That letter writer was Timothy McVeigh from Lockport, N.Y. Two years later, he blew up the Murrah federal building in Oklahoma City in what is now the second-worst act of terrorism ever committed on American soil.

What's startling to me are the ways that McVeigh's complaints were echoed in some of the fragmentary evidence that we have seen about the terrorists of September 11, and especially in the portrait of Mohammed Atta, the suspected mastermind of the operation and the pilot of the first plane to hit the World Trade Center.

Looking at these two men through the lens of gender may shed some light on both the method and the madness of the tragedies they wrought.

McVeigh was representative of the small legion of white supremacists—from older organizations like the John Birch Society, the Ku Klux Klan, and the American Nazi Party, to newer neo-Nazi, racist-skinhead, white-power groups like Posse Comitatus and the White Aryan Resistance, to radical militias.

These white supremacists are mostly younger (in their early 20s), lower-middle-class men, educated at least through high school and often beyond. They are the sons of skilled workers in industries like textiles and tobacco, the sons of the owners of small farms, shops, and grocery stores. Buffeted by global political and economic forces, the sons have inherited little of their fathers' legacies. The family farms have been lost to foreclosure, the small shops squeezed out by Wal-Marts and malls. These young men face a spiral of downward mobility and economic uncertainty. They complain that they are squeezed between the omnivorous jaws of global capital concentration and a federal bureaucracy that is at best indifferent to their plight and at worst complicit in their demise.

As one issue of The Truth at Last, a white-supremacist magazine, put it:

"Immigrants are flooding into our nation willing to work for the minimum wage(or less). Super-rich corporate executives are flying all over the world in search of cheaper and cheaper labor so that they can lay off their American employees. . . . Many young White families have no future! They are not going to receive any appreciable wage increases due to job competition from immigrants."

What they want, says one member, is to "take back what is rightfully ours."

Their anger often fixes on "others"—women, members of minority groups, immigrants, gay men, and lesbians—in part because those are the people with whom they compete for entry-level, minimum-wage jobs. Above them all, enjoying the view, hovers the international Jewish conspiracy.

What holds together these "paranoid politics"—antigovernment, anti-global capital but pro-small capitalist, racist, sexist, anti-Semitic, homopho-bic—is a rhetoric of masculinity. These men feel emasculated by big money and big government—they call the government "the Nanny State"—and they claim that "others" have been handed the birthright of native-born white men.

In the eyes of such downwardly mobile white men, most white American males collude in their own emasculation. They've grown soft, feminized, weak. White supremacists' Web sites abound with complaints about the "whimpering collapse of the blond male"; the "legions of sissies and weak-lings, of flabby, limp-wristed, nonaggressive, non-physical, indecisive, slack-jawed, fearful males who, while still heterosexual in theory and practice, have not even a vestige of the old macho spirit."

American white supremacists thus offer American men the restoration of their masculinity—a manhood in which individual white men control the fruits of their own labor and are not subject to emasculation by Jewish-owned finance capital or a black and feminist-controlled welfare state. Theirs is the militarized manhood of the heroic John Rambo, a manhood that celebrates their God-sanctioned right to band together in armed militias if anyone, or any government agency, tries to take it away from them. If the state and the economy emasculate them, and if the masculinity of the "others" is problem-atic, then only "real" white men can rescue America from a feminized, multi-cultural, androgynous melting pot.

Sound familiar? For the most part, the terrorists of September 11 come from the same class, and recite the same complaints, as American white supremacists.

Virtually all were under 25, educated, lower middle class or middle class, downwardly mobile. The journalist Nasra Hassan interviewed families of Middle Eastern suicide bombers (as well as some failed bombers them-selves) and found that none of them had the standard motivations ascribed to people who commit suicide, such as depression.

Although several of the leaders of Al Qaeda are wealthy—Osama bin Laden is a multimillionaire, and Ayman al-Zawahiri, the 50-year-old doctor thought to be bin Laden's closest adviser, is from a fashionable suburb of Cairo—many of the hijackers were engineering students for whom job opportunities had been dwindling dramatically. (Judging from the minimal information I have found, about one-fourth of the hijackers had studied engi-neering.) Zacarias Moussaoui, who did not hijack one of the planes but is the first man to be formally charged in the United States for crimes related to September 11, earned a degree at London's South Bank University. Marwan al-Shehhi, the chubby, bespectacled 23-year-old from the United Arab Emirates who flew the second plane into the World Trade Center, was an engineering student, while Ziad Jarrah, the 26-year-old Lebanese who flew the plane that crashed in Pennsylvania, had studied aircraft design.

Politically, these terrorists opposed globalization and the spread of Western values; they opposed what they perceived as corrupt regimes in several Arab states (notably Saudi Arabia and Egypt), which they claimed were merely puppets of American domination. "The resulting anger is naturally directed first against their rulers," writes the historian Bernard Lewis, "and then against those whom they see as keeping those rulers in power for selfish reasons."

Central to their political ideology is the recovery of manhood from the emasculating politics of globalization. The Taliban saw the Soviet invasion and westernization of Afghanistan as humiliations. Bin Laden's October 7 videotape describes the "humiliation and disgrace" that Islam has suffered "for more than 80 years." And over and over, Nasra Hassan writes, she heard the refrain: "The Israelis humiliate us. They occupy our land, and deny our history."

Terrorism is fueled by a fatal brew of antiglobalization politics, convoluted Islamic theology, and virulent misogyny. According to Ehrenreich, while these formerly employed or self-employed males "have lost their traditional status as farmers and breadwinners, women have been entering the market economy and gaining the marginal independence conferred by even a paltry wage." As a result, "the man who can no longer make a living, who has to depend on his wife's earning's, can watch Hollywood sexpots on pirated videos and begin to think the world has been turned upside down."

The Taliban's policies thus had two purposes: to remasculinize men and to refeminize women. Another journalist, Peter Marsden, has observed that those policies "could be seen as a desperate attempt to keep out that other world, and to protect Afghan women from influences that could weaken the society from within." The Taliban prohibited women from appearing in public unescorted by men, from revealing any part of their body, and from going to school or holding a job. Men were required to grow their beards, in accordance with religious images of Muhammad, yes; but also, perhaps, because wearing beards has always been associated with men's response to women's increased equality in the public sphere, since beards symbolically re-affirm biological differences between men and women, while gender equality tends to blur those differences.

The Taliban's policies removed women as competitors and also shored up masculinity, since they enabled men to triumph over the humiliations of globalization and their own savage, predatory, and violently sexual urges that might be unleashed in the presence of uncovered women.

All of these issues converged in the life of Mohammed Atta, the terrorist about whom the most has been written and conjectured. Currently, for example, there is much speculation about Atta's sexuality. Was he gay? Was he a repressed homosexual, too ashamed of his sexuality to come out? Such innuendoes are based on no more than a few circumstantial tidbits about his life. He was slim, sweet-faced, neat, meticulous, a snazzy dresser. The youngest child of an ambitious lawyer father and a pampering mother, Atta grew up shy and polite, a mama's boy. "He was so gentle," his father said. "I used to tell him, 'Toughen up, boy!'"

When such revelations are offered, storytellers seem to expect a reaction like "Aha! So that explains it!" (Indeed, in a new biography of Adolf Hitler, The Hidden Hitler, Lothar Machtan offers exactly that sort of explanation. He argues that many of Hitler's policies—such as the killing of longtime colleague and avowed homosexual Ernst Rohm, or even the systematic persecution and execution of gay men in concentration camps—were, in fact, prompted by a desire to conceal his own homosexuality.)

But what do such accusations actually explain? Do revelations about Hitler's or Atta's possible gay propensities raise troubling connections between homosexuality and mass murder? If so, then one would also have to conclude that the discovery of Shakespeare's "gay" sonnet explains the Bard's genius at explicating Hamlet's existential anguish, or that Michelangelo's sexuality is the decisive factor in his painting of God's touch in the Sistine Chapel.

Such revelations tell us little about the Holocaust or September 11. They do, however, address the consequences of homophobia—both official and informal—on young men who are exploring their sexual identities. What's relevant is not the possible fact of Hitler's or Atta's gayness, but the shame and fear that surround homosexuality in societies that refuse to acknowledge sexual diversity.

Even more troubling is what such speculation leaves out. What unites Atta, McVeigh, and Hitler is not their repressed sexual orientation but gender—their masculinity, their sense of masculine entitlement, and their thwarted ambitions. They accepted cultural definitions of masculinity, and needed someone to blame when they felt that they failed to measure up. (After all, being called a mama's boy, a sissy, and told to toughen up are demands for gender conformity, not matters of sexual desire.) Gender is the issue, not sexuality.

All three failed at their chosen professions. Hitler was a failed artist—indeed, he failed at just about every job he ever tried except dictator. McVeigh, a business-college dropout, found his calling in the military during the gulf war, where his exemplary service earned him commendations; but he washed out of Green Beret training—his dream job—after only two days. And Atta was the odd man out in his family. His two sisters both became doctors—one a physician and one a university professor. His father constantly reminded him that he wanted "to hear the word 'doctor' in front of his name. We told him, your sisters are doctors and their husbands are doctors and you are the man of the family."

Atta decided to become an engineer, but his degree meant little in a country where thousands of college graduates were unable to find good jobs. After he failed to find employment in Egypt, he went to Hamburg, Germany, to study architecture. He was "meticulous, disciplined, and highly intelligent, an ordinary student, a quiet, friendly guy who was totally focused on his studies," according to another student in Hamburg.

But his ambitions were constantly undone. His only hope for a good job in Egypt was to be hired by an international firm. He applied and was continually rejected. He found work as a draftsman—highly humiliating for someone with engineering and architectural credentials and an imperious and demanding father—for a German firm involved with razing low-income Cairo neighborhoods to provide more scenic vistas for luxury tourist hotels.

Defeated, humiliated, emasculated, a disappointment to his father and a failed rival to his sisters, Atta retreated into increasingly militant Islamic theology. By the time he assumed the controls of American Airlines Flight 11, he evinced a hysteria about women. In the message he left in his abandoned rental car, he made clear what mattered to him in the end. "I don't want pregnant women or a person who is not clean to come and say good-bye to me," he wrote. "I don't want women to go to my funeral or later to my grave." Of course, Atta's body was instantly incinerated, and no burial would be likely.

The terrors of emasculation experienced by lower-middle-class men all over the world will no doubt continue, as they struggle to make a place for themselves in shrinking economies and inevitably shifting cultures. They may continue to feel a seething resentment against women, whom they perceive as stealing their rightful place at the head of the table, and against the governments that displace them. Globalization feels to them like a game of musical chairs, in which, when the music stops, all the seats are handed to others by nursemaid governments.

The events of September 11, as well as of April 19, 1995 (the Oklahoma City bombing), resulted from an increasingly common combination of factors—the massive male displacement that accompanies globalization, the spread of American consumerism, and the perceived corruption of local political elites—fused with a masculine sense of entitlement. Someone else— some "other"—had to be held responsible for the terrorists' downward mobility and failures, and the failure of their fathers to deliver their promised inheritance. The terrorists didn't just get mad. They got even.

Such themes were not lost on the disparate bands of young, white supremacists. American Aryans admired the terrorists' courage and chastised their own compatriots. "It's a disgrace that in a population of at least 150 million White/Aryan Americans, we provide so few that are willing to do the same [as the terrorists]," bemoaned Rocky Suhayda, the chairman of the American Nazi Party. "A bunch of towel head/sand niggers put our great White Movement to shame."

It is from such gendered shame that mass murderers are made.

❧ ❧ ❧

Questions

1. List the out-groups hated by white supremacist groups in the United States. How do they jibe with the out-groups of Al-Qaeda and the Nazis?

2. Kimmel briefly discusses homosexuality. What is the relationship between homophobia and violence?

3. Kimmel concludes by highlighting the American Nazi Party's response to the September 11 attacks with their quote: "A bunch of towel head/sand niggers put our great White Movement to shame." Visit the Web sites of the American Nazi Party, the John Birch Society, the White Aryan Resistance, Posse Comitatus, or the Ku Klux Klan. What is their response to the September 11 attacks? Do they admire, respect, or lionize the attackers?

"The Night They Took Over": Misogyny in a Country-Western Gay Bar

CoReY W. Johnson
Diane M. Samdahl

The construction of the public sphere as men's space and the private sphere as women's space has been widely analyzed. The racial segregation of neighborhoods is readily documented. In this article, Johnson and Samdahl examine the segregation of space in a country-western gay bar through men's responses to "Lesbian Night."

☻ Introduction

"Thursday nights are Lesbian Nights," Paul said slurring each "s" in a very stereotypical effeminate way. "It's just the night they took over." I sit silently thinking about Paul's statement and then ask, "Well, does the climate change on Thursday nights?" Paul stops what he is doing and walks down to where I sit. He leans over onto the bar and in a serious tone says, "Yes! And I would say it to anybody. It is the night we have more shit broken; we have more fights, and more crazy behavior than any other night of the week." I raise my eyebrows in astonishment. "Really?" I say, pondering the interesting relevance his statement might have. "Seriously," Paul states, and he returns to his task of setting up the bar.

Scholars in leisure studies have advocated a need to extend research on marginalized populations beyond the examination of individuals to include examination of the structures that perpetuate and foster inequality (Aitchison, 1999; Kivel, 2000; Pedlar, 1995) to "develop richer understandings about the social construction of place and its political ramifications" (Stokowski, 2002,

Reprinted from *Leisure Sciences* 27, no. 4, 2005, by permission of Taylor and Francis.

p. 379). This paper addresses that concern. This study is part of a larger project, based on an ethnography of *Saddlebags*, a country-western gay bar. The goal of the larger project was to describe the culture of this bar and to explore how gay men confront and negotiate meanings of masculinity in that culture. In this paper we focus on gay men's misogynistic reactions to Thursday nights when lesbians "take over" the bar. Misogyny refers to a range of negative emotions for or actions toward women. These negative emotions/actions can range from intense hatred to more subtle forms of dislike, oppression, and marginalization. Regardless, misogyny is a political ideology like racism and anti-Semitism whereby women are viewed as inferior to men and thus should be dominated and/or controlled by men. In the spirit of ethnography, we switch between a narrative voice and an analytical voice in presenting this material; the pronoun "I" is always indicative of the first author.

❧ A Thursday Night at Saddlebags

It is after 10:00 p.m. and I am running a bit late according to my self-constructed, self-imposed, and self-monitored data collection agenda. Pulling my ID and Visa checkcard from my wallet, I slide them, along with some cash, into my right front pocket. I don't carry a wallet when I wear these jeans because it feels and looks so bulky. I grab my ethnographic tool kit, or in laymen's terms, my black book bag. I double check its contents (digital voice recorder, note cards, tapes, batteries, business cards, pens, and pencils) and head for the door, pausing to read the home-made sign that hangs near my book shelf. On a plain white 81/2 × 11 piece of paper written in dark black magic marker are my research questions. Familiar to me but strange to most, the sign reads: How does this gay bar serve as a leisure context for its gay male patrons? How do gay men in this gay bar negotiate hegemonic and counter-hegemonic gendered practices? What structures exist to facilitate and/or prohibit gendered practices by gay men in this gay bar? I feel tired as I reach for the door. The sign reminds me that I can't answer my research questions if I don't go collect more data.

Madge, my new-to-town lesbian friend, is waiting for me outside, underneath the red canopy, when I arrive at Saddlebags. "Sorry if I am late," I apologize. "Not to worry," Madge says, and we move inside, showing our identifications to Doris, the woman who works the door on Thursday nights (and during the course of my study, the only woman to be employed by Saddlebags). Doris greets me with a "hello honey," checks only Madge's ID, and then motions us inside.

*With my arm across the back of her waist, I motion Madge toward the line that
extends back from the bartenders' station. As we stand in line I catch the attention
of Paul, the bartender, and both Madge and I wave. Paul winks at me flirtatiously
and then goes back to serving the women who wait for their beer and drinks. After
waiting over 10 minutes, Madge and I finally procure our own cocktails and scoot
down the bar where Jared, a friend and bar regular, sits talking to a woman, a rare
instance for Jared. As we approach them I recognize his female friend and begin to
search my mind for her name. Jared saves me. "Eleanor, this is my friend Corey. He
is the one writing his dissertation on Saddlebags."*

*After a few moments of conversation, I discern that Madge is comfortable in
this new setting, Eleanor is interested in Madge, and Jared has been doing tequila
shots. Taking advantage of his inebriated state, I ask Jared if he wants to dance (the
only time he will dance is when he is intoxicated), hoping to test some theories I had
about movement on the dance floor. Jared graciously accepts my offer, and I beg
forgiveness as I depart from Eleanor and Madge, promising to return. Then holding
hands for both solidarity and balance, Jared and I leave the lesbians alone and work
our way toward the dance floor. On the way to the dance floor Jared leans up and
whispers in my ear, "I cannot believe I am going out onto the dance floor with this
school of fish." I let go of his hand and turning to scold I warn, "Behave yourself,
some of our best friends are lesbians." Jared shakes his head and reminds me, "They
might be your friends, but they aren't mine." Misogyny in the gay bar? I begin to
wonder why.*

◉ Theoretical Framework

Over the past several decades, feminist leisure researchers have made significant
advances adding gender to the agenda of leisure research (Henderson, 1994;
Henderson & Bialeschki, 1999; Shaw, 1994, 1999). The empirical and theoretical advances made in the light of feminism have not only exposed the andocen-
tric premises of early leisure theories but have also encouraged leisure scholars
to examine men and masculinity (cf. Henderson & Shaw, 2003; Wearing,
1998). This shift in focus encourages investigators to go beyond the lives of
women to examine broader sets of power relations that link masculinity and
femininity (Henderson, 1994; Samdahl, Jacobson, & Hutchinson, 2001; Shaw,
1999; Wearing, 1998). An important extension of this work has been the examination of gendered discourse that shapes the spaces and places of people's
leisure (Aitchison, 1999; Broom, Byrne, & Petkovic, 1992; Kirby & Hay, 1997;
Scraton & Watson, 1998; Skeggs, 1999; Stokowski, 2002; Wearing, 1998).

Though discourse and ideology are often used interchangeably and their precise meanings are widely debated by social scientists, we draw upon Purvis and Hunt's (1993) explanation where discourse or discursive practices are semiotic and social practices whereby meanings, truth-claims, and subjectivities are produced. Ideologies are the effects of that production in relation to domination or subordination. The following literature review illuminates some of the conceptual ideas that informed our thinking as we approached the study of gay masculinity in a country-western gay bar.

Masculinity

Most men are quite cognizant of the essentialized notion of what it means to be a "man;" however, men are not always successful in the execution of it. Yet, despite their success or failure at presenting an acceptable "performance" of manhood, mainstream culture provides a persuasive and often subversive set of dominant ideologies to inform and guide men's behavior (Butler, 1990; Connell, 1995).

Connell (1995) described *masculinity* as those practices in which men engage male social gender roles with the effects being expressed or "performed" through the body, personality, and culture. Masculinity has taken shape in relation to securing and maintaining dominance in western society (Connell, 1995; Wearing, 1998). Masculinity is typically grounded in a dialectical relationship with femininity, with masculine being valued over the feminine. Masculinity is not a static characteristic but a fluid construct organized within social relations. According to Connell, masculinity is not just an object of knowledge but the interplay between the agency of the individual and the structure of social institutions. Although masculinity can be performed in a variety of ways, this argument contends that men often feel obligated consciously or unconsciously to perform in specific ways that are dependent upon the current cultural climate. Those dominant ideological norms of masculinity are referred to as hegemonic masculinity.

Hegemonic Masculinity

Most people would agree that some socially constructed characteristics of masculinity are valued more than others. The value of those characteristics is often based on their relationship to dominant ideological messages. Hegemonic masculinity is the configuration of male gender practices that serve to legitimize patriarchy and heterosexuality, guaranteeing the dominant position of men and heterosexuals and the subordinate position of women and non-heterosexuals (Connell, 1995).

Connell (1995) used the term *hegemonic masculinity* to describe structures of practice that are constructed in social situations and that foster access to power for those who are male and heterosexual. Therefore, hegemonic masculinity is a powerful tool used to secure and maintain the current social order. Consequently, hegemonic masculinity is an elaborate performance of social authority and is not easy to challenge openly. Men who eventually choose to separate from hegemonic masculinity are choosing to confront a major dilemma of difference. What happens to men who cannot or do not conform to hegemonic masculinity?

*G*ay *M*asculinity

Gay men are sociologically fascinating because they consistently express such a paradoxical relationship to hegemonic masculinity, sometimes resisting and sometimes reinforcing dominant ideologies. Because gay men encounter a hegemonic masculinity that is based on heterosexuality, their everyday relations carry contradictory messages and an undercurrent of threat. Dominant groups such as male heterosexuals may use violence and fear as tactics to maintain their power and dominance as they enforce hegemonic masculinity. Those actions are aimed at punishing the betrayers of manhood—betrayers such as gay men.

Gay men, by their very existence, challenge the power structures of hegemonic masculinity in a variety of ways. One argument suggests that gay men give up their everyday masculine privileges and styles of interaction by claiming a non-heterosexual identity (Connell, 1995; Sedgwick, 1993). Sedgwick elaborated the politics of "coming out" in her influential essay *Epistemology of the Closet*. In this essay, Sedgwick illustrated how the categorical management of sexual identity creates a double bind for gay men because denouncing heterosexuality severs their link to hegemonic masculinity. Sedgwick wrote:

> Heterosexist and masculinist ethical sanctions [find] ready camouflage. If the new common wisdom that hotly overt homophobes are men who are 'insecure about their masculinity' supplements the implausible, necessary illusion that there could be a *secure* version of masculinity (known, presumably, by the coolness of its homophobic enforcement) and a stable, intelligible way for men to feel about other men in modern heterosexual

capitalist patriarchy, what tighter turn could there be to the screw of an already off-center, always at fault, endlessly blackmailable male identity ready to be manipulated into any labor of channeled violence.

What Sedgwick emphasizes in the above passage is the hindrance and vulnerability gay men encounter in trying to be "gay" and "men" at the same time.

Lehne (1998) discussed the double bind gay men encounter, suggesting that heterosexual relations with women are often the proving grounds for masculinity and that adequate sexual functioning with women is seen as proof of masculinity. Consequently, a lack of sex with women will inevitably damage the male gender identity. Accordingly, since gay male homosexual desire is not based on the desire for women, it serves as a direct challenge to the power of hegemonic heterosexual masculinity. In retaliation, hegemonic ideologies create messages that frequently use gay men as the antithesis of masculine, portraying them instead as feminine.

Gay men attempt to resist the stigma of homosexuality by enacting a variety of strategies. These strategies include renunciation or adoption of hyper-masculine qualities (Connell, 1995), and/or self-segregation (Johnson, 2000). As they negotiate the double bind of being gay and male, many gay men retain the idealized sexual and gendered messages connected with the symbolic power, strength, and self-worth maintained in hegemonic masculinity. Although not all men practice hegemonic masculinity, most men benefit from it. Therefore, when faced with giving up their masculine gender privilege for their (homo) sexual identity, some gay men repress or even deny the (homo) sexual identity. Others attempt to maintain their masculine gender privilege in spite of their gay identity, and unconsciously reinforce and intensify hegemonic heterosexual and masculine ideologies by engaging in the oppressive, monolithic practices associated with being a "man."

Although some activists would argue that gay men are forced to live in a world that does not acknowledge their existence, we contend that gay men live in a world that *requires* their existence in order to maintain definitional control of dominant ideologies (Foucault, 1978). These dominant ideologies allow heterosexual men to maintain control by reinforcing the structures that value heterosexual over homosexual and masculine over feminine, and link those traits together inextricably. Therefore, acknowledgement of the everyday life and experiences of gay men categorically situates gay men into an identity category that serves as a mechanism for both their oppression and the dominance and superiority of "men" (Kirby & Hay, 1997; Valentine, 1993). With these considerations in mind, gay men seem to occupy an interesting intersection for the study of gender and sexuality in contemporary society.

*G*ay *M*en in *L*eisure

While heterosexual ideologies often appropriate gay men as feminized males, a closer look at gay men in their everyday lives may help to better understand how gay men come to understand and negotiate the meaning of masculinity. One context where the negotiation of gay men's double bind might be readily evident is in their places of leisure (Aitchison, 1999; Kirby & Hay, 1997; Scraton & Watson, 1998; Skeggs, 1999; Wearing, 1998).

Although leisure studies scholars have begun to focus on the cultural ideologies fostered in the contexts of leisure, research examining gay men's leisure is noticeably absent. When gay men have been examined, their experiences are assumed to be the same as or similar to those of lesbians, bisexuals, and/or people questioning their sexuality (Caldwell, Kivel, Smith, & Hayes, 1998; Johnson, 2000; Kivel, 1996; Kivel & Kleiber, 2000). This blending of non-dominant populations highlights oppression and marginalization as the groups' common characteristics but also creates a framework that overlooks other important differences between these groups (Podmore, 2001; Valentine, 1993). A focused study of gay men's leisure is needed.

*T*he *I*mportance of *G*ay "*P*lace"

Wearing (1998) argued that leisure is often used to shift the goal posts of cultural domination and that leisure spaces are important locations where social control of individuals and strategies for political and social change are prevalent. Kivel (1996) recognized the need for understanding these differences and advocated for more theoretical work on lesbians and gay men, claiming that researchers "should not only focus on the individual, but should also focus on the cultural ideologies . . . to understand how leisure contexts contribute to a hegemonic process". Henderson and Frelke (2000) warned, "Individuals interested in leisure cannot ignore the control of space, the segregation of space, and the effective exclusion of certain social groups from certain leisure spaces and places at particular times".

Leisure spaces are dynamic settings defined by spatial and social circumstances (Slavin, 2004). Gay space, in particular, "is about power over against the power of straights. Being in the majority, for a change, puts you in the position of, '. . . the one in power' (Moran, Skeggs, Tyrer, & Corteen, 2003, p. 188). From this perspective, places like gay bars become sites where invisible populations become visible and make claims for legitimacy (Skeggs, 1999). Overt and covert practices in those sites reinforce alternative notions of ideology, power, and control in ways that validate and reinforce desired identities (Stowkowski, 2002). Therefore, gay places are more than locations where typical hetero-normative discourse is silenced. They also serve as locations where alternative discourses are created and nutured.

The gay bar is one of the most visible and accessible gay male leisure sites (Israelstam & Lambert, 1984). Since before the Stonewall riots in 1969, the gay bar has served as a pivotal place for gay male social life by providing a cultural environment where release and enjoyment can occur away from the heterosexualized locations of everyday life (D'Emilio, 1993; Skeggs, 1999). Even though gay men have become more visible in recent years (Vaid, 1995) and have created additional and alternative spaces and places for their leisure, the gay bar remains a central social institution and leisure context for gay men (Johnson, 2000).

Our study is drawn from an ethnography of a gay male country-western bar. It was driven by an interest in understanding gay men's negotiation and performance of masculinity in that setting, and it focuses specifically on gay men's reaction to Lesbian Night in this bar.

❧ *Feminist Ethnography*

Feminist ethnography was selected as the form of qualitative inquiry for this study because it offered the opportunity to engage in an analytic description and reconstruction of cultural scenes and cultural groups to both illuminate and criticize that culture's behavior, knowledge, and artifacts. As Stokowski (2002) advocated, to understand our role in the fabric of place, we must not only have factual background on the physical setting, but also develop an "abstract understanding of how place is organized and confirmed socially and culturally . . . and look to the role of language and discourse to develop richer understandings about the social construction of place and its political ramifications."

As a male using feminist ethnography, I could not shed my male power and privilege but instead was required to keep them it under close scrutiny. My goal was to "foreground the tensions involved in speaking with rather than *to/for* marginalized groups" (Lather, 1994, p. 107). In her recent essay on ethnography, Richardson (2000) wrote that the ethnographic life is not separable from the subjective self. She argued who researchers are, what they can be, what they can study, and how they write about what they study needs to be done from the perspective of ethical subjects who constantly check their motives and actions. Therefore, in my efforts to de-center myself as the conveyer of "truth," I used a variety of mechanisms to ensure trustworthiness (i.e., validity, reliability, and credibility) in my data and its representation. I used member checks with key informants and *Saddlebags* participants, I sought guidance from a community-based gay male advisory panel, and I engaged in peer debriefing with fellow feminists. Throughout this process I shared my data and interpretations with my advisor/mentor/second author, and our ongoing discussions helped refine and focus the analysis.

The results of this study originated from that process of constantly questioning my own assumptions and privileges in relation to the data and, in fact, reflect new understandings that resulted directly from that scrutiny. As Levinson (1998) wrote, "any male contribution to feminist research must engage in a more or less continuous reflexivity, a struggle to undermine and contradict the ever-emerging signs of gender privilege". In spite of my immersion in *Saddlebags* as a gay male ethnographer, I was initially unable to see the significance of what was occurring on Lesbian Nights. When discussion and debriefing with feminist colleagues led to that realization, my own experiences became the subject of critical self-reflection and provided additional insight into the misogynistic reactions to Lesbian Night at *Saddlebags*.

Site Selection

The specific bar selected for this ethnography was *Saddlebags* (a pseudonym), a country-western gay bar located in the downtown region of a major southern metropolitan city. *Saddlebags* is one of the few country-western gay bars in the country, thus shaping this ethnography both specifically and circumstantially to that gay country western culture. In a discussion of masculinity in relation to country-western imagery, Horrocks (1995) noted that "the western [image] is a true mythical system . . . constantly elaborated over time, until it has achieved the complexity and richness of more ancient mythologies. It provides a set of symbols, which are instantly recognizable". Those symbols usually aligned with "true manhood" and heterosexuality prevail in country-western bars through the décor, music, attire, and behaviors of bar patrons. Though *Saddlebags* was a gay bar, it mirrored these attributes and appeared like any heterosexual country-western bar in the region. With the strong hegemonic culture of masculinity already in place, *Saddlebags* was an interesting and appropriate selection for examining gay men's negotiation of gender.

Data collection and preliminary analysis on *Saddlebags* began on September 30, 2000, and continued until December 2, 2001. However, site visits to the bar and continued conversations with the bar's patrons and staff remained on-going through May 2002 as a means of ensuring the trustworthiness of my representation of *Saddlebags*' culture.

Data Collection Procedures

Using participant observation as the primary method of ethnography, I entered the social situation both to participate in activities appropriate to the culture and to observe the people, activities, and context of the social situation (Spradley, 1980). As the frequency of my participation increased, I funneled my observations from a macro focus on *Saddlebags* as a cultural context for leisure toward a micro focus on the cultural phenomenon and individual behaviors that were more relevant to my research questions. My goal was to create a written record of my observations, experiences, feelings, reactions, and reflections to serve as the primary data source for this study. Although there is no one way to create or maintain this written record, I found it quick and comfortable to speak my jottings into a digital voice recorder and then transform those jottings into expanded field notes.

In addition to the jottings and expanded field notes, I also maintained a research journal that documented the more personal experiences, ideas, mistakes, dilemmas, epiphanies, reactions, and thinking during my time studying *Saddlebags*. Unlike a researcher's diary that only documents the daily reflections of a researcher, my journal is a "messy" text (Marcus, 1998) that more accurately illustrated the reflective and reflexive processes of research. It contains personal entries about my time in the field, as well as the theoretical and methodological tensions encountered that exemplified and rationalized the decisions made. I also added response data from faculty, colleagues, and family who accompanied me to the site. Response data, according to St. Pierre (1999), is "others' response to what they imagine we are doing". These imaginations and observations are important as researchers attempt to validate their own perceptions and strive to understand how they are perceived in the culture. Included in my research journal also were physical renderings of the space, handwritten notes from meetings with faculty, business cards from people in the bar, napkins with new insights scrawled across the front, as well as other pieces of writing that ultimately advanced my understanding of what was going on in *Saddlebags*.

Although participant observation was a primary method for this ethnographic study and proved to be an invaluable tool, ethnography encourages a multi-instrument approach (Wolcott, 1999). Therefore, ethnographic and semi-structured interviews were used to collect additional data. Ethnographic interviewing, according to Spradley (1979), is a "series of friendly conversations into which the researcher slowly introduces new elements to assist informants to respond as informants". Ethnographic interviews typically occurred at the bar and allowed me to directly follow up on my observations. Though the ethnographic interviews were never audio-recorded, these conversations became part of my expanded field notes.

Although not necessarily typical in ethnography, semi-structured interviews with a variety of *Saddlebags*' participants were conducted. Using an interview guide, I conducted 9 semi-structured interviews with a total of 11 participants. Each interview lasted between one and three hours and was audio-recorded with the permission of the participant. Using purposeful sampling, I consciously selected gay men (and eventually women) based on their potential for offering insight and/or expanding on information I had been gathering through my participant observations. As Fetterman (1989) indicated, researcher judgment is the most appropriate way to select interview participants for ethnographic studies, as it allows the ethnographer to seek out the most appropriate members of a culture to serve as informants. These judgments, according to Creswell (1998), are grounded in a researcher's evolving understanding of the culture, the culture's demographics, and the diverse behaviors witnessed in the culture. Although gay men's masculinity was the focus of my study, gay men's reaction to Lesbian Night became a central aspect of my data. Thus, I eventually expanded my sample to include three lesbian women.

*D*ata *T*ransformation

As suggested by Creswell (1998) and Wolcott (1994, 1999), a three-stage process for formal data transformation was used by simultaneously constructing descriptions, conducting analysis, and making interpretations guided by the research questions. Description, according to Wolcott (1994), is the foundation on which qualitative research is built and therefore, is a primary concern for all ethnographers. It is important to keep in mind that the cultural description of *Saddlebags* is not an objective task but involves both the perception and interpretation of the researcher (Emerson, Fretz, & Shaw, 1995). Cultural description is a purposeful and theoretical form of data transformation.

The more formal analysis stage began as the data were interrogated to identify patterns of thought, behavior, and key events. In the early stages, a standard construct approach was used (Creswell, 1998) by conducting line-by-line readings of the expanded field notes and interview transcripts. After reading through these materials many times, open coding began. Several rounds of open coding allowed for the creation and application of abstract categories to the data and the use of those categories to compare, contrast, complexify, sort, reduce, refute, and refine patterned regularities, key events, cultural groups, and cultural signifiers. As this conceptualization process progressed, analytical memos were written to explore patterned themes and to connect the individual pieces of data across the entire set of data. Although open coding and analytical memoing generated an over- whelming number of interesting avenues for exploration, we used the research questions and theoretical framework to focus the analysis toward our purpose. After identifying Lesbian Night as a central theme of the study, data collection continued and focused coding began specifically on that theme. According to Emerson et al. (1995), focused coding analytically expands identified themes and "distinguishes differences and variations within the broader topic . . . to identify patterns and variations in relation- ships and in the ways that members understand and respond to conditions and contingencies in the social setting".

Descriptions and analysis next were used to construct the narrative vignettes (Van Maanen, 1988) that accompany each theme. The details of these tales were directly lifted from the field notes or from the transcripts of the semi-structured interviews. Although not descriptive of actual events, these tales are not fictional. Rather, they have been pulled together so that discrete pieces of data are organized around a theme that tells an analytic story (Emerson et al., 1995; Van Maanen, 1988). Each narrative uses time disjuncture and/or a re-sequencing of the data to create engaging stories and balance the tensions between analytic propositions and localized meanings (cf. Emerson et al., 1995; Van Maanen, 1988; Wolcott, 2001). In addition to altering time and the sequence of events, participants' physical and social characteristics were altered to ensure confidentiality. In several instances throughout the narratives, participants' feelings and/or emotions are cautiously ascribed. In every case where feelings and/or emotions are assigned, data exist to support that characterization.

After narrative construction, the second author and I outlined the major theoretical points we wanted to discuss. At this stage that we began to connect the data with the theoretical structure that framed this ethnographic work. As new ideas and understandings arose, we sought relevant theory to strengthen our emerging understandings of gay men's reaction to Lesbian Night at *Saddlebags*. The discussion below summarizes some of our key findings.

❧ Findings and Interpretation

Saddlebags is a place of community, despite the novelty that lies at the intersection of country-western ideologies and the gay men and lesbians who occupy it. We used Young's (1990) broad definition of community whereby people "share a common heritage, a common self-identification, a common culture, and a common set of norms". One of the bar employees indicated that *Saddlebags* "is a community center mixed with a bar." Another patron said, "It's hard for me to say *Saddlebags* is just a bar. *Saddlebags* is a part of people's every day lives . . . and that is weird to say about a bar, but *Saddlebags* is much more than a bar." So what is it that makes *Saddlebags* so much more?

One element that contributes to this sense of community is a definitive discourse at *Saddlebags* that attempts to convey the philosophy that "everyone is welcome." Darrin, a fairly new patron of *Saddlebags*, said, "It's a different environment than I've been exposed to before and it's one [that is] more inclusive rather than exclusive." Paul, a *Saddlebags* employee, referred to the diversity of the clientele, saying, "We get everything from a twenty-one year old just coming out to seventy-year old females that come to the bar . . . we have that type of clientele, we have that variety." This belief that everyone is welcome was ardently supported in spite of the fact that *Saddlebags* has primarily a white gay male clientele.

Although *Saddlebags* does regularly serve patrons of diverse backgrounds with respect to race, class, ability, and even sexual orientation, people seldom noted that when they spoke about "everyone being welcome." Instead, their comments focused mostly on gender. When asked who was or wasn't welcome at *Saddlebags*, one bar patron said, "Everybody is welcome. It don't matter if you are male, female, transsexual, whatever you are." Another patron said, "Men and women are there, it's not just one way or the other." Unless asked specifically about other demographic categories (e.g., race or ethnicity), characteristics beyond gender (and less frequently age) were simply not salient in their definitions of diversity. Thus, although the discourse that "everyone is welcome" seemed to convey an inclusive community, "everyone" appeared to refer primarily to sexual minorities. Young (1990) referred to this notion as a 'shared margin,' a community composed of people of marginalized sexual identities who come together to create an alternative space that welcomes and validates sexual diversity. However, as we will see, *Saddlebags* was not all that welcoming.

Where Are All the Lesbians? On Thursday's Nights They Are at Saddlebags

Researchers have described how lesbians, in the absence of their own permanent spaces, appropriate lesbian places in their communities (Bouthillette, 1997; Podmore, 2001; Rothen-berg, 1995). Wolfe (1997) noted that lesbian bars commonly "are not 'places' in the sense of a consistent physical location that one could design or decorate permanently" but instead consist of lesbian nights at other bars. In fact, even with the progress of the feminist and gay and lesbian social movements, the city in which *Saddlebags* is located with over 4 million people and more than 30 gay bars has only one consistent lesbian bar. That is not to say that women don't patronize, to varying degrees, the other gay bars in the city. However, in almost every instance those bars are dominated by a gay male clientele.

Based on knowledge of other gay bars in this city and information learned through this ethnography, *Saddlebags* appears to be one of the most lesbian-friendly mixed-gender gay bars in this metropolitan area. Several major factors influenced this friendliness, including *Saddlebags* being owned by two lesbians who previously operated a bar for lesbians but found that it wasn't as profitable as a bar for gay men. *Saddlebags* was the only gay male bar in the city that devotes an entire night to lesbians and as noted earlier, the "everyone is welcome" discourse refers directly to the inclusion of lesbians.

Although some lesbians are in the crowd most every night of the week, Thursday night at *Saddlebags* is know as "Lesbian Night." This one night of the week is when the number of lesbian women surpass the gay male clientele. Malcolm, a *Saddlebags* bartender, said, "We have a lot of women that come out on Thursday nights and then Friday, Saturday, and Sunday are busy, but primarily with men."

Saddlebags does not advertise Thursday night as Lesbian Night, even though this tradition is commonly known throughout the local gay and lesbian community. When asked how she knew Thursday nights were lesbian nights, Madge said, "A lot of it is word of mouth. There have also been different groups, like lesbian oriented groups . . . that have announced in on their web-sites and different locations." Katie said she enjoyed *Saddlebags* because of the diversity of the lesbian community that patronizes *Saddlebags* on Thursday nights. She said, "There is a quite a bit of [diversity]. You have very backwoods type of women and there's a range of butch/femme, and a lot of in between." Racial diversity also seemed to increase on Lesbian Nights, with a lot of gay men in attendance. Referring to the men, Eleanor said, "There is probably about—it is not a very large percent. It's probably about maybe fifteen percent [men]. But the ones that are there pretty much know the women and they are intermixed."

When questioned about *Saddlebags*, most lesbians who were interviewed described the bar in terms of community. Like the men, they reiterated the "everyone is welcome" discourse. One woman said:

> There is just so much community there. . . . People are there to interact with other people and the guys that seem to frequent *Saddlebags* like to interact with everybody and they just don't seem to have a lot of bias so it's just like interacting with anybody else. . . . And when I think about it now, there are more men at *Saddlebags* than women, but the people who ask me to dance are typically guys.

Speaking about Thursday nights Katie said, "I think for the most part everybody gets along great. You know it is all one giant happy country family, and you know Mama Wendy's [one of the bar owners] behind the counter."

These women espoused the discourse of community just the same as the men at *Saddlebags*. The women I spoke with seemed to be unaware of, or at least not concerned about, the antagonism that was generated when they took over the bar on Lesbian Night. However, what we saw in the gay male patrons' behaviors openly contradicted this belief that *Saddlebags* was a welcoming environment for lesbians.

"How Dare They Be Here": Gay Men React Negatively to Lesbian Night

Kurt feels a hard jerk near his elbow as a group of women maneuver past him in the crowd. His beer bottle slips through his fingers and crashes to the floor. Kurt leaps backward to avoid splashing beer, and then attempting to catch his balance he hits several of the men in his circle of conversation. Apologizing to Trey, Chuck, and

Cheeks for his inadvertent instability, he turns his head to determine the root of the accident. Cheeks points to the group of women who just passed as they continue to move toward the dance floor, offering no condolences for Kurt's loss. "Dumb Cunt," Kurt mutters to his friends.

In a matter of moments Lyle, one of the bar backs, arrives with a small broom, a dustpan, and a mop. The small group of men expand their circle to allow Lyle inside to clean up the mess. As Lyle sweeps the bits of glass and most of the liquid into the dustpan he chastises Kurt. "Sweetheart, do we need to cut you off?" Lyle asks sarcastically. "It wasn't his fault," Trey says, standing up for Kurt, "It is all these fucking dykes!" Lyle laughs and then looking up from the wet floor says, "Yep, once again Lesbian Night rears its ugly head," and he departs the group of men, returning to his work behind the bar.

As Lyle and Cheeks exit, leaving behind only a trace of the broken beer bottle, Chuck returns from the bar with a replacement beer for Kurt. Handing the beer to Kurt he jokingly says, "Now, hold onto this one." Despite Chuck's attempt to change the mood of the situation, Trey continues the lesbian baiting, "You know, I love my lesbian sisters, but get 'em all together and they have absolutely no respect at all, not even for each other! Lesbians are just so bitter." After a moment of scanning the large number of women in the room, Kurt says, "I just don't understand; why Thursdays?"

"Maybe lesbians don't work on Fridays," Trey quips. "The lesbian weekend begins today!"

"But why Saddlebags? Why do they like it here so much?" Kurt inquires more seriously.

"I don't really know," Chuck responds.

"Other bars in town don't have a lesbian night. We should take it away," Trey states.

"Take away what?" asks Chuck.

"Lesbian Night," Trey states boldly. "We should take away Lesbian Night."

"Where else can lesbians go in the city?" Chuck asks.

Trey replies, "Well, I don't know. They have their own places from what I understand!"

"Really, where?" Chuck asks.

"Do I look like I care?" Trey asks, cocking his head and presenting the palm of his hand toward Chuck in a circular motion. All three men laugh at Trey's campy exhibition. As their conversation steers away from the lesbians that inundate their evening they begin to move toward the dance floor for the next set of line dances. Hating line dances, Chuck leans against the rail to watch as Trey and Kurt take their places on the front right-hand corner of the dance floor.

Lesbians and Gay Men: Can't We All Just Get Along?

Some men spoke about Thursday nights with a sense of tolerance, even though they displayed markedly less enthusiasm than when discussing other aspects of the bar. Dirk spoke about going to *Saddlebags* on Thursday nights, saying, "There is not much difference, other than the fact that it's more ladies there than men. I've found that, you know, gay women seem to be just as nice as gay men pretty much." When Malcolm was asked if Thursday nights felt different he said, "Well, a lot of [lesbians] have attitude, but a lot of the guys do too. I mean I treat everybody equally . . . if they are a hard ass or something like that I just try to find out what the problem is . . . but everybody is friendly."

Despite the lukewarm reactions described above, most men reacted to Lesbian Night with animosity. When Dave was asked if he would take an out-of-town guest to the bar on Thursday nights he said:

> If it were a gay man, no! Gay men are like flipped out if there are like more than two [lesbian] women in a place, you know two women in a bar. They are like, "Oh god there is all these lesbians everywhere." So I would probably tell them that, if it were a Thursday night, that there would be a lot of lesbians everywhere or whatever.

When Paul was asked why gay men hated Lesbian Night, he said:

> I don't think that they have even thought about it. They just are like, this bar belongs to us . . . it is just a feeling that they have. So anytime there is a bunch of women out at the bar they will be like 'where are all these women coming from?' and 'how dare they be here!'

However, gay men's unhappiness has not kept Lesbian Night from happening. Over the span of this study Lesbian Night grew in popularity so much that some lesbians began to say it was "too crowded" and that they would rather come on a different night.

Gay men and lesbians were often observed interacting in a presumably enjoyable or mutually beneficial manner. However, men rarely if ever shared stories about meaningful interactions with lesbians. When asked David said, "There is just some level of friendly rivalry. I mean gay men are gay men and they just bitch about stuff, you know they just bitch." Not satisfied with the explanation that all gay men are "bitchy," we explored the data more carefully to identify instances where gay men talked positively about their relationships with lesbians, or talked about Lesbian Night in a positive manner. In fact, the field notes included no stories by gay men about positive interactions with lesbians, beyond my own reflections on personal relationships with lesbians that I recorded while examining this issue.

We began to ask more difficult questions of the data: If gay men didn't want lesbians in the bar, how were they reacting? Malcom, a regular *Saddlebags* patron, commented that the men who showed up on Lesbian Night are "those that are regulars and that just *tolerate* it." Many gay patrons, however, simply stayed away from the bar on that night. For example, Brian didn't go on Thursday nights because "usually there are guys in there . . . but [Thursday] is a completely different crowd, it makes you feel like you are in a lesbian bar." Kirby said, "I am not coming in on Thursday. It's Lesbian Night. I am not dealing with it." During the early stages of participant observation I also avoided the bar on Lesbian Night. It was not until this phase of data analysis that I realized my bias and understood the rich data I was missing by not visiting the bar on Thursday nights.

Misogynistic Discourse: Privileging Men over Women

In spite of the voiced opinion that everyone is welcome, a definite misogynistic discourse was perpetuated by gay men in *Saddlebags*. Although some men made derogatory comments that referred specifically to lesbians, most of the comments about Lesbian Night referred to *women*—a reference to gender not to sexual orientation. With our goal of understanding how gay men confront and negotiate masculinity within this bar, this misogynistic discourse about Lesbian Night was particularly relevant. By "Othering" lesbians, gay men seemed to be suppressing the commonalty of a non-heterosexual orientation that they shared with lesbians, and reaffirming the dominant heteronormative discourse that privileges men over women.

Situated in the context of power relations, Othering is used to distinguish between insiders and outsiders to achieve and maintain, in this case, male power. De Beauvior (1952) developed the concept of Othering as she focused on the dialectic relationship between men and women, demonstrating that the Other represents some kind of threat or danger to the subject. Two distinct but partially overlapping sub-themes were identified in how gay men Other lesbians in relation to Lesbian Night: women's occupation of space, and women's economic contribution to the sustainability of the bar.

Occupation of Space

Similar to findings by Moran et al. (2003), we found that gay men at *Saddlebags* used their bodies and perceptions of personal space to mark social boundaries and boundary violations. Many men reported that women do not have proper regard for others as they navigate within the bar. Jared said, "They bump into me, and just keep going without an apology." Though I did not specifically probe for men's reactions to being bumped by other men, my observations suggest that this *does* occur with some frequency yet was generally tolerated and frequently welcomed as flirtation. My data included no instances of men complaining about other men invading their social space.

Much of the discourse around the occupation of space focused on the dance floor, perhaps because dancing is a central activity at the bar. Malcolm said, "I've heard a lot of people comment on the women's dancing; I wouldn't say all of them, but there is a percentage, you know, that bump into you and they don't apologize." This opinion was expressed by other gay patrons as well who said that lesbians dance in a way that results in gay men and lesbians "constantly running into each other."

I asked Dirk and Darrin, "You guys go on Thursdays? What is that like?" Dirk replied, "A bunch of lesbians that don't know how to dance." Turning to Darrin I asked, "Do you believe that is true, Darrin?" He expressed his agreement, saying, "I've been once or twice on Thursday. I would say, generally speaking that the guys do know how to dance a little better than the women." Intrigued, I asked, "How do you know or why do you say that?" Dirk explained:

> Because one time I went there on a Thursday night and we danced. There's a specific order on the dance floor because everybody dances in a circular motion. . . . Lesbians are all over the place it seems. . . . I was like, you know, with Darrin trying to steer him around all these, you know, lesbian at twelve-o'clock, you know, all 5′2″ and 230 pounds.

Reflecting on what he was saying Dirk added, "This is so totally stereotypical and it's completely rude to categorize the [m], but its fun [laughs]. Not all lesbians suck at dancing."

Women seemed to use space differently at *Saddlebags*. Reflecting on some of the comments gay men made about women's use of space, Eleanor who was one of the lesbian women who patronized *Saddlebags* said, "Although I wouldn't use some of the terminology they use, I think that they are somewhat accurate and/or justified in making those comments because I think that does happen."

Even if these perceptions about women's occupation of space were true, gay men's reaction to it was interesting. Studies of gender differences (Wearing, 1998) report that boys are less protective of the personal space around them. If true, men would be *more* tolerant of being jostled or bumped in a crowded public space. The fact that this complaint was raised in conjunction with Lesbian Night and only with reference to women, rather than other nights when the bar is undoubtedly more crowded, implies that the complaint is driven by misogynistic reactions to the presence of women rather than the simple invasion of personal space that inevitably occurs in a crowd.

It is also intriguing that gay men reacted to the invasion of personal space by discounting women in general. Alternative explanations such as the fact that Thursday night brought a lot of newcomers who had less experience dancing and did not know the cultural norms of the bar could conceivably produce antagonism against strangers or against novice dancers. Instead, gay men focused on gender and phrased their reaction within misogynistic statements about the presence of women at *Saddlebags*.

Though the men attributed this problem to the presence of women, Eleanor offered an alternative explanation. She explained that many of the "older" lesbians had a longer history with *Saddlebags* and had a cultural investment in the bar. In contrast, most of the younger lesbians who showed up on Lesbian Night were rude and did not know how to dance. Madge agreed with Eleanor's assessment that the problems were most visible with women new to the bar, but she added:

> But there is some sexism there too in the sense that we are begrudging our sense of community and since the other nights are usually predominantly men, I see a bit of a double standard there. Do we feel the same way about the men [who aren't that familiar with *Saddlebags*] coming in here on Friday and Saturday nights, that just come here to cruise?

Madge's insight about the double standard effectively highlighted the misogyny present in gay men's antagonistic response to lesbians in *Saddlebags*. Men noticed the presumably inappropriate way that lesbians occupied space in part *because* those actions were by women. They did not mention comparable behaviors by men. Whereas gay men framed the problem as due to the presence of women, lesbians attributed it to younger women who did not know the norms of the bar. Because the lesbians had an alternative explanation and saw this as a problem due to a smaller subset of women, served to highlight the misogynistic nature of gay men's response in blaming women in general.

Contributing to the Economic Sustainability of Saddlebags

Sitting on the corner of the bar surrounded by several other women, Eleanor waves her twenty-dollar bill into the air, indicating to Jack that she want to buy another round of shots. "Be right there baby," Jack hollers to Eleanor as he finishes making a round of cocktails for the woman standing at the front of his line. Then punching pre-programmed drink-price keys on his cash register Jack calls out, "Two Corona, One Amstel Light, and three kamikaze shooters—twenty-four fifty." The woman in line holding a twenty-dollar bill raises her eyebrows in astonishment as Jack calls out the number, and then she feverishly searches her jean pockets for more money. In a matter of seconds her hands emerge with a five-dollar bill and she hands both the twenty and the five to Jack, passing the beers and shooters to her friends—one man and one woman—who stand behind her in line. Jack places her two quarters change on the bar, but she has already turned and walked away. Jack rolls his eyes and shakes his head back and forth. Jared, the next man in line, notices Jack's "two-bit tip" and says, "What the hell is that?" Jack replies, "Girl, you know lesbians—they don't drink gin and they don't tip." Then, without inquiry Jack places an Icehouse on the counter and he and Jared exchange money for the beer. Jared leaves a two-dollar tip on the bar.

In addition to women's use of space, another issue that was prevalent in gay men's discussion of Lesbian Night was women's perceived stinginess in spending and tipping at the bar. Gay men felt that women did not contribute their fair share to the profitability and sustainability of *Saddlebags*. Male regulars were often referred to in terms of their economic contribution to "keeping *Saddlebags* open." For example, "He owns stock in *Saddlebags*" or, "Since Terry won't be in town this weekend, *Saddlebags* might as well close their doors." These statements highlight the symbolic status awarded to male patrons who spent generously at the bar.

Although male patrons were seen to contribute significantly to the economic success of *Saddlebags*, I never heard a comment that acknowledged women's economic contributions. Instead, gay men commented on the perceived *lack* of contribution made by women at the bar. One gay patron said, "I have heard some women at *Saddlebags* bring liquor and keep it in their car and thereby circumvent having to go to the bar." He immediately followed this statement with an explanation that, "While I don't drink, I still buy coffee and bottled water to contribute to the success of the bar." The significance of tipping was made apparent by one patron who after complaining that women do not tip said, "They just don't take care of our boys [the bartenders]." Jack, one of the bartenders, agreed:

> Well, [women] don't tip as well and I'm sure you've heard that because I've served like four beers and they would leave me a quarter, maybe not leave me anything, maybe leave a dollar when normally you would've sold each one and you would have got a dollar a piece. So, you might make half of what you would normally make if it was all men . . . I mean, most of your nights are all men and you know what you make and then suddenly when it's all women you all of a sudden make a lot less . . . I mean it's [proof].

Similar to perceptions about occupation of space, comments about tipping were attributed to gender instead of any other relevant characteristic. For example, the level of tipping could easily be associated with a patron's loyalty and commitment to the bar. Women clearly visited *Saddlebags* less frequently than men. The weekly occurrence of Lesbian Night highlighted the limited nature of their patronage. Many of the gay men, on the other hand, were "regulars" who were at the bar several nights a week. These men shared a close sense of community and felt loyalty to the bartenders. They grossly overtipped the bartenders because, as David said, they wanted "the boys to do well for themselves." When these men commented on women's lack of tipping they overlooked lesbians like Eleanor who was a "regular" and who left substantial tips for her bartender. Likewise, no mention was made of the many men who left small tips or made few purchases from the bar.

Of equal interest, however, was the fact that economic sustainability was framed only as a function of individual behavior—men spent money, women did not. Contextual aspects of the bar (e.g. all bartenders were male) were never mentioned in relation to spending behaviors. A clearly visible culture of flirtation and sexual banter occurred between gay male regulars and the bartenders. Bartenders knowingly engaged in this behavior because it brought larger tips. This style of interaction did not occur with women, with whom the bartenders were friendly but not flirtatious. Men who commented on gender differences in spending inevitably framed this as a personal inadequacy of women without acknowledging how the bartenders "worked" men into giving larger tips.

When analyzed in this fashion, comments about spending appeared to be statements about the perceived nature of women rather than sincere concerns about the economic viability of the bar. Since the men who made those comments tended to be regulars who took pride in their own lavish spending and tipping, their remarks served to validate their own loyalty to *Saddlebags* while Othering women for behaviors that were simply not fostered in that environment.

❧ *Discussion*

Much like the research of Aitchison (1999), Binnie and Skeggs (2004), and Slavin (2004), this study of *Saddlebags* illustrates how a gay space can serve as a site of community for gay men. Like Skeggs (1999), we found that gay male leisure space offered a respite from normative heterosexuality. However, it also retains a culture of hegemonic masculinity. In *Saddlebags*, gay men did not develop new images and ideologies that differed from the cultural prescriptions of what a man is supposed to be. Instead, we saw support for Connell's (1995) argument that even gay men perform masculinity in ways that maintain their male privilege.

Gay men's practice of Othering lesbians was perhaps the most subversive and disturbing social practice witnessed in *Saddlebags*. Situated in the context of power relations, Othering occurs when dialectic relationships are used to distinguish between insiders and outsiders (cf. de Beauvoir, 1952; Wittig, 1993). The other often represents some kind of a threat or danger to the Subject. In *Saddlebags* it was women, not heterosexuals, who represented that threat or danger for gay men. Obviously, they wanted *Saddlebags* to be a gay *male* space.

Gay men and lesbians are implicated in each other's lives and brought together through shared discrimination that stems from normative heterosexuality. Gay bars have often been portrayed as contexts where gay men and lesbians can distance themselves from heterosexual discourses that Other them. However, assuming that shared discrimination brings gay men and lesbians together into a unified community is too simplistic (Young, 1990). This study showed that gay men, though seeking reprieve from heterosexual discourse, actively engaged in misogynistic practices to protect and maintain *Saddlebags* as a male-dominated space.

As Sedgwick (1993) noted, gay men have a complex and often contested relationship with masculinity. This relationship was clearly visible in *Saddlebags*. Although the safety of the gay bar protected gay men from the normative heterosexuality of the outside world, these men clearly claimed and enacted a form of masculinity that privileged male over female, tenaciously retaining masculine authority and power by engaging in a discourse that put down women *as women*. These findings highlight the dialectical relationships between gay and straight, male and female, and demonstrate the importance of studying *gender* as distinct from sexual orientation.

Wearing (1998) spoke of leisure as an important context for social control, and Kivel (1996) called for examination of leisure's contribution to cultural ideologies that foster inequity. This ethnography of a gay bar clearly illustrated both factors by showing how control and resistance are entangled in an intricate and complex relationship within this leisure setting. On one level *Saddlebags* represented an escape for both gay men and lesbians from the heterosexual discourse that shapes most of our society. On another level, however, *Saddlebags* was a microcosm of the gender inequities that stem from that same heterosexual discourse. Lesbian Night not only illustrates how gay men reaffirmed their masculinity, it also shows that leisure spaces are complex and dynamic locations where cultural discourse is simultaneously resisted and embraced.

References

AITCHISON, C. (1999). New cultural geographies: The spatiality of leisure, gender and sexuality. *Leisure Studies, 18,* 19–39.

BINNIE, J. & SKEGGS, B. (2004). Cosmopolitan knowledge and the production and consumption of sexualized space: Manchester's gay village. *The Sociological Review, 52*(1), 39–63.

BOUTHILLETTE, A. (1997). Queer and gendered housing: A tale of two neighbourhoods in Vancouver. In G. Ingram, A. Bouthillette, & Y. Retter (Eds.), *Queers in space: Communities, public places, sites of resistance* (pp. 213–232). Seattle, WA: Bay Press.

BROOM, D., BYRNE, M., & PETKOVIC, L. (1992). Off cue: Women who play pool. *Australian & New Zealand Journal of Sociology, 28*(2), 175–191.

BUTLER, J. (1990). *Gender trouble: Feminism and the subversion of identity.* New York: Routledge.

CALDWELL, L. L., KIVEL, B. D., SMITH, E. A., & HAYES, D. M. (1998). The leisure context of adolescents who are lesbian, gay male, bisexual and questioning their sexual identities: An exploratory study. *Journal of Leisure Research, 30*(3), 341–355.

CONNELL, R. W. (1995). *Masculinities.* Cambridge, UK: Polity Press.

CRESWELL, J. W. (1998). *Qualitative inquiry and research design: Choosing among five traditions.* Thousand Oaks, CA: Sage Publications.

DE BEAUVOIR, S. (1952). *The Second Sex.* New York: Alfred A. Knopf.

D'EMILIO, J. (1993). Capitalism and gay identity. In H. Abelove, M. A. Barale, & D. M. HALPERINE (EDS.), *The Lesbian and Gay Studies Reader* (pp. 467–478). New York: Routledge.

EMERSON, R. M., FRETZ, R. I., & SHAW, L. L. (1995). *Writing ethnographic fieldnotes.* Chicago: University of Chicago Press.

FETTERMAN, D. M. (1989). *Ethnography: Step by step.* Thousand Oaks, CA: Sage Publications.

FOUCAULT, M. (1978). *The history of sexuality* (1st American ed.). New York: Pantheon Books.

HENDERSON, K. A. (1994). Perspectives on analyzing gender, women, and leisure. *Journal of Leisure Research, 20*(2), 119–137.

HENDERSON, K. A. & BIALESCHKI, M. D. (1999). Markers of meanings: Feminist perspectives on leisure research. In E. L. Jackson & T. L. Burton (Eds.), *Leisure Studies: Prospects for the twenty-first century* (pp. 167–176). State College, PA: Venture Publishing.

HENDERSON, K. A. & FRELKE, C. E. (2000). Space as a vital dimension of leisure: The creation of place. *World Leisure, 3*, 18–24.

HENDERSON, K. A. & SHAW, S. M. (2003). *Leisure research about gender and men: The weaker link?* Paper presented at the meeting of the National Recreation and Park Societies Leisure Research Symposium, St. Louis, MO. National Park and Recreation Association. Ashburn.

HORROCKS, R. (1995). *Male myths and icons: Masculinity in popular culture.* Basingstoke: Macmillan. Israelstam, S. & Lambert, S. (1984). Gay bars. *Journal of Drug Issues, 14*(4), 637–653.

JOHNSON, C. W. (2000). Living the game of hide and seek: Leisure in the lives of gay and lesbian young adults. *Leisure, 24*(2), 255–278.

KIRBY, S. & HAY, I. (1997). (Hetero) sexing space: Gay men and "straight" space in Adelaide, South Australia. *Professional Geographer, 49*(3), 295–305.

KIVEL, B. D. (1996). *In on the outside, out on the inside: Lesbian/gay/bisexual youth, identity, and leisure.* Unpublished manuscript, University of Georgia.

KIVEL, B. D. (2000). Leisure experience and identity: What difference does difference make? *Journal of Leisure Research, 32*(1), 79–81.

KIVEL, B. D. & Kleiber, D. A. (2000). Leisure in the identity formation of lesbian/gay youth: Personal, but not social. *Leisure Sciences, 22*, 215–232.

LATHER, P. (1994). Critical inquiry in qualitative research: Feminist and post-structural perspectives. In B. F. Crabtree (Ed.), *Collaborative research in primary care* (pp. 103–114). Thousand Oaks, CA: Sage Publications.

LEHNE, G. K. (1998). Homophobia among men: Supporting and defining the male role. In M. S. Kimmel & M. A. Messner (Eds.), *Men's lives* (4th ed., pp. 237–249). Boston, MA: Allyn and Bacon.

LEVINSON, B. A. (1998). How can a man do feminist ethnography of education? *Qualitative Inquiry, 4*(3), 337–368.

MARCUS, G. (1998). *Ethnography through thick and thin.* Princeton, NJ: Princeton University Press.

MORAN, L. J., SKEGGS, B., TYRER, P., & CORTEEN, K. (2003). The formation of fear in gay space: The 'straights' story. *Capital & Class, 80*, 173–199.

Pedlar, A. (1995). Relevance and action research in leisure. *Leisure Sciences, 17*, 133–140.

Podmore, J. A. (2001). Lesbians in the crowd: Gender, sexuality and visibility along Montreal's Boul. St-Laurent. *Gender, Place and Culture, 8*(4), 333–355.

Purvis, T. & Hunt, A. (1993). Discourse, ideology, discourse, ideology, discourse, ideology . . . . *The British Journal of Sociology, 44*(3), 473–499.

Richardson, L. (2000). Evaluating ethnography. *Qualitative Inquiry, 6*(2), 253–255.

Rothenberg, T. (1995). 'And she told two friends': Lesbians creating urban social space. In D. Bell & G. Valentine (Eds.), *Mapping desire: Geographies of sexualities* (pp. 165–181). London: Routledge.

Samdahl, D. M., Jacobson, S., & Hutchinson, S. (2001). When gender is problematic: Leisure and gender negotiation for marginalized women. In J. White & S. Clough-Todd (Eds.), *Women's Leisure Experiences: Ages, Stages and Roles* (pp. 139–146). Eastbourne, UK: Leisure Studies Association.

Scraton, S. & Watson, B. (1998). Gendered cities: Women and public leisure space in the 'postmodern city.' *Leisure Studies, 17*, 123–137.

Sedgwick, E. K. (1993). Epistemology of the closet. In H. Abelove, M. A. Barale, & D. M. Halperin (Eds.), *The Lesbian and gay studies reader* (pp. 45–61). New York: Routledge.

Shaw, S. M. (1994). Gender, leisure and constraint: Toward a framework for the analysis of women's leisure. *Journal of Leisure Research, 26*(1), 8–22.

Shaw, S. M. (1999). Gender and leisure. In E. L. Jackson & T. L. Burton (Eds.), *Leisure studies: Prospects for the twenty-first century* (pp. 271–282). State College, PA: Venture Publishing.

Skeggs, B. (1999). Matter out of place: Visibility and sexualities in leisure spaces. *Leisure Studies, 18*, 213–232.

Slavin, S. (2004). Drugs, space, and sociality in a gay nightclub in Sydney. *Journal of Contemporary Ethnography, 33*(3), 265–295.

Spradley, J. P. (1979). *The ethnographic interview.* New York: Holt Rinehart and Winston.

Spradley, J. P. (1980). *Participant observation.* New York: Holt Rinehart and Winston.

St. Pierre, B. (1999). The work of response in ethnography. *Journal of Contemporary Ethnography, 28*, 266–288.

Stokowski, P. A. (2002). Languages of place and discourses of power: Constructing new senses of place. *Journal of Leisure Research, 34*(4), 368–382.

Vaid, U. (1995). *Virtual equality: The mainstreaming of gay and lesbian liberation.* New York: Anchor Books.

Valentine, G. (1993). (Hetero) sexing space: Lesbian perceptions and experiences of everyday spaces. *Environment and Planning D: Society & Space, 11*, 395–413.

Van Maanen, J. (1988). *Tales of the field: On writing ethnography.* Chicago, IL: University of Chicago Press.

Wearing, B. (1998). *Leisure and feminist theory.* Thousand Oaks, CA: Sage Publications.

Wittig, M. (1993). One is not born a woman. In H. Abelove, M. A. Barale, & D. M. Halperin (Eds.), *The lesbian and gay studies reader* (pp. 103–109). New York: Routledge.

Wolcott, H. F. (1994). *Transforming qualitative data: Description, analysis, and interpretation.* Thousand Oaks, CA: Sage Publications.

Wolcott, H. F. (1999). *Ethnography: A way of seeing.* Walnut Creek, CA: AltaMira Press.

Wolcott, H. F. (2001). *Writing up qualitative research* (2nd ed.). Thousand Oaks, CA: Sage Publications.

Wolfe, M. (1997). Invisible women in invisible places: The production of social space in lesbian bars. In G. Ingram, A. Bouthillette, & Y. Retter (Eds.), *Queers in space: Communities, public places, sites of resistance.* Seattle, WA: Bay Press.

Young, I. M. (1990). The ideal community and the politics of difference. In L. J. Nicholson (Ed.), *Feminism/Postmodernism.* London: Routledge.

● ● ●

Questions

1. Define "misogyny." Characterize the "misogynistic discourse" of the men at Saddlebags.

2. Explain the significance, meanings, and need for "gay space" in a society dominated by heterosexuals. Is gay space synonymous with "lesbian space"?

3. How can the notion that "everyone is welcome" exist alongside antagonism toward lesbians at Saddlebags?

4. Analyze the specific strategies gay men used to "other" lesbians at the bar.

5. Formulate an explanation for gay men's performances of masculinity in relation to lesbians.

6. Were you surprised by gay men's responses to the presence of lesbians? Why or why not?

Becoming Bisexual

Martin S. Weinberg, Colin J. Williams
and Douglas W. Pryor

*In a society that promotes heterosexuality, people often take sexual orienta-
tion and identify for granted. Specifically, many people rarely question the
socialization process by which heterosexual individuals arrive at their
sexual orientation and identity. This is not true for homosexuality or bisexuality, however. In these cases, the general public and research community
take an interest in what leads some individuals to develop an "alternative"
sexual identity and orientation. In this selection, the authors address this
topic by asking how people realize that a bisexual identity is a viable alternative, how people establish their bisexual identity, and how people manage
the stigma associated with this orientation.*

Becoming bisexual involves the rejection of not one but two recognized categories of sexual identity: heterosexual and homosexual.
Most people settle into the status of heterosexual without any struggle over
the identity. There is not much concern with explaining how this occurs;
that people are heterosexual is simply taken for granted. For those who find
heterosexuality unfulfilling, however, developing a sexual identity is more
difficult.

How is it then that some people come to identify themselves as "bisexuals"? As a point of departure we take the process through which people
come to identify themselves as "homosexual." A number of models have
been formulated that chart the development of a homosexual identity
through a series of stages.[1] While each model involves a different number of
stages, the models all share three elements. The process begins with the
person in a state of identity confusion-feeling different from others, struggling with the acknowledgment of same-sex attractions. Then there is a
period of thinking about possibly being homosexual—involving associating
with self-identified homosexuals, sexual experimentation, forays into the
homosexual subculture. Last is the attempt to integrate one's self-concept

and social identity as homosexual—acceptance of the label, disclosure about being homosexual, acculturation to a homosexual way of life, and the development of love relationships. Not every person follows through each stage. Some remain locked in at a certain point. Others move back and forth between stages.

To our knowledge, no previous model of bisexual identity formation exists. In this [selection] we present such a model based on the following questions: To what extent is there overlap with the process involved in becoming homosexual? How far is the label "bisexual" clearly recognized, understood, and available to people as an identity? Does the absence of a bisexual subculture in most locales affect the information and support needed for sustaining a commitment to the identity? For our subjects, then, what are the problems in finding the "bisexual" label, understanding what the label means, dealing with social disapproval from two directions, and continuing to use the label once it is adopted? From our fieldwork and interviews, we found that four stages captured our respondents' most common experiences when dealing with questions of identity: initial confusion, finding and applying the label, settling into the identity, and continued uncertainty.

◉ The Stages

Initial Confusion

Many of the people interviewed said that they had experienced a period of considerable confusion, doubt, and struggle regarding their sexual identity before defining themselves as bisexual. This was ordinarily the first step in the process of becoming bisexual.

They described a number of major sources of early confusion about their sexual identity. For some, it was the experience of having strong sexual feelings for both sexes that was unsettling, disorienting, and sometimes frightening. Often these were sexual feelings that they said they did not know how to easily handle or resolve.

> In the past, I couldn't reconcile different desires I had. I didn't understand them. I didn't know what I was. And I ended up feeling really mixed up, unsure, and kind of frightened. (F)

> I thought I was gay, and yet I was having these intense fantasies and feelings about fucking women. I went through a long period of confusion. (M)

Others were confused because they thought strong sexual feelings for, or sexual behavior with, the same sex meant an end to their long-standing heterosexuality.

> I was afraid of my sexual feelings for men and . . . that if I acted on them, that would negate my sexual feelings for women. I knew absolutely no one else who had . . . sexual feelings for both men and women, and didn't realize that was an option. (M)

> When I first had sexual feelings for females, I had the sense I should give up my feelings for men. I think it would have been easier to give up men. (F)

A third source of confusion in this initial stage stemmed from attempts by respondents trying to categorize their feelings for, and/or behaviors with, both sexes, yet not being able to do so. Unaware of the term "bisexual," some tried to organize their sexuality by using the readily available labels of "heterosexual" or "homosexual"—but these did not seem to fit. No sense of sexual identity jelled; an aspect of themselves remained unclassifiable.

> When I was young, I didn't know what I was. I knew there were people like Mom and Dad—heterosexual and married—and that there were "queens." I knew I wasn't like either one. (M)

> I thought I had to be either gay or straight. That was the big lie. It was confusing. . . . That all began to change in the late 60s. It was a long and slow process. . . . (F)

Finally, others suggested they experienced a great deal of confusion because of their "homophobia"—their difficulty in facing up to the same-sex component of their sexuality. The consequence was often long-term denial. This was more common among the men than the women, but not exclusively so.

> At age seventeen, I became close to a woman who was gay. She had sexual feelings for me. I had some . . . for her but I didn't respond. Between the ages of seventeen and twenty-six I met another gay woman. She also had sexual feelings towards me. I had the same for her but I didn't act on . . . or acknowledge them. . . . I was scared. . . . I was also attracted to men at the same time. . . . I denied that I was sexually attracted to women. I was afraid that if they knew the feelings were mutual they would act on them . . . and put pressure on me. (F)

I though I might be able to get rid of my homosexual tendencies through religious means—prayer, belief, counseling—before I came to accept it as part of me. (M)

The intensity of the confusion and the extent to which it existed in the lives of the people we met at the Bisexual Center, whatever its particular source, was summed up by two men who spoke with us informally. As paraphrased in our field notes:

The identity issue for him was a very confusing one. At one point, he almost had a nervous breakdown, and when he finally entered college, he sought psychiatric help.

Bill said he thinks this sort of thing happens a lot at the Bi Center. People come in "very confused" and experience some really painful stress.

ℱinding and 𝒜pplying the ℒabel

Following this initial period of confusion, which often spanned years, was the experience of finding and applying the label. We asked the people we interviewed for specific factors or events in their lives that led them to define themselves as bisexual. There were a number of common experiences.

For many who were unfamiliar with the term bisexual, the discovery that the category in fact existed was a turning point. This happened by simply hearing the word, reading about it somewhere, or learning of a place called the Bisexual Center. The discovery provided a means of making sense of long-standing feelings for both sexes.

Early on I thought I was just gay, because I was not aware there was another category, bisexual. I always knew I was interested in men and women. But I did not realize there was a name for these feelings and behaviors until I took Psychology 101 and read about it, heard about it there. That was in college. (F)

The first time I heard the word, which was not until I was twenty-six, I realized that was what fit for me. What it fit was that I had sexual feelings for both men and women. Up until that point, the only way that I could define my sexual feelings was that I was either a latent homosexual or a confused heterosexual. (M)

Going to a party at someone's house, and finding out there that the party was to benefit the Bisexual Center. I guess at that point I began to define myself as bisexual. I never knew there was such a word. If I had heard the

160

word earlier on, for example as a kid, I might have been bisexual then. My feelings had always been bisexual. I just did not know how to define them. (F)

Reading *The Bisexual Option* . . . I realized then that bisexuality really existed and that's what I was. (M)

In the case of others the turning point was their first homosexual or heterosexual experience coupled with the recognition that sex was pleasurable with both sexes. These were people who already seemed to have knowledge of the label "bisexual," yet without experiences with both men and women, could not label themselves accordingly.

The first time I had actual intercourse, an orgasm with a woman, it led me to realize I was bisexual because I enjoyed it as much as I did with a man, although the former occurred much later on in my sexual experiences. . . . I didn't have an orgasm with a woman until twenty-two, while with males, that had been going on since the age of thirteen. (M)

Having homosexual fantasies and acting those out. . . . I would not identify as bi if I only had fantasies and they were mild. But since my fantasies were intensely erotic, and I acted them out, these two things led me to believe I was really bisexual. . . . (M)

After my first involved sexual affair with a woman, I also had feelings for a man, and I knew I did not fit the category dyke. I was also dating gay-identified males. So I began looking at gay/lesbian and heterosexual labels as not fitting my situation. (F)

Still others reported not so much a specific experience as a turning point, but emphasized the recognition that their sexual feelings for both sexes were simply too strong to deny. They eventually came to the conclusion that it was unnecessary to choose between them.

I found myself with men but couldn't completely ignore my feelings for women. When involved with a man I always had a close female relationship. When one or the other didn't exist at any given time, I felt I was really lacking something. I seem to like both. (F)

The last factor that was instrumental in leading people to initially adopt the label bisexual was the encouragement and support of others. Encouragement sometimes came from a partner who already defined himself or herself as bisexual.

Encouragement from a man I was in a relationship with. We had been together two or three years at the time—he began to define as bisexual. . . . [He] encouraged me to do so as well. He engineered a couple of three-somes with another woman. Seeing one other person who had bisexuality as an identity that fit them seemed to be a real encouragement. (F)

Encouragement from a partner seemed to matter more for women. Occasionally the "encouragement" bordered on coercion as the men in their lives wanted to engage in a *ménage à trois* or group sex.

I had a male lover for a year and a half who was familiar with bisexuality and pushed me towards it. My relationship with him brought it up in me. He wanted me to be bisexual because he wanted to be in a threesome. He was also insanely jealous of my attractions to men, and did everything in his power to suppress my opposite sex attractions. He showed me a lot of pictures of naked women and played on my reactions. He could tell that I was aroused by pictures of women and would talk about my attractions while we were having sex. . . . He was twenty years older than me. He was very manipulative in a way. My feelings for females were there and [he was] almost forcing me to act on my attractions. . . . (F)

Encouragement also came from sex-positive organizations, primarily the Bisexual Center, but also places like San Francisco Sex Information (SFSI), the Pacific Center, and the Institute for Advanced Study of Human Sexuality, all of which were described earlier.[2]

At the gay pride parade I had seen the brochures for the Bisexual Center. Two years later I went to a Tuesday night meeting. I immediately felt that I belonged and that if I had to define myself that this was what I would use. (M)

Through SFSI and the Bi Center, I found a community of people . . . [who] were more comfortable for me than were the exclusive gay or heterosexual communities. . . . [It was] beneficial for myself to be . . . in a sex-positive community. I got more strokes and came to understand myself better. . . . I felt it was necessary to express my feelings for males and females without having to censor them, which is what the gay and straight communities pressured me to do. (F)

Thus our respondents became familiar with and came to the point of adopting the label bisexual in a variety of ways: through reading about it on their own, being in therapy, talking to friends, having experiences with sex partners, learning about the Bi Center, visiting SFSI or the Pacific Center, and coming to accept their sexual feelings.

Settling into the Identity

Usually it took years from the time of first sexual attractions to, or behaviors with, both sexes before people came to think of themselves as bisexual. The next stage then was one of settling into the identity, which was characterized by a more complete transition in self-labeling.

Most reported that this settling-in stage was the consequence of becoming more self-accepting. They became less concerned with the negative attitudes of others about their sexual preference.

> I realized that the problem of bisexuality isn't mine. It's society's. They are having problems dealing with my bisexuality. So I was then thinking if they had a problem dealing with it, so should I. But I don't. (F)

> I learned to accept the fact that there are a lot of people out there who aren't accepting. They can be intolerant, selfish, shortsighted and so on. Finally, in growing up, I learned to say "So what, I don't care what others think." (M)

> I just decided I was bi. I trusted my own sense of self. I stopped listening to others tell me what I could or couldn't be. (F)

The increase in self-acceptance was often attributed to the continuing support from friends, counselors, and the Bi Center, through reading, and just being in San Francisco.

> Fred Klein's *The Bisexual Option* book and meeting more and more bisexual people . . . helped me feel more normal. . . . There were other human beings who felt like I did on a consistent basis. (M)

> I think going to the Bi Center really helped a lot. I think going to the gay baths and realizing there were a lot of men who sought the same outlet I did really helped. Talking about it with friends has been helpful and being validated by female lovers that approve of my bisexuality. Also the reaction of people who I've told, many of whom weren't even surprised. (M)

> The most important thing was counseling. Having the support of a bisexual counselor. Someone who acted as somewhat of a mentor. [He] validated my frustration. . . . helped me do problem solving, and guide[d]

me to other supportive experiences like SFSI. Just engaging myself in a supportive social community. (M)

The majority of the people we came to know through the interviews seemed settled in their sexual identity. We tapped this through a variety of questions. Ninety percent said that they did not think they were currently in transition from being homosexual to being heterosexual or from being heterosexual to being homosexual. However, when we probed further by asking this group "Is it possible, though, that someday you could define yourself as either lesbian/gay or heterosexual?" about 40 percent answered yes. About two-thirds of these indicated that the change could be in either direction, though almost 70 percent said that such a change was not probable.

We asked those who thought a change was possible what it might take to bring it about. The most common response referred to becoming involved in a meaningful relationship that was monogamous or very intense. Often the sex of the hypothetical partner was not specified, underscoring that the overall quality of the relationship was what really mattered.

> Love. I think if I feel insanely in love with some person, it could possibly happen. (M)

> If I should meet a woman and want to get married, and if she was not open to my relating to men, I might become heterosexual again. (M)

> Getting involved in a long-term relationship like marriage where I wouldn't need a sexual involvement with anyone else. The sex of the . . . partner wouldn't matter. It would have to be someone who I could commit my whole life to exclusively, a lifelong relationship. (F)

A few mentioned the breaking up of a relationship and how this would incline them to look toward the other sex.

> Steve is one of the few men I feel completely comfortable with. If anything happened to him, I don't know if I'd want to try and build up a similar relationship with another man. I'd be more inclined to look towards women for support. (F)

Changes in sexual behavior seemed more likely for the people we interviewed than changes in how they defined themselves. We asked "Is it possible that someday you could behave either exclusively homosexual or exclusively heterosexual?" Over 80 percent answered yes. This is over twice as many as those who saw a possible change in how they defined themselves, again showing that a wide range of behaviors can be subsumed under the same label. Of this particular group, the majority (almost 60 percent) felt that there was nothing inevitable about how they might change, indicating that it could be in either a homosexual or a heterosexual direction. Around a quarter, though, said the change would be to exclusive heterosexual behavior and 15 percent to exclusive homosexual behavior. (Twice as many women noted the homosexual direction, while many more men than women said the heterosexual direction.) Just over 40 percent responded that a change to exclusive heterosexuality or homosexuality was not very probable, about a third somewhat probable, and about a quarter very probable.

Again, we asked what it would take to bring about such a change in behavior. Once more the answers centered on achieving a long-term monogamous and involved relationship, often with no reference to a specific sex.

> For me to behave exclusively heterosexual or homosexual would require that I find a lifetime commitment from another person with a damn good argument of why I should not go to bed with somebody else. (F)

> I am a romantic. If I fell in love with a man, and our relationship was developing that way, I might become strictly homosexual. The same possibility exists with a woman. (M)

Thus "settling into the identity" must be seen in relative terms. Some of the people we interviewed did seem to accept the identity completely. When we compared our subjects' experiences with those characteristic of homosexuals, however, we were struck by the absence of closure that characterized our bisexual respondents—even those who appeared most committed to the identity. This led us to posit a final stage in the formation of sexual identity, one that seems unique to bisexuals.

Continued Uncertainty

The belief that bisexuals are confused about their sexual identity is quite common. This conception has been promoted especially by those lesbians and gays who see bisexuality as being in and of itself a pathological state. From their point of view, "confusion" is literally a built-in feature of "being" bisexual. As expressed in one study:

> While appearing to encompass a wider choice of love objects . . . [the bisexual] actually becomes a product of abject confusion; his self-image is that of an overgrown young adolescent whose ability to differentiate one

form of sexuality from another has never developed. He lacks above all a sense of identity. . . . [He] cannot answer the question: What am I?[3]

One evening a facilitator at a Bisexual Center rap group put this belief in a slightly different and more contemporary form:

> One of the myths about bisexuality is that you can't be bisexual without somehow being "schizoid." The lesbian and gay communities do not see being bisexual as a crystallized or complete sexual identity. The homosexual community believes there is no such thing as bisexuality. They think that bisexuals are people who are in transition [to becoming homosexual] or that they are people afraid of being stigmatized [as homosexual] by the heterosexual majority.

We addressed the issue directly in the interviews with two questions: "Do you *presently* feel confused about your bisexuality?" and "Have you *ever* felt confused. . . ?" For the men, a quarter and 84 percent answered "yes," respectively. For the women, it was about a quarter and 56 percent.

When asked to provide details about this uncertainty, the primary response was that *even after having discovered and applied the label "bisexual" to themselves, and having come to the point of apparent self-acceptance, they still [were confused by] their sexual identity.* One reason was the lack of social validation and support that came with being a self-identified bisexual. The social reaction people received made it difficult to sustain the identity over the long haul.

While the heterosexual world was said to be completely intolerant of any degree of homosexuality, the reaction of the homosexual world mattered more. Many bisexuals referred to the persistent pressures they experienced to relabel themselves as "gay" or "lesbian" and to engage in sexual activity exclusively with the same sex. It was asserted that no one was *really* bisexual, and that calling oneself "bisexual" was a politically incorrect and inauthentic identity. Given that our respondents were living in San Francisco (which has such a large homosexual population) and that they frequently moved in and out of the homosexual world (to whom they often looked for support) this could be particularly distressing.

> Sometimes the repeated denial the gay community directs at us. Their negation of the concept and the term bisexual has sometimes made me wonder whether I was just imagining the whole thing. (M)

> My involvement with the gay community. There was extreme political pressure. The lesbians said bisexuals didn't exist. To them, I had to make

up my mind and identify as lesbian. . . . I was really questioning my identity, that is, about defining myself as bisexual. . . . (F)

For the women, the invalidation carried over to their feminist identity (which most had). They sometimes felt that being with men meant they were selling out the world of women.

I was involved with a woman for several years. She was straight when I met her but became a lesbian. She tried to "win me back" to lesbianism. She tried to tell me that if I really loved her, I would leave Bill. I did love her, but I could not deny how I felt about him either. So she left me and that hurt. I wondered if I was selling out my woman identity and if it [being bisexual] was worth it. (F)

A few wondered whether they were lying to themselves about their heterosexual side. One woman questioned whether her heterosexual desires were a result of "acculturation" rather than being her own choice. Another woman suggested a similar social dimension to her homosexual component:

There was one period when I was trying to be gay because of the political thing of being totally woman-identified rather than being with men. The Women's Culture Center in college had a women's studies minor, so I was totally immersed in women's culture. . . .

Lack of support also came from the absence of bisexual role models, no real bisexual community aside from the Bisexual Center, and nothing in the way of public recognition of bisexuality, which bred uncertainty and confusion.

I went through a period of dissociation, of being very alone and isolated. That was due to my bisexuality. People would ask, well, what was I? I wasn't gay and I wasn't straight. So I didn't fit. (F)

I don't feel like I belong in a lot of situations because society is so polarized as heterosexual or homosexual. There are not enough bi organizations or public places to go to like bars, restaurants, clubs. . . . (F)

For some, continuing uncertainty about their sexual identity was related to their inability to translate their sexual feelings into sexual behaviors. (Some of the women had *never* engaged in homosexual sex.)

Should I try to have a sexual relationship with a woman? . . . Should I just back off and keep my distance, just try to maintain a friendship? I question whether I am really bisexual because I don't know if I will ever act on my physical attractions for females. (F)

167

I know I have strong sexual feelings towards men, but then I don't know how to get close to or be sexual with a man. I guess that what happens is I start wondering how genuine my feelings are. . . . (M)

For the men, confusion stemmed more from the practical concerns of implementing and managing multiple partners or from questions about how to find an involved homosexual relationship and what that might mean on a social and personal level.

I felt very confused about how I was going to manage my life in terms of developing relationships with both men and women. I still see it as a difficult lifestyle to create for myself because it involves a lot of hard work and understanding on my part and that of the men and women I'm involved with. (M)

I've thought about trying to have an actual relationship with a man. Some of my confusion revolves around how to find a satisfactory sexual relationship. I do not particularly like gay bars. I have stopped having anonymous sex. . . . (M)

Many men and women felt doubts about their bisexual identity because of being in an exclusive sexual relationship. After being exclusively involved with an opposite-sex partner for a period of time, some of the respondents questioned the homosexual side of their sexuality. Conversely, after being exclusively involved with a partner of the same sex, other respondents called into question the heterosexual component of their sexuality.

When I'm with a man or a woman sexually for a period of time, then I begin to wonder how attracted I really am to the other sex. (M)

In the last relationship I had with a woman, my heterosexual feelings were very diminished. Being involved in a lesbian lifestyle put stress on my self-identification as a bisexual. It seems confusing to me because I am monogamous for the most part, monogamy determines my lifestyle to the extremes of being heterosexual or homosexual. (F)

Others made reference to a lack of sexual activity with weaker sexual feelings and affections for one sex. Such learning did not fit with the perception that bisexuals should have balanced desires and behaviors. The consequence was doubt about "really" being bisexual.

On the level of sexual arousal and deep romantic feelings, I feel them much more strongly for women than for men. I've gone so far as questioning myself when this is involved. (M)

I definitely am attracted to and it is much easier to deal with males. Also, guilt for my attraction to females has led me to wonder if I am just really toying with the idea. Is the sexual attraction I have for females something I constructed to pass time or what? (F)

Just as "settling into the identity" is a relative phenomenon, so too is "continued uncertainty," which can involve a lack of closure as part and parcel of what it means to be bisexual.

We do not wish to claim too much for our model of bisexual identity formation. There are limits to its general application. The people we interviewed were unique in that not only did all the respondents define themselves as bisexual (a consequence of our selection criteria), but they were also all members of a bisexual social organization in a city that perhaps more than any other in the United States could be said to provide a bisexual subculture of some sort. Bisexuals in places other than San Francisco surely must move through the early phases of the identity process with a great deal more difficulty. Many probably never reach the later stages.

Finally, the phases of the model we present are very broad and somewhat simplified. While the particular problems we detail within different phases may be restricted to the type of bisexuals in this study, the broader phases can form the basis for the development of more sophisticated models of bisexual identity formation.

Still, not all bisexuals will follow these patterns. Indeed, given the relative weakness of the bisexual subculture compared with the social pressures toward conformity exhibited in the gay subculture, there may be more varied ways of acquiring a bisexual identity. Also, the involvement of bisexuals in the heterosexual world means that various changes in heterosexual lifestyles (e.g., a decrease in open marriages or swinging) will be a continuing, and as yet unexplored, influence on bisexual identity. Finally, wider societal changes, notably the existence of AIDS, may make for changes in the overall identity process. Being used to choice and being open to both sexes can give bisexuals a range of adaptations in their sexual life that are not available to others.

Endnotes

[1]Vivien C. Cass, "Homosexual Identity Formation: Testing a Theoretical Model." *Journal of Sex Research* 20 (1984), pp. 143–167; Eli Coleman, "Developmental Stages of the Coming Out Process." *Journal of Homosexuality* 7 (1981/2), pp.

31–43; Barbara Ponse, *Identities in the Lesbian World: The Social Construction of Self* (Westport, CT: Greenwood Press, 1978).

[2]Martin S. Weinberg, Colin J. Williams, and Douglas Pryor, "Telling the Facts of Life: A Study of a Sex Information Switchboard." *Journal of Contemporary Ethnography* 17 (1988), pp. 131–163.

[3]Donald Webster Cory and John P. Leroy, *The Homosexual and His Society* (New York: The Citadel Press, 1963), p. 61.

◉ ◉ ◉

Questions

1. Why do you think that heterosexuality is normative in our society and being bisexual is an "alternative" sexual orientation? How is this related to some of the problems of living that bisexuals face?

2. According to the authors, what are the four stages that a person goes through in becoming bisexual?

3. What relationship do "significant others" play in establishing and reinforcing the bisexual identity? What role do significant others play in the discarding of the bisexual identity?

4. What are the major sources of initial confusion regarding one's sexual identity?

5. What is the relationship between one's sexual behavior and one's sexual identity?

6. Are there any differences between men and women in the development of a bisexual identity (especially regarding the stage of continued uncertainty)? If so, what might account for these differences?

Reaching Out to the Down Low

CHRISTOPHER LISOTTA

This article from The Advocate, *a magazine for gay, lesbian, bisexual, and transgender people, shows how complicated human sexuality can be. Christopher Lisotta offers insight into the lives of black men who identify themselves as straight and have wives or girlfriends but who also have random, often unprotected sex with men on the sly. Lisotta also describes what health groups are trying to do to get these men to use safer sex practices to protect not only themselves, but their intimate partners.*

Most visitors to Hollywood would never notice the Study, a gay bar tucked into a side street about two miles east of Grauman's Chinese Theatre. On a recent Sunday night, however, the place is packed with mostly African-American and Latino men who squeeze by each other along the aging paneled walls. A song by Lauryn Hill bleeds into a Madonna classic as customers play pool, chat up the bartenders, or watch sports.

The Study is a place to find a quick same-sex hookup, although many of the men here say they don't consider themselves to be gay at all. They keep their sex with other men a secret, refusing even to tell their wives or girlfriends.

A man named Ezel, a volunteer with Minority AIDS Project who declines to give his last name, is staffing a table in a corner of the bar, offering free condoms and information on STDs to help educate patrons about safer sex. He is bisexual, although his new 24-year-old wife has no idea he sleeps with men. "She's open-minded, but I don't think she'd be *that* open-minded," says Ezel, who calls the men he sleeps with "associates" and never has boyfriends. "I meet people at work, on the bus, and on the street. You meet people in casual, everyday contact, just as you would a female."

Ezel prefers effeminate men and always insists on safer sex. "I consider that whenever I have intercourse with another man that I have a wife to go home to. But if I were to take something home to her, be it HIV, gonorrhea,

---

Reprinted by permission from *The Advocate*, August 17, 2004.

or chlamydia, it's going to be a question of, How did this happen?" he says. "As I become more comfortable with my sexuality, it will eventually be something I will express to her."

By now most Americans are familiar with the term "on the down low"—at least those who read national newspapers or watch the Oprah Winfrey show. In April the talk show featured men who identify as straight and have wives or girlfriends but also have random, often unprotected sex with men on the sly. The women in Winfrey's studio audience were furious that they were being kept in the dark and ran a high risk of contracting HIV from their supposedly monogamous husbands and boyfriends.

One of Winfrey's most controversial guests was author J.L. King, whose book *On the Down Low: A Journey Into the Lives of "Straight" Black Men Who Sleep With Men* is stirring up controversy among African-Americans because most see black men in very specific ways, images that have been cultivated by and co-opted from hip-hop stars and rap videos. Fearful of being shunned by their families, friends, and churches, men who desire other men sexually stay in the closet.

Even with the increased media attention, health groups are fighting an uphill battle to convince men on the down low to practice safer sex. They are blanketing bars, clubs, and bathhouses with prevention information and starting support groups in an effort to curb rising HIV rates, which are disproportionately high among straight black women, in part due to the down-low culture. In light of this, outreach efforts are truly a matter of life and death. According to various AIDS groups, African-Americans make up just 12% of the U.S. population but account for more than half of all new HIV diagnoses. Black women make up 72% of new HIV infections among American women. African-American women have an AIDS rate 23 times greater than that of white women, and African-American men have a rate nine times greater than that of white men. Among blacks, AIDS is the leading cause of death for women age 25–34 and men age 35–44.

Men living on the down low are not exclusively to blame for these figures, but they are certainly exacerbating the situation. "We need to talk about whether we should be using condoms in this relationship. We need to talk about safer-sex interventions," says Stephen Simon, AIDS coordinator for the city of Los Angeles and an openly bisexual black man. "Saying 'spy on your man; he might be sleeping around on you' is not getting us there. The goal seems to be to find a man you can make sure won't sleep with another man, and that's just a preposterous goal."

Another problem that safer-sex advocates run into when they speak with men of color, says openly gay television producer Maurice Townes, is that "our society, America, has only shown the world that gay equals white, that AIDS equals white, so that anything that comes on television or in the media that's gay, it's always been white. Outside of *To Wong Foo* and *Six Feet Under,* there is nothing that is black and gay." Townes and business partner Kevin F. Allen have created a DVD series titled *The Closet,* which follows several African-American men who have sex with men, and they hope to deal with issues of bisexuality and the down-low culture in a positive way. The series has been popular among gay men and straight black women.

Back at the Study, "Terrance," a 33-year-old black man who has just broken up with his fiancée following her discovery that he also dates men, points out a man across the parking lot whom he has dated in the past. Terrance recently found out that his cousin is gay and has been talking to him regularly about his sexuality. "I want love, I want commitment, I want intimacy," he explains. "But I'm not sure if that will be with a man or a woman. I haven't figured it out yet."

In Los Angeles a group of African-American men have established what may be the next step in helping men determine their sexuality and perhaps embrace safer sex more fully. In 1999, Jeffrey King founded In the Meantime, a group that explores the mental, physical, and spiritual needs of African-American men, particularly those who consider themselves gay, bisexual, or "same-gender-loving"—a term popular with members. On Tuesday nights the group gathers in the bottom-floor meeting room of a cavernous disco popular among gay, lesbian, bisexual, and transgendered people of color. The meetings draw a wide variety of people—retirees, businessmen, and college students mix easily—and might feature a guest speaker or a discussion about a book or HIV awareness. In the Meantime also sponsors men's retreats and a telephone hotline and has organized cross-cultural events to reach out to other populations.

Simon, a regular at the Tuesday meetings who declines to give his last name, says the group "can bridge these community gaps, bridge the gap between the old-school gay and lesbian community. They don't have an agenda that says 'Same-gender-loving is good, gay is bad—pick one.' They don't have an agenda that says 'You're either black or gay—prioritize.' They, I think, allow the space for people to self-identify a lot more comfortably."

While many black men completely shun gay sex, Latinos often consider it culturally acceptable to have gay sex on the side provided that one assumes the top or dominant role. There is much more discrimination against men who take receptive roles.

On a recent Tuesday near downtown Los Angeles, men are lining up, waiting for a bathhouse to open—at noon. Once it opens, it becomes crowded with a racially diverse group of men: older guys, 20-somethings, skinny club types, gym rats, and overweight men. As they cruise the hallways—occasionally darting into rooms to have sex—some peer into the third-floor TV lounge. About half a dozen men in towels are, for now at least, forgoing sex to have a safer-sex discussion in Spanish, organized by Bienestar Human Services, a Southern California outreach group for Latinos.

Two Bienestar staffers hover over condoms, dildos, and literature about STDs. The group is getting animated. The conversation touches on issues of machismo and cultural expectations, topics that few of the men have ever discussed with anyone. These men don't want to reveal information about themselves; they are there for sex only. Victor Martinez, director of prevention and education for Bienestar's GLBT unit, explains that the group can't talk about Latinos as one monolithic entity in trying to identify people at risk. For example, he says, Latinos from the Caribbean tend to be more comfortable talking about sexuality than those from Central America.

"We have immigrants; we also have families who have been living here for generations and generations," Martinez says. "For monolingual Spanish speakers, the 'down low' is not in the vocabulary. However, for some groups that are more acculturated, it is getting more popular."

Also, some new immigrants are turning to sex to make money. Bienestar has learned that home improvement centers and lumberyards—where itinerant Latino day laborers congregate looking for work—have become popular cruising spots where workers can exchange sex just as easily as other services for money. The results for their unsuspecting female partners at home are the same as in African-American households: an exponentially increased risk of HIV infection. "They go back to their families and their houses and give the virus to their [wives and girlfriends]," Martinez says. "And what we see here at Bienestar, most of the female clients have been infected by their primary male partner."

Townes has always considered himself gay and never lived life on the down low. Still, he sees what's happening in his community.

"This has been going on forever in every culture," he says. "It's always been looked down upon to be homosexual. Men who were ashamed of it have done everything in their power to hide. These men are in denial. They are lying to their intimate partners, their sexual partners, and they are lying to the person that they see in the mirror."

◉ ◉ ◉

Questions

1. What is the meaning of the term "on the down low" ?

2. Why do men who identify themselves as straight and have wives or girl-friends sometimes have unprotected sex with men on the sly? What are the potential dangers of this practice to these men and their intimate partners?

3. Compare the perspectives of black men and Latino men on the accept-ability of having same-sex sexual encounters.

4. Describe what is being done by health groups to get men on the down low to use safer sex practices.

Why Suzie Wong Is Not a Lesbian: Asian and Asian American Lesbian and Bisexual Women and Femme/Butch/Gender Identities

JEEYEUN LEE

In this article, JeeYeun Lee analyses the intersections of race, gender, and sexuality to explain why Asian and Asian-American women are unlikely to be labeled as lesbians. Showing how Asian gender norms differ from white, Western gender norms, she identifies the pitfalls of using white norms as the standard for evaluation. Only by examining race, gender, and sexuality together can we understand the unique position of Asian women. When multiple sets of stereotypes come together, there may be no place in our imaginations for certain kinds of people to exist. This fact provides yet another example of the problems with stereotypes: They make people who don't fit them invisible.

*L*ately, some commentators of lesbian life have noted the prevalence of what Lillian Faderman calls "neo-butch/femme," where women appear to be playing with femme and butch roles "with a sense of lightness and flexibility."[1] These writers are worried by the seemingly de-politicized nature of this carefree attitude:

> [T]he "fluidity" school seems to champion a celebratory approach, a refusal to consider any deeper, or problematic, elements. "Gender play" is all the rage, but, in all this, where is a feminist consciousness and challenge to gender divisions and inequalities?[2]

Reprinted from *Queer Studies: A Gay, Bisexual, & Transgender Anthology*, edited by Brett Beemyn and Mickey Eliason, (1996), by permission of New York University Press.

This characterization of femme/butch as an apolitical lifestyle is itself somewhat glib. While it is true that many lesbian and bisexual women in certain regions of the U.S. do describe their gender/sexual styles as play, the reasons that women play with gender have deeper significance than just frivolous masquerade and have more to do with living the complex intersections of sex, appearance, anatomy, sexuality, race, and culture. In particular, for women of color who "play" with gender, relationships to gender identities are complicated by racial and cultural differences that affect both how their genders are perceived and how they shape their genders. In this essay, I specifically want to explore some of these factors that affect Asian and Asian American lesbian and bisexual women.

First, let me clarify some terms that form the bounds of my discussion I use "gender" to address both femme/butch dynamics and ideas about femininity and masculinity. These two frameworks are not quite the same, and the definitions of these terms are highly contested. Let me make a working definition here: I use "femininity" and "masculinity" to talk about the alignment of behavior with anatomy in a framework of compulsory heterosexuality; that is, I use these terms to refer to heterosexually based gender norms. I use "femme" and "butch" to refer to gender/sexual styles among lesbian and bisexual women, styles that have historical and cultural variations and roots.[3] The two frameworks are not absolutely distinct, yet neither are they exactly similar. Indeed, the crux of the debate about femme/butch dynamics is precisely the extent to which they are imitations (or appropriations) of heterosexual genders. I do not intend to engage in this debate here; for the purposes of this article, I will use "femme/butch" when discussing lesbian and bisexual women's communities and "feminine/masculine" for heterosexual contexts.[4]

Another clarification concerns my interchangeable use of both "Asian" and "Asian American," although I do restrict my analysis to women of Asian descent living in the U.S. On the one hand, since the 1960s, Asian American groups have insisted on being recognized as "American," in order to defy dominant views of Asians as perpetual foreigners as well as to provide an alternative to the loaded term "Oriental." On the other hand, many first-generation Asian Americans do not identify as Americans. Also, many people of all generations who originate from nations that have endured colonial subjugation in the past and/or neo-colonial relationships in the present, such as the Philippines, reject Americanness: to a certain extent, these people have already been forcibly made "American" in their own homelands. In addition, racial stereotypes do not distinguish between Asian and Asian American, as they are based on phenotype and imagined cultural traits. For all these reasons, I will use both "Asian" and "Asian American" interchangeably. I also debated whether including women of Pacific Islander descent would be truly inclusive or merely tokenizing. Since much of my analysis involves specifically Orientalist constructions of Asian women that are substantially different from those of Pacific Islander women,[5] I decided it would be hypocritical to extend my discussion to include Pacific Islanders in name only. However, I do believe that many of the other factors that I discuss here also affect Pacific Islander lesbian and bisexual women.

Related to this issue is my use of "we" and "our" throughout this article, to refer to Asian and Asian American lesbian and bisexual women. I do this in order to deconstruct the myth of objectivity in the social sciences, but I realize that this has the danger of falling into an identity politics that relies on some mythic vision of a monolithic "community" that comes together naturally. This is hardly the case, either in theory or in fact; as the APLN (Asian Pacifica Lesbian Network)[6] 1989 national retreat and 1993 West Coast retreat showed, there is still an implicit center that marginalizes many people. As was stated at the latter retreat, this "community" can only work as a coalition, and it is in this sense that I use "we": to acknowledge those who are joined by common political agendas. However, I also realize that my use of "we" has the danger of being appropriated by others to view me as a native informant and tokenize me as speaking for a constituency, especially when there is so little on this topic in the legitimated world of research and writing This is a risk that I consciously face and can only hope to deflect through a constant reiteration of the diversity in this coalitional identity.

In this essay, I want to explore some factors that affect Asian and Asian American lesbian and bisexual women's femme/butch/gender identities. I am particularly interested in those factors that reflect the racial and cultural differences that influence how we shape gender and how our genders are perceived by mainstream and lesbian communities. One of these factors is a particular strain of Orientalist discourse in the U.S. that constructs Asian women of various ethnicities as hyperfeminine, exotic, passive objects of white heterosexual male desire.[7] In an environment where we are constantly confronted by such expectations, our presentations of gender are decidedly not neutral. Another factor is the prevailing image in lesbian communities of what a lesbian looks like, an image that is constructed as white and butch, making invisible lesbian and bisexual women of color and femme women of all races. This invisibility is compounded especially for femme and feminine-looking Asian women, who often find themselves judged in light of the above-mentioned Orientalist discourse that can only construe them as heterosexual. In addition, all of this is complicated by our awareness of different cultural norms for gender. For Asian and Asian American women, ideas about what it means to be masculine or feminine are influenced not only by dominant U.S. norms but also by our perceptions of various Asian cultural standards of gender.

I do not want to present these forces as having all-powerful effects on Asian women's gender identities, and in fact, some of the women I interviewed for this work were not aware of the existence of some of these factors. However, gender is not an individual choice that lies completely outside of societal discourses and practices. I want to examine these various forces in a way that accounts for both determination and agency; while not all women experience these pressures to equal degrees, they form part of the terrain on which our genders are mapped.

I want to emphasize that these are only a few of the many forces that affect gender identities. I focus on these to show how the consideration of racial and cultural differences affects analyses of gender and femme/butch identities for lesbian and bisexual women. Whether Asian and Asian American lesbian and bisexual women consciously respond to these forces or not, our gender identities do not resonate solely in the context of compulsory heterosexuality: they are also affected by histories and practices of racialization and ethnocentrism and differences in cultural standards. Critics must also start to investigate the particularities of white women's gender identities, white lesbian and bisexual women's concepts of femme and butch are also specifically shaped and interpreted in light of what is deemed appropriate for white women in mainstream and lesbian/bisexual communities.[8]

Part of my research for this article consisted of interviews with ten Asian and Asian American lesbian and bisexual women. These women are in no way representative of the diversity of all those who identify as such. I tried to interview a group diverse in age, immigration status, ethnicity, mixed-race heritage, bisexual/lesbian identification, and femme/butch identification but did not have sufficient resources to achieve the diversity and outreach I would have liked. I am of course not trying to generalize these women responses as representative of all Asian American lesbian and bisexual women; I do not view these interviews as subject matter to be dissected or as proof of my views, but rather as anecdotal illustrations of the kinds of factors that I am examining.

❧ Lotus Blossoms and American Orientalisms

Images of Asian women, however, have remained consistently simplistic and inaccurate . . . There are two basic types: the Lotus Blossom Baby (a.k.a. China Doll, Geisha Girl, shy Polynesian beauty), and the Dragon Lady (Fu Manchu's various female relations, prostitutes, devious madames . . . The Lotus Blossom Baby, a sexual-romantic object, has been the prominent type throughout the years. These "Oriental flowers" are utterly feminine, delicate, and welcome respites from their often loud, independent American counterparts. Many of them are the spoils of the last three wars fought in Asia.[9]

In the world's media, the stereotypes are being perpetuated. We're geisha girls, we're Suzie Wong, or whatever, just somebody to exploit sexually. And also somebody really sexual in bed. That we're really meek and passive but once you get us in bed, we're wildcats (O.M.).[10]

Many of the women I spoke to were familiar with the above stereotypes, citing not only their encounters with film images but also with male strangers on the streets who hailed them as "mama-san" or "china girl." However, before I discuss these images and the impact they have on Asian lesbian and bisexual women's gender identities, I want to utter a word of caution. In *Critical Terrains: French and British Orientalisms,* Lisa Lowe argues persuasively that there are a multiplicity of discourses about the East that can all be called Orientalist while differing wildly in their purposes, their referents (which part of the East they are talking about), and the reasons for their development.

[M]uch as I wish to underscore the insistence of these power relations, my intervention resists totalizing orientalism as a monolithic, developmental discourse that uniformly constructs the Orient as the Other of the Occident. . . . I argue for a conception of orientalism as heterogeneous and contradictory; to this end I observe, on the one hand, that orientalism consists of an uneven matrix of orientalist situations across different cultural and historical sites, and on the other, that each of these orientalisms is internally complex and unstable.[11]

My analysis of Orientalist constructions of Asian women is thus not only specific to twentieth-century U.S. dominant discourses—what I call American Orientalisms, following Toni Morrison's coining of "American Africanism"[12]—but also points to the internal diversity of these constructions. Not only is there the "Lotus Blossom," but also the "Dragon Lady," as Renee E. Tajima and others note, as well as news anchors, Olympic figure skaters, model minorities, store owners, and other variations.

Here I want to focus on American Orientalist constructions of the Lotus Blossom image, primarily of East and Southeast Asian women, as it is depicted in and reified through various representations, institutions, and practices. This is obviously a very broad topic, so I will only discuss a few aspects here. It has been noted that many Orientalist discourses portray the East as feminine in and of itself, with the men emasculated and the women hyperfeminized.[13] For instance, David Henry Hwang's play M. Butterfly turns on this notion; in a much quoted passage, the character Song Liling comments "The West thinks of itself as masculine—big guns, big industry, big money—so the East is feminine—weak, delicate, poor...but good at art, and full of inscrutable wisdom—the feminine mystique."[14] This type of Orientalist discourse constructs Asian women of various ethnicities as hyperfeminine, passive, eroticized objects of white heterosexual male desire.[15] Similarly, one assessment of portrayals of Asian women in mainstream film mentions "Hollywood's skewed representations of Asian women: sleek, evil goddesses with slanted eyes and cunning ways, or smiling, sarong-clad South Seas 'maidens' with undulating hips, kinky black hair, and white skin darkened by makeup. . . . If we are 'good,' we are childlike, submissive, silent, and eager for sex . . . or else we are tragic victim types."[16]

Aside from representations in film, literature, and other media, other U.S. institutions and practices that participate in this discourse are the sectors of the sex industry that sell racialized sex and the mail-order bride business.[17] Hwang comments on some of these practices:

> "Yellow Fever"—Caucasian men with a fetish for exotic Oriental women. I have often heard it said that "Oriental women make the best wives." . . . This mythology is exploited by the Oriental mail-order bride trade which has flourished over the past decade. American men can now send away for catalogues of "obedient, domesticated" Asian women looking for husbands. Anyone who believes such stereotypes are a thing of the past need look no further than Manhattan cable television, which advertises call girls from "the exotic east, where men are king; obedient girls, trained in the art of pleasure."[18]

In addition, U.S. involvement in Asia helps to reinforce these American Orientalist constructions; this includes the sex industry around U.S. military bases, sex tourism in Thailand, the Philippines, South Korea, and other parts of Asia, and wars in Asia and the consequent phenomenon of Asian war brides.[19] Connie Chan describes this historical context:

> During the U.S. involvement with the Philippines wars, Japan and China in World War II, and more recently, the Korean and Vietnamese Wars, Asian women were perceived by American soldiers as prostitutes and sexual objects who provided rest and recuperation from the war zones. This perception was not restricted to Western soldiers overseas, but was portrayed and perpetuated through film and other media in the United States and Europe. . . . As a result of these war and media images, Asian women have suffered from a cultural stereotype of being exotic, subservient, passive, sexually attractive and available.[20]

Although I do not agree with this strict cause-and-effect model, it does appear that U.S. participation in wars has been significant in reifying this particular American Orientalist image of Asian women.

How does this construction of Asian women as models of heterosexual femininity par excellence impact on Asian lesbian and bisexual women? How do we deal with and/or challenge the stereotypes of passivity, hyperfemininity, and eroticization that are meant to be in service of white heterosexual male desire? Among the women I interviewed, those who were familiar with this discourse thought that it affected their lives whether they conformed to it or not. For example, one feminine-looking woman states:

> I hate seeing Asian women with a white man. I hate it, I just hate it. . . . I guess it feels especially weird, because every time I see that, I know that's what I'm looked as. That's how people see me, as somebody who should be with a white man. Which means I'm heterosexual. Which means I can't possibly want my own brothers, let alone my own sisters. Or that [I can possibly be] butch. I mean, you know, shit (O.M.)

This woman finds that she is circumscribed by a narrow conception of "the Asian woman," where her appearance alone is enough to trigger very specific and limited expectations about her behavior, her sexuality, and her gender attributes. Some of the consequences of fulfilling certain aspects of this particular Orientalist construction can be significant:

> To go back to the exoticism of Asian women, even in a domestic violence situation with an Asian woman, you get race-baited. . . . I think that I'm seen as someone who can be beaten on, as an Asian woman, 'cause the stereotype that I'm weak, I'm passive, that I'm sort of like a lily flower, and I can be beaten on, and stomped on, and attacked and abused. And that is

seen by, I'm sure it's seen by men, I know it's seen by men, I know it's seen by women, I know it's seen by sisters, other sisters. That's happened. I also see, I do see, that maybe Asian women do experience a lot of violence because of that stereotype of us, in the heterosexual world, in the queer world, you know, we'll get raped because we're exoticized, abused because were seen as weak and passive, and silent. (O.M.)

I think women who are feminine get harassed a lot, every day on the street. I mean I used to have long hair, you know, when I was in high school, and I would get shit all the time. . . . Course that was in Denver too, and there aren't that many Asians. But women get a lot of shit, just walkin' the streets, just being out there, just being out there; it's constant and it never stops. (L.D.)

Being femme and feminine seems to lead to greater vulnerability to harassment from men. Because this Orientalist image is so strongly heterosexual, Asian women are viewed as a more-than-appropriate object of male attention, and because the image is so passive and docile, Asian women are seen as an easy target. Yet equally significant are the reactions when a woman does not fulfill these stereotypes.

Growing up as a butch, or as a Chinese butch, and what that means as far as when people see Asian women and the stereotypes of them being docile, submissive, long hair, kind of, like, eroticized, demoralized—I don't fit those descriptions as far as being Asian, so it's very different. When I talk butch/femme, I also have to talk about my Asian identification. Because it all plays into that. Because—I'll give you a typical day: I'm walking down the street, Southern California. Because I'm also mixed, I also get this assumption by people in the military that my father is a soldier who went over to Vietnam and fell in love with, or captured, a Vietnamese woman. . . . Then they trip on the fact that it wasn't just a Vietnam story, and then they trip on the fact that, all of a sudden, through the conversation, they figure out that I'm in a woman's body, and then it goes like, men, if they can't come on to you, then they want to kick your ass. If you challenge them, then you're in a fist fight, and you know, you're subjected to a lot of violence because you don't feel like being mentally, emotionally, or physically oppressed. So, I also have to bring race into that. I get a lot of "you slant-eyed slut," blah, blah, blah. (J.M.)

How does that translate into people's choices, to the extent that they have a choice, about marking themselves as gendered beings? I think considerations like this often have much to do with our gender presentations. Being feminine might mark one as an easy target, but it is apparent that being more butch isn't necessarily safer or easier: people are beaten up for defying, as well as for complying with, the dominant stereotypes. This is true for women in general, but the discourse that casts Asian women as particularly feminine, weak, and passive leaves us more vulnerable to both violence and backlash.

I present these stories about harassment from men because they seem to constitute a significant aspect of the American Orientalist image of Asian women. However, I do not want to make it sound as if we are always and solely reacting to this image. Our gender identities have many aspects and are shaped by many forces; and how we are viewed by men is often the least of our concerns. In fact, one woman, an immigrant from Singapore, stresses that her gender identification has nothing to do with reacting to these images:

> I've never seen this Suzie Wong image; I don't even know what it means. . . . I've never thought of, like, "Oh, Asian women are supposed to be passive or whatever," you know, so it doesn't affect [me]. Even without knowing that, I'm still butch, you know. It's not because I'm trying to fight off this stereotype that I'm butch. (J.U.)

Yet I discuss this Orientalist discourse here as an example of how gender is always racialized; any analysis of femme/butch and gender identities must be complicated by a consideration of racial specificities. These images affect us to varying degrees—whether we react to them, choose to ignore them, or are simply unaware of them—but they do form part of the environment in which our gender identities are perceived and judged.

❧ Looking like a "Lesbian"

> If you're really, really, really, really, really stupid, and think the whole world is completely heterosexual, and that every single woman with long hair, no matter how she acts, is heterosexual, then you could probably assume that I'm heterosexual. . . . And I think it has a lot to do with, not only because I have long hair, but because I'm an Asian woman, and the stereotype of an Asian woman with long hair. In their eyes, I cannot be anything but a heterosexual woman. Which is fucked up, you know, because I can be many things, and I am. (O.M.)

Another factor that affects Asian lesbian and bisexual women's gender identities is the archetypal figure of the lesbian as butch. Although this image varies in different lesbian and bisexual women's communities, butchness usually serves as the visible marker of lesbian difference.[21] As Arlene Istar states:

In the lesbian community, though, botches *are* our image of dykes. Butchness is the hub of our lesbian universe. Lesbians are never described as women who wear dresses and high heels, or have long nails or hair, or as women who dislike sports. Oh, we all know there are lesbians like that, but somehow they are different, not like "us," somehow not authentic.[22]

Even in the era of "neo-butch/femme," where there is more flexibility in and tolerance for a range of lesbian styles than in earlier decades, the butch is still more recognizable and is accepted as the typical lesbian. People know and rely on the butch image as the visual definition of lesbian even as they question it.

I don't think I have anything, show anything, or wear anything that makes me look like a lesbian. . . . That's kind of a weird thing to say, because what does a lesbian look like? . . . [T]hey look like us! How do you look like a lesbian? But there is a definite distinct thing that people are saying. You know, "She doesn't look like a lesbian": she's not wearing Birkenstocks, she's not carrying a backpack, her hair's too long, or she's not wearing triangle earrings. You know, there's always something. (S.U.)

The image of the butch also serves to define a queerness that is conflated with lesbianism, since the stereotypical representation of bisexual women is as femmes. That is, the usual equation is queer = lesbian = butch, excluding self-defined femmes, feminine-looking women, and bisexual women of all genderings. Many stereotypes associated with femme women are also applied to bisexual women: that they are inauthentic lesbians who want to pass as straight, that they are not feminists and not politicized, that they are indeed weak, duped, apolitical, and traitorous. Many femme-identified women describe their encounters with this exclusion and devaluation, both in the past and also sometimes in the present, in the anthology *The Persistent Desire: A Femme-Butch Reader*.[23] Lisa Walker, in an article decrying these assumptions, addresses the accusation that femme women want to pass as straight women, supposedly garnering some heterosexual privilege as a result of fulfilling traditional visual norms of femininity:

The glorification of the butch as authentic lesbian is based on her "blatant" representation of sexual deviance, and this in turn implies ambiguity and confusion around the femme's sexual identity. The femme's adaptation of what has been historically defined as a "feminine" sexual style is tacitly constructed as evidence of her desire to pass for straight and not of her desire for other women.[24]

Bisexual women offer similar accounts of exclusion and denigration in anthologies such as *Bi Any Other Name: People Speak Out* and *Closer to Home:*

Bisexuality and Feminism.[25] I want to make clear that bisexuality and femme styles *are* accepted to varying degrees by lesbians, and that the attitudes described above are not held by a monolithic bloc of lesbians. However, it is equally clear that these attitudes still exist.

For Asian American lesbian and bisexual women, these stereotypical assumptions are compounded by various racialized discourses. The American Orientalist construction of Asian women as Lotus Blossoms, as subservient, feminine, heterosexual women, influences both femme and butch identities. L.D. notes that in the shadow of this image, it is often hard for Asian butches to be recognized as butch:

> [Y]ou talked about the subservient Asian woman, I think that definitely carries over in the mainstream dyke community. I don't think that a lot of people take us seriously. . . . [I]f you talk about, like, butch and femme, it's like Asian women aren't real butches, we're just pretending to be, but we could never aspire to gain that recognition because we're still considered followers.

For femme Asian women who look recognizably feminine and Asian, this confluence of various discourses works to almost completely erase their existence as lesbians and bisexuals. One explanation for this dynamic is offered by Walker, who views this as the result of the intersection of various erasures: not only are femmes invisible as lesbians, but in addition, the sexualities of women of color are often not seen or differentiated.

> If we pursue the racist logic of this layered invisibility and add to it the invisibility of the lesbian femme, it follows that the woman of color who identifies as femme may be triply erased. That is to say, while a butch woman of color might not be recognized as a lesbian because she is not white, she might be perceived as lesbian because her sexual style is considered "blatant." A femme woman of color, on the other hand, will probably not be recognized as lesbian, first because she is not white and then because she is not butch.[26]

Although this analysis is seductive in its logic, it is a little simplistic when one considers the prominent stereotype of black lesbians as butch bulldaggers. The gender identities of bisexual and lesbian women of color are not formed by a simple addition or layering of racist, *then* sexist, *then* homophobic logic. Discourses do not work as sums, they work as particularities. For femme Asian women, it is a *specific* racializing discourse of gender that constructs them as feminine and heterosexual and serves to make them invisible. One woman stated:

I guess that's one reason why I'm so in your face and out about being a dyke. . . . It's just, like, the eye of the other looking at me; they always see a heterosexual woman, and that *pisses* me off like nothing else. And a lot of it has to do with how I carry myself in a cultural context. I'm a Cambodian lesbian, and this is how I look. And I'm invisible as a lesbian because I look in a cultural way—that is, where I have long hair, you know—and I *despise* that invisibility, because it's their ignorance that makes me invisible. And not the way I look, necessarily, you know. I think even if you have short hair and you're an Asian woman, you have a hard time, because the idea of being anything but heterosexual is so far from anybody's mind. You have long hair, it's doubly that way. . . . I know other sisters of color . . . who have the same problem. Pushed into [a femme role] by the lesbian world, labeled a femme, when they might not be, and always assumed heterosexual by the straight world. So you're invisible both in the gay world and in the straight world. You know? So we make a lot of noise. To compensate. (O.M.)

Asian women who are both bisexual *and* feminine or femme occupy an even more overdetermined position that renders them extremely invisible as queers. The assumption of normative heterosexuality embedded in American Orientalist discourse colludes with the image of the lesbian as butch and the stereotype of bisexuals as swinging straights to virtually erase the very existence of femme bisexual Asian women.

◉ Cultural Norms of Gender

J.L.: [So] when you identify as a butch, it's more from a different cultural stance than white American?

J.M.: It's got a different "slant" to it.

Another factor that affects the gender identities of Asian and Asian American lesbian and bisexual women is our awareness of various Asian cultural norms of gender. I do not wish to imply that there are monolithic, unchanging norms for any given "culture" that Asian lesbian and bisexual women know "correctly" and authentically, but rather that we experience pressures that we feel are different from those exerted by the dominant standards of the U.S. white middle class. It is our *perceptions* of these cultures and their gender norms that we respond to. These different ideas about masculinity and femininity intersect in complicated ways with U.S. norms, sometimes contradicting them, sometimes overlapping with them, and differ according to specific class backgrounds, occupations, U.S. regional differences, and a host of other factors. They affect not only how we are perceived as masculine or feminine by the mainstream but also how we are viewed as butch or femme in lesbian communities. Thus, as Lyndall MacCowan notes, "we need to be aware of the nuances that arise from different classes and cultures. What is butch to a Jewish lesbian is not necessarily butch to a lesbian from Philadelphia's mainline [sic], a lesbian from Harlem, or a lesbian from Thailand."[27] Yet most lesbian communities make evaluations according to white American hegemonic norms for gender and white lesbian standards for femme/butch identities, thus distorting, or simply being unaware of, the cultural differences. For some of my interviewees, certain behaviors or appearances that they felt were masculine, feminine, or not gendered according to their Asian cultural backgrounds were rendered femme or butch in mainstream lesbian contexts and thus interpreted in ways that they hadn't intended.

For example, J.M. states that, as a butch, her models for masculinity include those of her Chinese culture:

> And for me, I also wanted to put out, because I'm Asian, I don't necessarily have all of the—although I do, I would say I do have more of a macho defense mode towards men—[but] I don't have the same butch thinking that perhaps a white dyke butch would have. 'Cause, for one, in my culture, the Asian men, they cook. So I cook . . . because the men in my family cook. . . . And I would also say that in my culture . . . when I say my culture, I mean mostly my Chinese culture—the Cantonese heterosexual roles, the men are much softer. They're more softer, very family-oriented. . . . It's not the same [as white western heterosexual roles]. It's just not the same. So therefore butch/femme isn't the same. In my head.

B.T., on the other hand, feels that since her models for femininity are those of a southern Philippine culture with standards that she cannot fulfill, she never feels truly feminine.

> I have a different reality about being female, based on my size. I think that it really does affect my perception of myself as feminine or masculine, you know, it makes me never believe that the feminine comes off perfectly. . . . I know that my image of myself as not a successful femme is very much tied into being culturally Filipino and genetically mixed. . . . If I were raised as culturally Filipino from Manila, I also wouldn't have as much of a problem. Because there's more Spanish blood in the North, and there's more European blood in general up there, because it's a big city, and there's more milk, so people are growing taller. And, in general, there's like at least a one to two inch height difference between people from the North and people

from the South. But I'm from the South. . . . In some part of my head I equate grace and femininity with petite. And so it's not just, like, height, it's petiteness, it's everything about it. And so, when I'm in a room full of women, I cannot perceive myself that way. I cannot perceive myself as feminine. I feel like a drag queen.

Others adhere to a culturally significant form of gender that they consciously embrace as expressing their cultural differences but find that, in U.S. lesbian contexts, their cultural differences are interpreted as reflecting a femme identity. For example, Kaushalya Bannerji writes:

> As a lesbian of Indian origin with an active relationship to India and to my family, I was struck by the conformity to androgyny that appeared to be the norm of white lesbian beauty. . . . My breasts, hips, and long hair were not seen by everyone as symbols integral to my identity as an Indian woman; they were reinterpreted by white lesbians as manifestations of my being a "femme."[28]

Similarly, O.M. expresses her dissatisfaction with being labeled femme for traits that she experiences as being more "cultural" than "gendered":

> Long hair is a stereotypical femme look, but void of the cultural context. For me, as a Cambodian immigrant, to have long hair is a cultural identity. It's also something I like. But it doesn't mean I'm femme, based on the way I wear my hair. . . . I'm very nurturing . . . and very affectionate— . . . of course, all that being me, being the individual that I am—but I think that it has a lot to do with my culture. You know, Cambodian people are very affectionate people. Of course I'm gonna be affectionate, and of course, you know, Cambodian women, a lot of women, are very nurturing, and my mother's very nurturing, and I learn from my mother to be a nurturer, and I see that as a very powerful powerful thing, very creative and very powerful female thing to be a nurturer. But I think it's pegged as femme.

Some women feel that there are differences in cultural norms, not only for gender in general, but also for what constitutes appropriate femme/butch roles in same-sex relationships. For some Asian lesbian and bisexual women who are closely tied to Asian communities or lived until recently in Asia, it appears that their gender identities respond not so much to white lesbian femme/butch roles as to their own norms for femme/butch and how these identities resonate in Asian communities.[29]

> I've heard that sometimes, from this one woman, for her [femme/butch] is a construction. It's definitely heterosexually based; she totally acknowledges that. It's partially based on familial acceptance. . . . That she expects that

because she's butch, her family will accept her going out with a femme. And because in her family, there're basically very masculine men and very feminine women, she sees herself, if she's gonna be dating women, she's identifying with a masculine role. So, that kind of construction, it fits into her family. (B.T.)

Moreover, in their conscious reasons for not wanting to be traditionally feminine, Asian women may be reacting more to what they perceive to be Asian cultural norms of femininity than to white mainstream standards, which might actually be perceived as more liberating.

[In] a lot of cultures that are from Asia or perhaps even from other of color cultures, I think women's roles and women's identities are still very much . . . placed in a very, more clearly defined, sexist context. . . . You don't want to be in that more traditional role. It's like a box. It's like you suddenly don't have arms, you know? You wanna be able to walk around with these arms, and you really need to move them and to use them. And from an identity perspective it's, like, in order to do that, what do you do? You reject, you reject, you push away any perception . . . of you being perceived as being like this objectified, passive, Asian female woman. (G.M.)

Although such descriptions of Asian cultures may seem a little extreme, I cannot compare them to some "objective" view to see how "correct" they are. Instead, I assume that, insofar as these are conscious interpretations, such perceptions of Asian gender norms have a distinct impact on gender identities. This awareness of different cultural standards for gender constitutes another part of the environment that affects how Asian lesbian and bisexual women shape gender identities. In these and myriad other ways, we react to what we perceive to be Asian norms for femininity and Asian ideas about femme/butch roles. Yet, inevitably, we also react to the myopia of mainstream heterosexuals and white lesbians and bisexuals, who interpret our appearances and behaviors according to white hegemonic standards for femininity and masculinity and white lesbian ideas about femme/butch identities. It is important for analyses of gender not to fall into the same shortcomings, but to examine closely how the specificities of cultural differences affect gender, not only for women of color, but also for white women.

❧ Conclusion

What I have discussed here are a few of the factors that affect the gender identities of Asian and Asian American lesbian and bisexual women, in terms of how we shape them and how they are perceived in the U.S. by mainstream and lesbian/bisexual communities. I have specifically focused on those factors that reflect racial and cultural differences, to show that gender analyses *must* include a complex account of racialization. Asian women are affected by American Orientalist images that portray us in a specifically racialized construction of gender, as hyperfeminine, submissive, eroticized objects of white heterosexual male desire. This "heterosexualization" and the forces of femme invisibility and devaluation work to exclude us from the dominant visual definition of lesbians as butch and converge to make femme and feminine-looking Asian women especially invisible. In addition, our adherence to or rejection of what we perceive to be Asian cultural standards are often misinterpreted and compared to mainstream U.S. standards of masculine/feminine and lesbian standards of femme/butch. Asian American lesbian and bisexual women interact with these forces in different ways, sometimes consciously responding to them, sometimes choosing to ignore them, sometimes simply being unaware of them.

However we respond or not, I believe that these factors form a significant part of the environment in which our gender is perceived and judged. Because they intersect in different ways and resonate differently in different circumstances, our gender identities have no simple or single meanings. Thus, when we "play" with gender, our playing has significant effects. Due to discourses around race and our lack of white privilege, we have less room to maneuver; we thus often end up challenging serious societal forces that are meant to control our appearances and behaviors, and ultimately our place in society. Our playing with gender disrupts, not only compulsory heterosexuality and traditional gender norms, but also discourses of race and racialized gender.

> I like to challenge people's idea of what things are, because I feel like my whole existence has been constant, constant contradiction to a lot of different things. The role of me being with a white man, I contradicted that a long time ago. I date women of color! That's the total opposite. Of having long hair, whatever, of being seen as whatever way of being with women, the way I am being femme in a different way, I challenge that, being very outspoken and loud Asian woman, as opposed to being quiet and passive, you know? I figure if you can't see me as a lesbian, I don't need to change the way I look to fit your definition of a lesbian. *You* need to change your definition of what a lesbian looks like to include me, with my hair, or Jee, with short hair, you know? And I think that's revolutionary. To challenge other people's ideas and not conform to their ideas is revolutionary. So if a butch with short hair says to me, "Well, you're just being a white man's woman,"

you know, I'm like, "No, I'm challenging your idea of what a lesbian looks like, of what a lesbian is."(O.M.)

I believe that the specification of racial and cultural differences and how they impact on gender must be more fully explored not only for other women of color but also for white women and white femme/butch identities. Just as there are discourses that construct images of Asian women and other women of color, there are specific discourses that construct white women in certain ways. The gender identities of white lesbians and bisexual women are also shaped by racially specific forces that prescribe how they should act out their gender and affect how they are perceived. This changes the ways in which hegemonic norms of gender can be challenged; since the limits of what is seen as allowable are different, strategies to resist them must also be different.

I want to end by stating that despite the heavy emphasis I have placed on some of the specific factors that affect the gender identities of Asian lesbians and bisexual women, these forces are neither monolithic nor all-powerful. They may constitute certain limitations and pressures, but they are also permeable, self-contradictory, and multiple. Indeed, were they not so, there would be no possibility of challenging them. The gender identities of Asian lesbians and bisexual women often use these contradictions and are formed in the gaps of these discourses and practices. I do not believe that our challenges to dominant structures of race, gender, and sexuality are formed fully outside these structures; that would be to imagine some pure space of marginality that is somehow untainted by all dominant discourses. Yet neither do I believe that this dooms us to the impossibility of changing them. The possibilities for resistance lie in the inconsistencies inherent in the multiple and self-contradictory nature of discourses. Our interventions in our gender identities do not completely destroy the hegemonic Orientalist constructions of Asian women, of femme Asian invisibility, of white standards for femme/butch, but they do shift the ground on which these are built.[30]

Appendix: Backgrounds of the Interviewees

I would like to thank the women I interviewed, although I did not use all of their interviews directly, they were all extremely generous with their time and honesty and helped me to clarify many of my ideas. I hope that our conversations and this essay will spark more discussions of this topic within the community. The following are descriptions of the interviewees by age, ethnic

background, approximate class background, immigration status, bisexual/
lesbian identification, and femme/butch identification.

A.D. is a second-generation, butch-identified Chinese American lesbian
and describes her class background as upper middle class. She is twenty-six
years old.

B.T. is twenty-six years old and of Filipino and white heritage, the white
part being "English, Irish, Welsh, and Scottish, American white mix, mutt."
Her class background in the U.S. is middle to upper middle class; she was
born in the U.S. but lived in the Philippines until the age of six. She identifies
as bi, as opposed to bisexual, and thinks she is both femme and butch in different ways.

C.H. is a thirty-nine-year-old Indian lesbian who came to the U.S. from
India at the age of seventeen. She describes her class background as upper
middle class in India and immigrant working class in the U.S. She does not
identify as either femme or butch.

C.W. is a forty-three-year-old third-generation Chinese American lesbian who identifies as neither femme nor butch.

G.M. is a twenty-eight-year-old second-generation Chinese American
lesbian, who does not identify as either femme or butch.

J.M. is a butch-identified lesbian of mixed Cantonese and
Polish/English/Germanic heritage. The Cantonese side of her family has
resided in the U.S. for three generations. She is twenty-nine years old.

J.U. is twenty-two years old. She is of Chinese heritage and came to the
U.S. from Singapore when she was seventeen. She describes her class background as having been middle to upper middle class in Singapore. She identifies as a lesbian and views herself as fairly butch.

L.D. is thirty-three years old, a second-generation American of Chinese
and Mexican heritage. She is lesbian-identified, of working class background,
and a tradeswoman. She identifies as a top, but not as a butch.

O.M. is a twenty-seven-year-old Cambodian lesbian who came to the
U.S. as a refugee when she was nine. She identifies as working-class and does
not identify as either femme or butch.

S.U. is a second-generation American of Asian Indian and Japanese heritage. She is thirty-three years old and states that her class background is
working to middle class. She is a lesbian who describes herself as fairly
femme.

*E*ndnotes

[1]Lillian Faderman, "The Return of Butch and Femme: A Phenomenon in Lesbian Sexuality of the 1980s and 1990s," *Journal of the History of Sexuality* 2, no. 4 (1992): 592. The writers I refer to are Arlene Stein, "All Dressed Up, but No Place to Go? Style Wars and the New Lesbianism," in *The Persistent Desire: A Femme-Butch Reader,* ed. Joan Nestle (Boston: Alyson, 1992), 431–39; Inge Blackman and Kathryn Perry, "Skirting the Issue: Lesbian Fashion for the 1990s, *Feminist Review* 34 (Spring 1990): 67–78; and Susan Ardill and Sue O'Sullivan, "Butch/Femme Obsessions," *Feminist Review* 34 (Spring 1990): 79–85. Sue-Ellen Case's "Towards a Butch-Femme Aesthetic," *Discourse: Journal for Theoretical Studies in Media and Culture* 11, no. 1 (1988–89): 55–73, also characterizes femme/butch roles as play and camp, but defends it as such.

[2]Ardill and O'Sullivan, "Butch/Femme Obsessions," 79.

[3]For more detailed and complex self-definitions and histories of femme/butch identities, see Nestle, *The Persistent Desire;* Lillian Faderman, *Odd Girls and Twilight Lovers: A History of Lesbian Life in Twentieth-Century America* (New York: Penguin Books, 1991); Madeline Davis and Elizabeth Lapovsky Kennedy, "Oral History and the Study of Sexuality in the Lesbian Community: Buffalo, New York, 1940–1960," *Feminist Studies* 12, no. 1 (1986): 7–26; and Davis and Kennedy, *Boots of Leather, Slippers of Gold: The History of a Lesbian Community* (New York: Routledge, 1993). For a brief historical overview of the changing practices of femme/butch in U.S. lesbian communities since the 1970s, see Faderman, "The Return of Butch and Femme," although I am uncomfortable with some of its totalizing generalizations.

[4]I deliberately use "femme/butch," as opposed to the usual "butch/femme," following the subtitle of Joan Nestle's anthology, *The Persistent Desire: A Femme-Butch Reader.* Of this decision, she states in her introduction:

> As feminists, we continue to fight back with a femme proclamation of independence. I subtitled this anthology "A Femme-Butch Reader" to herald this new voice in identity politics and break the traditional rhythms of the phrase and image. Femmes are the Lavender Menace within our community. (18)

I believe this reclamation of femme is long overdue, of which this deliberate change in terminology is a modest but important part.

[5]See J. Kehaulani Kauanui and Ju Hui "Judy" Han, "'Asian Pacific Islander': Issues of Representation and Responsibility," *Moving the Mountains: Asian American Women's Journal* (1993): 24–25.

[6]The name of this network has subsequently been changed to "Asian and Pacific Islander Lesbian and Bisexual Women's Network," or APLBN.

[7]Suzie Wong, a character in the 1960 film "The World of Suzie Wong," is a Chinese prostitute in Hong Kong who falls in love with a white man from the U.S. I invoke her here as the paradigmatic image of the submissive, exotic Asian woman.

[8]See Ruth Frankenberg, *White Women, Race Matters: The Social Construction of Whiteness* (Minneapolis University of Minnesota Press, 1993), although she focuses more explicitly on race than gender.

[9]Renee E. Tajima, "Lotus Blossoms Don't Bleed: Images of Asian Women," in *Making Waves: An Anthology of Writings by and about Asian American Women,* ed. Asian Women United of California (Boston Beacon Press, 1989), 309.

[10]Initials refer to interviewees. See appendix for background descriptions of the interviewees.

[11]Lisa Lowe, *Critical Terrains: French and British Orientalisms* (Ithaca, NY: Cornell University Press, 1991), 4–5.

[12]Toni Morrison, *Playing in the Dark: Whiteness and the Literary Imagination* (New York: Random House, 1992).

[13]This dynamic is also found rather blatantly in gay men's communities, where gay Asian men are often feminized in this way. See Daniel Tsang, "M. Butterfly Meets the Great White Hope," *Informasian* 6, no. 3(1992): 3–4; and Richard Fung, "Looking for My Penis: The Eroticized Asian in Gay Video Porn," in *How Do I Look? Queer Film and Video,* ed. Bad Object-Choices (Seattle: Bay Press, 1991), 145–60.

[14]David Henry Hwang, *M. Butterfly* (New York: Penguin Books, 1986), 83.

[15]L. Hyun-Yi Kang, "The Desiring of Asian Female Bodies: Interracial Romance and Cinematic Subjection," *Visual Anthropology Review* 9, no. 1 (1993): 5–21, discusses the representations of relationships between Asian women and white men in three mainstream Hollywood films, noting how the alleged focus on the Asian women characters is deflected by their portrayal as objects of white heterosexual male desire.

[16]Jessica Hagedorn, "Asian Women in Film: No Joy, No Luck," *Ms.* 4, no. 4 (January 1994): 74.

[17]See Alice Mayall and Diana E. H. Russell, "Racism in Pornography," in *Making Violence Sexy: Feminist Views on Pornography,* ed. Diana E. H. Russell (New York: Teachers College Press, 1993), 167–77; and Venny Villapando, "The Business of Selling Mail-Order Brides," in *Making Waves,* 318–26.

[18]Hwang, *M. Butterfly,* 98.

[19]See Brenda Stoltzfus and Saundra Pollock Sturdevant, *Let the Good Times Roll: Prostitution and the U.S. Military in Asia* (New York: New Press, 1993); and Elaine Kim,

"Sex Tourism in Asia: A Reflection of Political and Economic Inequality," *Critical Perspectives* 2, no. 1(1984): 214–32.

[20] Connie S. Chan, "Asian-American Women: Psychological Responses to Sexual Exploitation and Cultural Stereotypes," *Women and Therapy* 6, no. 4 (1987): 34–35.

[21] The hegemonic heterosexual imagination also subscribes to this lesbian-as-butch image but, in addition, often portrays lesbians as very feminine, usually in order to make lesbianism either titillating or unthreatening or both. This is apparent in many film representations and in heterosexual pornography. Thanks to Caroline Streeter for bringing this to my attention.

[22] Arlene Istar, "Femme-Dyke," in *The Persistent Desire,* 378.

[23] See especially Joan Nestle, "Butch-Fem Relationships: Sexual Courage in the 1950's," *Heresies* 12 (1981): 21–24; Amber Hollibaugh and Cherrie Moraga, "What We're Rollin Around in Bed With: Sexual Silences in Feminism," in *Powers of Desire: The Politics of Sexuality,* ed. Ann Snitow, Christine Stansell, and Sharon Thompson (New York: Monthly Review, 1983), 394–405; and the following articles in Nestle, *The Persistent Desire:* Nestle, "The Femme Question"; Madeline Davis, Amber Hollibaugh, and Joan Nestle, "The Femme Tapes"; Lyndall MacCowan, "Re-Collecting History, Renaming Lives Femme Stigma and the Feminist Seventies and Eighties"; Paula Austin, "Femme-inism"; Mykel Johnson, "Butchy Femme."

[24] Lisa M. Walker, "How to Recognize a Lesbian: The Cultural Politics of Looking like What You Are," *Signs: Journal of Women in Culture and Society* 18, no. 4 (Summer 1993): 882.

[25] Loraine Hutchins and Lani Kaahumanu, eds., *Bi Any Other Name: Bisexual People Speak Out* (Boston: Alyson, 1991); and Elizabeth Reba Weise, ed., *Closer to Home: Bisexuality and Feminism* (Seattle: Seal Press, 1992).

[26] Walker, "How to Recognize a Lesbian," 886.

[27] MacCowan, "Re-Collecting History," 323.

[28] Kaushalya Bannerji, "No Apologies," in *A Lotus of Another Color: An Unfolding of the South Asian Gay and Lesbian Experience,* ed. Rakesh Ratti (Boston: Alyson, 1993), 60–61.

[29] See also Marivic R. Desquitado, "A Letter from the Philippines," in *The Persistent Desire,* 295–98, for a description of femme/butch identities in the Philippines.

[30] My understanding of this theory of hegemony comes from Lowe, *Critical Terrains.*

☙ ☙ ☙

Questions

1. List the stereotypes of Asian women and of lesbians that Lee identifies.

2. How do stereotypes operate to make Asian lesbians (and bisexual women) invisible? How are Asian women "heterosexualized"?

3. What does this analysis tell us about the ways that gender and sexuality are "racialized"?

4. Examine the sexual stereotypes associated with women from other race/ethnic groups. Would these stereotypes make women of those races or ethnicities more likely to be identified as possible lesbians, or less likely?

5. How might these stereotypes influence the developing sexual identities of Asian women?

6. Explain why feminine women, even if they are not Asian, have a difficult time being seen as lesbians.

☙ References

Ardill, Susan, and Sue O'Sullivan. "Butch/Femme Obsessions" *Feminist Review* 34 (Spring 1990): 79–85.

Austin, Paula. "Femme-inism." *The Persistent Desire: A Femme-Butch Reader.* Ed. Joan Nestle. Boston: Alyson, 1992. 362–66.

Bannerji, Kaushalya. "No Apologies." *A Lotus of Another Color: An Unfolding of the South Asian Gay and Lesbian Experience.* Ed. Rakesh Ratti. Boston: Alyson, 1993. 59–64.

Blackman, Inge, and Kathryn Perry. "Skirting the Issue: Lesbian Fashion for the 1990s" *Feminist Review* 34 (Spring 1990): 67–78.

Case, Sue-Ellen. "Towards a Butch-Femme Aesthetic." *Discourse Journal for Theoretical Studies in Media and Culture* 11, no. 1(1988–89): 55–73.

Chan, Connie S. "Asian-American Women: Psychological Responses to Sexual Exploitation and Cultural Stereotypes." *Women and Therapy* 6, no. 4 (1987): 33–38.

Davis, Madeline, Amber Hollibaugh, and Joan Nestle. "The Femme Tapes." *The Persistent Desire: A Femme-Butch Reader.* Ed. Joan Nestle. Boston: Alyson, 1992. 254–67.

Davis, Madeline, and Elizabeth Lapovsky Kennedy. "Oral History and the Study of Sexuality in the Lesbian Community: Buffalo, New York, 1940–1960." *Feminist Studies* 12, no. 1 (1986): 7–26.

____. *Boots of Leather, Slippers of Gold: The History of a Lesbian Community.* New York: Routledge, 1993.

Desquitado, Marivic R. "A Letter from the Philippines." *The Persistent Desire: A Femme-Butch Reader.* Ed. Joan Nestle. Boston: Alyson, 1992. 295–98.

Faderman, Lillian. *Odd Girls and Twilight Lovers: A History of Lesbian Life in Twentieth-Century America.* New York: Penguin Books, 1991.

____. "The Return of Butch and Femme: A Phenomenon in Lesbian Sexuality of the 1980s and 1990s." *Journal of the History of Sexuality* 2, no. 4 (1992): 578–96.

Frankenberg, Ruth. *White Women, Race Matters: The Social Construction of Whiteness.* Minneapolis: University of Minnesota Press, 1993.

Fung, Richard. "Looking for My Penis: The Eroticized Asian in Gay Video Porn." *How Do I Look? Queer Film and Video.* Ed. Bad Object-Choices. Seattle: Bay Press, 1991. 145—60.

Hagedorn, Jessica. "Asian Women in Film: No Joy, No Luck." *Ms.* 4, no. 4 (January 1994): 74—79.

Hollibaugh, Amber, and Cherrie Moraga. "What We're Rollin Around in Bed With: Sexual Silences in Feminism." *Powers of Desire: The Politics of Sexuality.* Ed. Ann Snitow, Christine Stansell, and Sharon Thompson. New York: Monthly Review, 1983. 394–405.

Hutchins, Loraine, and Lani Kaahumanu, eds. *Bi Any Other Name: Bisexual People Speak Out.* Boston: Alyson, 1991.

Hwang, David Henry. *M. Butterfly.* New York: Penguin Books, 1986.

Istar, Arlene. "Femme-Dyke." *The Persistent Desire: A Femme-Butch Reader.* Ed. Joan Nestle. Boston: Alyson, 1992. 378–83.

Johnson, Mykel. "Butchy Femme." *The Persistent Desire: A Femme-Butch Reader.* Ed. Joan Nestle. Boston: Alyson, 1992. 395–98.

Kang, L. Hyun-Yi. "The Desiring of Asian Female Bodies: Interracial Romance and Cinematic Subjection." *Visual Anthropology Review* 9, no. 1 (1993): 5–21.

Kauanui, J. Kehaulani, and Ju Hui Han. "'Asian Pacific Islander': Issues of Representation and Responsibility." *Moving the Mountains: Asian American Women's Journal* (1993): 24–25.

Kim, Elaine. "Sex Tourism in Asia: A Reflection of Political and Economic Inequality." *Critical Perspectives* 2, no. 1 (1984): 214–32.

Lowe, Lisa. *Critical Terrains: French and British Orientalisms.* Ithaca, NY: Cornell University Press, 1991.

MacCowan, Lyndall. "Re-Collecting History, Renaming Lives: Femme Stigma and the Feminist Seventies and Eighties." *The Persistent Desire: A Femme-Butch Reader.* Ed. Joan Nestle. Boston: Alyson, 1992. 299–328.

Mayall, Alice, and Diana E. H. Russell. "Racism in Pornography." *Making Violence Sexy: Feminist Views on Pornography.* Ed. Diana E. H. Russell. New York: Teachers College Press, 1993: 167–77.

Morrison, Toni. *Playing in the Dark: Whiteness and the Literary Imagination.* New York: Random House, 1992.

Nestle, Joan. "Butch-Fem Relationships: Sexual Courage in the 1950's." *Heresies* 12 (1981): 21–24.

____. "The Femme Question." *The Persistent Desire: A Femme-Butch Reader.* Ed. Joan Nestle. Boston: Alyson, 1992. 138–46.

____. "Flamboyance and Fortitude: An Introduction." *The Persistent Desire: A Femme-Butch Reader.* Ed. Joan Nestle. Boston: Alyson, 1992. 13–20.

____, ed. *The Persistent Desire: A Femme-Butch Reader.* Boston: Alyson, 1992.

Stein, Arlene. "All Dressed Up, but No Place to Go? Style Wars and the New Lesbianism." *The Persistent Desire: A Femme-Butch Reader.* Ed. Joan Nestle. Boston: Alyson, 1992. 431–39.

Stoltzfus, Brenda, and Saundra Pollock Sturdevant. *Let the Good Times Roll: Prostitution and the U.S. Military in Asia.* New York: New Press, 1993.

Tajima, Renee E. "Lotus Blossoms Don't Bleed: Images of Asian Women." *Making Waves: An Anthology of Writings by and about Asian American Women.* Ed. Asian Women United of California. Boston: Beacon Press, 1989. 308–17.

Tsang, Daniel. "M. Butterfly Meets the Great White Hope." *Informasian* 6, no. 3(1992): 3–4.

Villapando, Venny. "The Business of Selling Mail-Order Brides." *Making Waves: An Anthology of Writings by and about Asian American Women.* Ed. Asian Women United of California. Boston: Beacon Press, 1989. 318–26.

Walker, Lisa M. "How to Recognize a Lesbian: The Cultural Politics of Looking like What You Are." *Signs: Journal of Women in Culture and Society* 18, no. 4 (Summer 1993): 866–90.

Weise, Elizabeth Reba, ed. *Closer to Home: Bisexuality and Feminism.* Seattle: Seal Press, 1992.

Rural Lesbians' Strategies for Coming Out to Health Care Professionals

KATHLEEN A. TIEMANN, SALLY A. KENNEDY AND MYRNA P. HAGA

Many journalists in the U.S. popular press address how the lack of health insurance keeps some people from seeking timely care. Others advocate for a national health-care plan. In this selection, the authors explore a different but related issue: what problems face lesbians who live in rural areas, and how and why these women manage knowledge of their sexual identities when seeking medical care. The women in this study worried about how health-care and insurance providers' knowledge of their sexual orientation might exclude them from access to health care, subject them to disapproval, or result in inappropriate treatment. As you read this article, think about how such fears would affect whether you would seek care if you needed it.

If lesbians are often difficult to see (Eliason & Randall, 1991; Eliason, Donelan & Randall, 1992; Hitchcock & Wilson, 1992; Robertson, 1992), then rural lesbians are even more "invisible." Because of this invisibility, rural health care practitioners may not

"Rural Lesbians' Strategies for Coming Out to Health Care Professionals," by Kathleen A. Tiemann, Sally A. Kennedy and Myrna P. Haga, reprinted from *Journal of Lesbian Studies*, vol. 2, no. 1, 1998, pp. 61–75.

realize that they have lesbian patients and, as a result, they may be unprepared to meet lesbians' health care concerns. Moreover, because doctors, nurses and other helping professionals often accept the same stereotypes about lesbians that are held by the general public (Stevens, 1992), they may unwittingly create a situation in which lesbians are unable or unwilling to speak about themselves and their health care needs (Falco, 1991; Harris, 1996; Noble, 1996; Potter, 1985; Raboy, 1996; Rankow, 1996; Tiemann, Kennedy & Haga, 1997; Waitkevicz, 1996). In this article, we provide lesbians from rural areas with the opportunity to describe their experiences with members of the health care community and the protective strategies they used during these interactions.

❧ Participants and Method

A nonrandom sample of 8 rural lesbians was recruited by the investigators and by a student who knew lesbians who might be interested in participating in this research project. Five of the women lived in communities of fewer than 8,000 residents. However, these towns were within 80 miles of a "large" city of 50,000 people where the other three women lived. All had sought, and reported on, health care services they had received from providers who practiced in this city of 50,000 people.

It is important to recognize that the term "rural" does not simply refer to areas that are sparsely populated; there is a *gemeinschaft* that is shared by rural residents. To live in a rural community means that people believe that their neighbors share their values and way of life. Moreover, because their social spheres overlap, rural residents know who their neighbors are and much of what they do. This creates a paradox. On the one hand, because rural residents take for granted that their neighbors are just like them, differences often go unrecognized because they are not expected. On the other hand, when differences are intentionally or unintentionally revealed, it is a serious matter.

Those who do not conform to the norms of the rural community, like lesbians, face predictable sanctions. They are gossiped about, shunned, ostracized, encouraged to leave, and they may face acts of violence. Thus, to protect themselves and to keep their sexual orientation from becoming their master status, lesbians may try to remain closeted and, therefore, "invisible." All of the lesbians in our study were well aware of this rural *gemeinschaft* and had felt its effects on their lives.

Interviews were scheduled by phone for times and locations that suited the participants. All interviews were audiotaped and lasted between two and one-half to four hours. Participants provided detailed information about coming out, identity development, family interactions, health care experiences, and other issues. Here we focus exclusively on their interactions with physicians, therapists, counselors and psychiatrists.

Each interview was transcribed and health care stories were highlighted in the transcripts. After all of the health care stories were highlighted, the content and context of the stories were analyzed so that similarities and differences in reported experiences could be discerned. It was from this process that the four strategies of coming out to health care providers emerged.

At the time the interviews were conducted, the participants ranged in age from their early 20's through their mid-40's. Five women were in committed lesbian relationships of 8 to 18 years, two were partnered with women for 1 to 7 years, and one woman was single but dating. Two respondents had children. One woman and her lesbian partner chose to have a child together while the other woman had a child during her heterosexual marriage. These women were well educated: four had bachelors degrees, three had masters degrees or its equivalent, and one respondent was a full-time college student. The student held a part-time job and the other participants were employed full-time in professional and managerial occupations appropriate to their level of education. Despite their occupational levels, the median yearly income was $24,000 with a range from $10,000 to $50,000.

❧ Coming Out to Health Care Professionals

. . .

Some lesbians do not reveal information about their sexual orientation to health care professionals for fear of rejection, ridicule, disrespect and inappropriate treatment (Stevens, 1992; Stevens, 1994; Trippet & Bain, 1992). These are not idle fears. Stevens (1994) reported that the health care interaction stories told by lesbians from San Francisco were overwhelmingly negative. They felt unsafe, fearful and vulnerable in health care facilities and were sometimes treated disrespectfully. If it was difficult and dangerous for lesbians to disclose their sexual orientation to health care professionals given the relative anonymity provided in urban areas, how difficult must it be to make this disclosure for rural lesbians?

Health care professionals should assume that they will come into contact with sexual minority clients during their careers (Falco, 1991; Trippet & Bain, 1992) and that clients will be at different stages of self-acceptance as lesbian, gay, bisexual or transgendered people (Coleman, 1982; Falco, 1991; Hammersmith & Weinberg, 1973). Urban lesbians who came out to health care practitioners in one study were reportedly more comfortable with their sexual identity than those who did not come out. However, once they revealed their sexual orientations, they had "feelings of being 'exposed,' 'embarrassed,' and 'less anonymous' and of a 'void' in the relationship" (Robertson, 1992 p. 160). It is vital for health care professionals to provide a positive response when a client discloses her sexual orientation. Doing so not only helps a patient accept herself and her sexual orientation (Falco, 1991; Fassinger, 1991; Gentry, 1992; E.J. Rankow, 1995), but it may help create an environment in which she is more likely to seek routine health care in the future (Gentry, 1992; Stevens, 1992; Stevens & Hall, 1990).

Protective Strategies

The ways the rural lesbians in our study disclosed their sexual orientation to health care professionals varied, although there were four main protective strategies. The four strategies that emerged through content analysis of transcribed interviews were "screening," "unplanned disclosure," "planned disclosure," and "non-disclosure." These protective strategies are similar to those reported by Stevens (1994) and by Hitchcock and Wilson (1992) in their studies of multiethnic and socio-economically diverse lesbians in San Francisco. However, the lesbians we interviewed perceived higher risks and costs associated with the use of particular protective strategies. Because negative attitudes about lesbians and gays are normative in rural locales (Herek, 1991), being a known lesbian is potentially hazardous to one's health.

Screening

The first strategy used by our participants is "screening." The goal in screening is to locate a health care practitioner who is sensitive to lesbians and knowledgeable about their health care needs in the event that they intentionally or accidentally disclose their sexual orientation. This technique is most effective when seeking routine health care as there is time to do adequate research (Stevens, 1994).

Women who screen use two main techniques. One is to gather information about other lesbians' experiences with a particular health care worker before making an appointment. This, of course, is chancy as it means coming out and seeking contact with the lesbian community. For example, "Jody" said, "I've always scoped them out . . . so I really haven't ever had bad experiences with mental health professionals." "Tina" was more specific when she said that she and her lesbian friends talk to each other about which practitioners are "safe" to see and which ones are not.

A second means to locate a safe health care professional is to ask for a referral from a health care provider who is lesbian-friendly. For example, when "Mary" needed a new physician, she asked her psychiatrist, for a referral. . . . "Laura" has had negative interactions with many health care professionals, but particularly with mental health professionals. She now carefully screens all of her health care providers and advocates an aggressive approach toward mental health practitioners who are unqualified to work with lesbian clients because of their hostility and lack of knowledge about lesbians and their lives. As she put it,

> The bad therapist should be outed. . . . The problem is that you have to be in a community . . . to hear that information . . . I wish the APA would get really tough on regulating some of these assholes out of it.

As Laura noted, lesbians in rural areas, like their heterosexual counterparts, might be unaware of the lesbian community around them and the support and assistance it might provide. The "invisibility" of the lesbian community is enhanced by the fact that lesbians are not distinguishable from other women unless they choose to reveal their sexual orientation (Eliason et al., 1992; Eliason & Randall, 1991; Hitchcock & Wilson, 1992; Robertson, 1992). . . . Participants commented on the isolation they face in rural communities and how locating or establishing a lesbian community in these areas was risky. According to Laura,

> We don't have the community support [because] it's not as large a group of gay or lesbian people. . . . You can't very well have much [of] a support group or anything else going on when there's like two of ya for how many miles. . . . Everybody is so closeted anyway because they're so scared of getting beat up that they don't want to talk about it. So then you're even closeted to people of your own kind.

Therefore, even if a lesbian locates the lesbian community, she may be unsure of how to join it or she may fear reprisals for doing so. The limited visibility of and access to the lesbian community in rural areas cuts some lesbians off from important information about health care practitioners and from a social support system that could help them cope with health care concerns and with other problems of living.

A problem that all rural residents share is limited access to appropriate health care professionals in their region. Jody illustrated this problem when she noted that there were only three psychiatrists from which she could choose. This difficulty is compounded for a lesbian as she may have to make difficult choices about her health care needs. She may ignore a health care concern (Potter, 1985); if she can afford it, she may drive long distances for treatment from a sympathetic and knowledgeable practitioner, go to a health care provider who is uninformed about lesbian health issues or who treats her disrespectfully (Potter, 1985; Stevens, 1992; Stevens, 1994), rely on informal help from family or friends (D'Augelli, 1989; D'Augelli & Hart, 1987); or she may pursue health care locally but hide her sexual orientation as she does so (Hitchcock & Wilson, 1992; Potter, 1985; Stevens, 1994).

While they are not without risk, the screening strategies described by our participants increase the probability that a lesbian will receive a positive response if she comes out to a health care professional because practitioners who are known to be unsupportive, hostile or unqualified to treat lesbians are avoided whenever possible. Screening, in one of its forms, was used by everyone we interviewed even if they did not intend to disclose their sexual orientation. The heavy reliance on screening may be a result of the high level of education attained by our subjects. Those with less formal education may feel unable to successfully use this strategy. Nonetheless, screening is a protective strategy that helped lesbians feel safer when dealing with an often unfriendly health care community.

Unplanned Disclosure

Unplanned disclosure, the second strategy used by the lesbians in this study, was rather risky. Patients did not intend to reveal their lesbianism to their health care provider; their disclosure was prompted by a triggering event during their visit. Women who made unplanned disclosures reported a range of responses from health care practitioners. However, even the most favorable responses were inadequate. ["Marsha's"] story illustrates a common type of inappropriate response that some lesbians face when they make an unplanned disclosure of their lesbianism to a health care professional. Marsha made an appointment with a neurologist because she had severe headaches, memory losses, and lost track of time for 10 or 15 seconds. While taking her medical history, the neurologist asked Marsha why she did not use birth control:

> I thought, "Well, hell. I'll give this a try and see what happens." I said, "I'm a lesbian." From that point on his treatment of me was completely different. And he immediately decided that I should take the MMPI . . . [and that] a clinical psychologist should see me . . . His physical exam of me was so sloppy! . . . The minute I mentioned I was a lesbian then it was all over with. He did not entertain my symptoms as being valid at all. Everything that was wrong with me was because I was a lesbian. And I got up and I said, "I'm sorry. I don't need to be treated this way" and I walked right out.

Marsha took a calculated risk with her disclosure especially since this doctor was one of only two neurologists in the area. To Marsha's dismay, the result of her honesty was an inappropriate response from the doctor. Marsha responded as she did because she is a well-educated woman and a health care professional. A less informed patient may not have responded so assertively in these circumstances. As Marsha discovered after seeking assistance elsewhere, her symptoms were caused by a classic case of spinal compression; they were not due to her lesbian identity nor did she need mental health care.

Like Marsha, Jody made an unplanned disclosure of her sexual orientation. She described an "incredibly funny" incident with her allergist which further portrays the heterosexism and the stereotypes about lesbians that seem to flourish among some members of the medical community.

> He was going on and on about yeast infections . . . and I final-
> ly just said, "Dr.—, I'm a lesbian." And he said, "Oh, my dear.
> You know you are really a very good looking woman." . . .
> And he was going to give me a shot for it! He figured it [les-
> bianism] was part of a yeast allergy. And he thought it would
> "take care of my social problem as well," is the way he put it.
> I said, "You know, I really don't regard it as a problem." "Oh!"
> he said. . . . A few years prior . . . I wouldn't have told him.

Jody saw a practitioner that she knew had unconventional ideas
before making an appointment because she knew what kind of health
care she needed. Despite his "understanding" of the etiology of lesbianism, his belief in the stereotype that lesbians are unattractive, and
his opinion that a lesbian sexual orientation can be converted into a
heterosexual one through injections (and that alcoholics can be
"cured" in a similar way), he is considered eccentric, but competent.
Jody's experience may be unusual, but the lack of information among
health care providers about lesbians and how their sexual orientation
may affect their reason for seeking treatment is not (D'Augelli, 1989;
D'Augelli & Hart, 1987; Falco, 1991; Stevens, 1992; Trippet & Bain,
1993).

Not all of our respondents reported unfavorable responses from
physicians when they disclosed their sexual orientation. Mary's spon-
taneous disclosure of her sexual orientation to her female physician
was one of the more positive ones reported by our subjects.
Mary said,

> She's asking about all the risk factors for cervical cancer . . .
> and instead of trying to lie, I said, "I'm a lesbian." [She said,]
> "That's neat. Are you in a relationship?" She seems to have
> some information about lesbians . . . It's like some people
> don't . . . have to . . . think about how they're going to
> respond so that they can seem like they're okay with who
> you are.

While "that's neat" is a more positive response than those reported by
Marsha, Jody or other participants, it still leaves much to be desired.

Why is Mary's lesbian identity neat? Is it because Mary trusted her physician enough to disclose this information? Is it because the doctor expected to be educated about lesbianism by Mary, or is it neat for some other reason? While this response is more affirming than those that many lesbians receive from health care practitioners, it is still inadequate and troubling.

All of the women in our study who made unplanned disclosures of their sexual orientation to female physicians received positive reactions. However, the responses from male physicians were uniformly negative. The correlation between the sex of the health care provider and the type of response they gave to patients who disclosed their sexual orientation is consistent with reports offered by more diverse samples of urban lesbians (Hitchcock & Wilson, 1992; Stevens, 1994; Trippet & Bain, 1993). However, unlike their urban counterparts, rural lesbians have fewer health care professionals from which to choose if they encounter one who responds negatively to disclosure of their sexual orientation. The negative responses of male physicians reported here and elsewhere shed light on women's preferences for knowledgeable female health care providers over male health care professionals regardless of their sexual orientation (Stevens, 1992; Trippet & Bain, 1990; Trippet & Bain, 1993).

Planned Disclosure

The third strategy, planned disclosure, was used by women who felt that it was either necessary or desirable to reveal their sexual orientation to a health care practitioner. Like those who relied on screening, women who planned to disclose their sexual orientation gathered information about the health care professional so that they could determine how she or he might respond when they disclosed their sexual orientation. Some screening activities were completed before they made an appointment. Indeed, making an appointment was often dependent upon the results of what they learned. Other information could only be gathered while in the waiting room and during the woman's interaction with the health care provider.

The physical environment of an office or clinic can make clients feel at ease. Many of our participants mentioned how difficult it was for them to feel safe or accepted when office decorations and informational pamphlets were restricted to depictions of intact, heterosexual, European-American families (E.J. Rankow, 1995; Stevens, 1995). They defined this as disrespectful of any client who did not fit this narrow categorization. Moreover, the phrasing of questions and the available response categories on intake forms were described as biased and inappropriate to describe these women's lives. There was no way, for example, to indicate that they had a same-sex partner and that they had some concerns that were not shared by heterosexual women.

The behavior of the staff when clients are present also affects clients' perceptions of safety. Laura reported how she heard staff members at one human service agency tell gay jokes to their colleagues. They were seemingly unconcerned about being overheard by clients who were in the waiting room. This incident created an unsafe environment for their clients in general, but was especially painful to Laura as a lesbian.

During the office visit, close regard was paid to what the health care professional did and to how she or he responded to the patient and to her questions. Attention to these details and her "gut feelings" during the interaction helped determine whether a client disclosed her sexual orientation. For example, . . . Jody carefully studied her psychiatrist to determine how he would respond to the disclosure of her sexual orientation. She described how difficult it was for her when she came out to him even after seeing him twice a week for two years:

> I called him and said, "This is real important and I need to come in and talk to you." So he found a half hour slot for me . . . And so I sat down and . . . just blurted it out. . . . And he said, "Oh, Jody . . . You know we've wasted a lot of time." I said, "I guess so but I just really just couldn't tell you that." And he said, "Did you think that I would think differently about you?" And I said, "I guess not really, but that I would feel different, you know? I mean it was like I needed to get

to a place myself where it was okay with me before I could tell you."

Jody's psychiatrist was supportive of her sexual orientation, but he also expressed disappointment that she took two years to disclose it to him. We cannot know if he reflected on whether his behavior kept Jody from disclosing her lesbianism earlier in their professional relationship. We also cannot know how keeping her sexual orientation secret affected the appropriateness of the care she received nor whether it has changed how Jody's psychiatrist interacts with his other clients. What is clear, however, is that her psychiatrist missed a crucial therapeutic issue at Jody's expense.

Women who embraced the protective strategy of planned disclosure proceeded with caution. Like their urban counterparts, they worried about how knowledge of their sexual orientation might affect their clinical treatment (Stevens, 1994). They were also concerned with how their lesbianism would be judged and how that judgment might affect future interactions with, and access to, this and other health care practitioners (Robertson, 1992), especially if this information was recorded in their files (Gentry, 1992; Lucas, 1992). These are significant concerns in rural communities where health care professionals know one another, the availability of practitioners is limited, and many people have access to clients' files.

Non-Disclosure

"Non-disclosure" comprised the fourth protective strategy used by the lesbians in our study. Some of the lesbians we interviewed took pains to hide their sexual orientation not only from their health care provider, but also from others with whom they regularly interacted. This decision is at least partly related to residing in a rural community. Six of the eight women specifically commented on the danger of being a known or suspected lesbian. According to "Carol," "When you're out in rural [state] you better not let everybody know you're a lesbian or you might get killed." Laura was so concerned about her safety that she did not have newsletters, magazines, books, or anything else that could be "incriminating" sent to her through the mail because:

> If somebody else reads it because they're nosy, and they will, you get 50 million questions . . . I've had violent crimes done to several friends of mine in [a larger town of 32,000]. They . . . [had] windows shot out of their cars, guys being beat up, things like this. That frightens me.

These safety concerns were generalized to the medical community by our subjects. Urban lesbians who participated in studies by Gentry (1992) and Lucas (1992) reported fear that their sexual orientation would be recorded in their medical files where anyone at the facility could read it. This concern takes on special significance in small towns where private matters may quickly become public knowledge. . . .

"Cathy" . . . revealed how, as a college student who was struggling with her lesbian identity, she had to summon up her courage to call the local mental health center's hotline for information.

> All I was looking for was . . . a group or something like that. [The hotline staff] kept on trying to get me into help, and at that point it was even such a risk for me to make that phone call . . . Once you are out in a small rural area . . . word spreads and people think it's their right to let everybody know . . . [You may] literally be run out of the community.

When Mary temporarily lived in a town of a few hundred people, she put her safety concerns this way:

> If someone thought you were gay and you went to a bar, they'd shoot you . . . If you look at them wrong or if they thought you were coming on to their girlfriend, male or female, they'd pull their pistol out or they'd beat you. . . . You just need to be real low key.

These concerns for physical safety keep some lesbians from disclosing their sexual orientation and from seeking the support and information that is available through the lesbian community. Mary's many negative experiences with helping professionals and her fear of retaliation and mistreatment have made her leery of coming out to most health care providers. On the few occasions that she has disclosed her sexual orientation, it was preceded by extensive research. Even then she only disclosed her sexual orientation after many favorable interactions with a health care provider with whom she felt very safe.

In some cases, the health care provider facilitated the protective strategy of non-disclosure. Recall how Jody's psychiatrist ignored her sexual orientation until she brought it up two years after beginning work with him despite the fact that it affected the clinical treatment she received. Mary reported a similar situation. She saw a counselor at a college psychological services center when she was an undergraduate. While her counselor understood the importance of facilitating Mary's self-acceptance, she never addressed Mary's lesbianism.

> I was in my first [lesbian] relationship . . . I talked about . . . [it as] being special . . . but she never brought up . . . being lesbian . . . I'm sure she knew that I was lesbian long before I accepted it.

Like Jody, Mary saw no problem with her clinician's failure to address her sexual orientation. Indeed, she was appreciative that her counselor did not directly address her sexual orientation. Unfortunately, this therapeutic decision helped Mary deny both her social and her personal identity as a lesbian and its possible effects on her life, including her life-long problem with recurrent depression (Falco, 1991; Fassinger, 1991).

The protective strategy of non-disclosure had both costs and benefits for these women. While this strategy allowed some lesbians to seek the health care they needed without fear of reprisal, it also meant that they may not have received appropriate care. For example, when used with mental health professionals non-disclosure kept some lesbians from directly revealing their sexual orientation. As a result, their therapy may have been hindered. Non-disclosure required vigilance and extraordinary energy on their parts so that their actual sexual orientation was not inadvertently revealed to health care providers.

Moreover, lesbians' fears of reprisal from other residents of the rural areas in which they lived, should their sexual orientation become known, kept them from seeking help from the lesbian community around them.

☙ Discussion

Coming out is not a single event; it is an ongoing process in the lives of lesbians. It is motivated by the need for self-validation, acceptance by others, to meet potential partners, by the need for medical intervention for health care concerns and for help with problems of living (Trippet & Bain, 1993; Potter, 1985). Disclosure of one's sexual orientation in a heterosexist medical system to homophobic health care professionals can have a detrimental effect on a woman's self-esteem, her future help-seeking behavior and on her physical safety (L. Rankow, 1996; Stevens, 1992; Stevens, 1995; Trippet & Bain, 1993). Similarly, not coining out and presenting an inaccurate self to others also has costs.

The rural lesbians we interviewed emphasized the importance of using protective strategies so that they could feel safe in their interactions with members of health care professions. They stressed that most helping professionals needed further education so that they could move beyond stereotypes about lesbians, provide appropriate responses to coming out, and so that they could adequately address lesbians' health care concerns. Participants also underscored the need for all health care professionals to reflect upon their feelings about lesbians, their ability to competently treat them in their practices, and their ability to effectively refer them to other practitioners.

The results of this study are not generalizable because of the methodological problems associated with sampling a population that is relatively "invisible." Additionally, our informants may be more homogeneous than those included in other studies on the basis of race and education. Indeed, their relatively high level of education may have enhanced their ability to effectively strategize about selecting health care practitioners and determining whether they could safely disclose their sexual orientation to them. These concerns notwithstanding, the stories these women told provide a glimpse into the health care concerns faced by lesbians who live in and seek medical care in rural communities.

References

Coleman, E. (1982). Developmental stages of the coming out process. *Journal of Homosexuality, 7,* 31–43.

D'Augelli, A.R. (1989). Lesbian women in a rural helping network: Exploring informal helping resources. *Women and Therapy, 8,* 119–130.

D'Augelli, A.R., & Hart, M.M. (1987). Gay women, men, and families in rural settings: Toward the development of helping communities. *American Journal of Community Psychology, 15,* 79–93.

Eliason, M.J., & Randall, C.E. (1991). Lesbian phobia in nursing students. *Western Journal of Nursing, 13,* 363–374.

Eliason, M., Donelan, C. & Randall, C. (1992). Lesbian stereotypes. *Health Care for Women International, 13,* 131–144.

Falco, K.L. (1991). *Psychotherapy with lesbian clients: Theory into practice.* New York: Brunner/Mazel.

Fassinger, R.E. (1991). The hidden minority: Issues and challenges in working with lesbian women and gay men. *The Counseling Psychologist, 19,* 157–176.

Gentry, S.E. (1992). Caring for lesbians in a homophobic society. *Health Care for Women International 13,* 173–180.

Hammersmith, S.K., & Weinberg, M.S. (1973). Homosexual identity: Commitment, adjustment, and significant others. *Sociometry, 36,* 56–79.

Harris, A. (1996). The invisibility of lesbians with AIDS. In G. Vida (Ed.), *The new our right to love: A lesbian resource book* (pp. 108–111). New York: Touchstone.

Herek, G.M. (1991). Stigma, prejudice, and violence against lesbians and gay men. In J.C. Gonsiorek and J.D. Weinrich (Eds.), *Homosexuality: Research and implications for public policy.* Newbury Park, CA: Sage.

Hitchcock, J.M., & Wilson, H.S. (1992). Personal risking: Lesbian self-disclosure of sexual orientation to professional health care providers. *Nursing Research, 41,* 178–183.

Lucas, V.A. (1992). An investigation of the health care preferences of the lesbian population. *Health Care for Women International, 13,* 221–228.

Noble, R.E. (1996). Chemical dependency: The journey home. In G. Vida (Ed.), *The new our right to love: A lesbian resource book* (pp. 102–104). New York: Touchstone.

Potter, S. (1985). Social work, traditional health care systems and lesbian invisibility. *Feminist Perspectives on Social Work and Human Sexuality, 20,* 59–68.

Raboy, B. (1996). Getting pregnant through donor insemination. In G. Vida (Ed.), *The new our right to love: A lesbian resource book* (pp. 99–102). New York: Touchstone.

Rankow, E.J. (1995). Lesbian health issues for the primary care provider. *The Journal of Family Practice, 40,* 486–493.

Rankow, L. (1996). Breast and cervical cancer among lesbians. In G. Vida (Ed.), *The new our right to love: A lesbian resource book* (pp. 96–99). New York: Touchstone.

Robertson, M.M. (1992). Lesbians as an invisible minority in the health services arena. *Health Care for Women International, 13,* 155–163.

Stevens, P.E. (1992). Lesbian health care research: A review of the literature from 1970 to 1990. *Health Care for Women International, 13,* 91–120.

Stevens, P.E. (1994). Protective strategies of lesbian clients in health care environments. *Research in Nursing & Health, 17,* 217–229.

Stevens. P .E. (1995). Structural and interpersonal impact of heterosexual assumptions on lesbian health care clients. *Nursing Research, 44,* 25–30.

Stevens, P.E., & J.M. Hall. (1990). Abusive health care interactions experienced by lesbians: A case of institutional violence in the treatment of women. *Response: To the Victimization of Women and Children, 13,* 23–27.

Tiemann, K.A., Kennedy, S.A. & Haga, M.P. (1997). Lesbian's experiences with helping professionals. *Affilia, 12,* 84–95.

Trippet, S.E., & Bain, J. (1990). Preliminary study of lesbian health concerns. *Health Values, 14,* 30–36.

Trippet, S.E., & Bain, J. (1992). Reasons American lesbians fail to seek traditional health care. *Health Care for Women International, 13,* 145–153.

Trippet, S.E., & Bain, J. (1993). Physical health problems and concerns of lesbians. *Women & Health, 20,* 59–71.

Waitkevicz, H.J. (1996). Lesbian health issues. In G. Vida (Ed.), *The new our right to love: A lesbian resource book* (pp. 93–95). New York: Touchstone.

❧ ❧ ❧

Questions

1. Briefly describe the four protective strategies used by rural lesbians.

2. Why were the women in this study concerned about revealing their sexual orientation to health-care providers? Do you think these are realistic concerns? Why or why not?

3. Has a health-care professional ever blamed your symptoms on your sexual orientation or tried to change your orientation with an injection or a prescription? Why or why not?

4. What can health-care providers do to create safer environments for their minority patients?

5. What do you think should be done to improve the care received by lesbians, gay men, bisexuals, and other sexual minorities?

Masculinity as Homophobia: Fear, Shame, and Silence in the Construction of Gender Identity

Michael S. Kimmel

When most people think about gender, they think about men and women. Recent findings on masculinity, however, suggest that gender is also very much about men's relationships with each other. Kimmel, in fact, argues that men's need to prove their masculinity to other men creates a variety of problems, including homophobia. This article offers a model for understanding the relationship between gender and sexuality. What does it mean, in the context of a patriarchal society, for many men to experience masculinity as a source of fear, shame, and silence? Consider the implications of this kind of experience for men.

"Funny thing," [Curley's wife] said "If I catch any one man, and he's alone, I get along fine with him. But just let two of the guys get together an' you won't talk. Jus' nothin' but mad." She dropped her fingers and put her hands on her hips. "You're all scared of each other, that's what. Ever'one of you's scared the rest is goin' to get something on you."

John Steinbeck, *Of Mice and Men* (1937)

We think of manhood as eternal, a timeless essence that resides deep in the heart of every man. We think of manhood as a thing, a quality that one either has or doesn't have. We think of manhood as innate, residing in the particular biological composition of the human male, the result of androgens or the possession of a penis. We think of manhood as a transcendent tangible property that each man must manifest in the world, the reward presented with great ceremony to a young novice by his elders for having

Reprinted from *Theorizing Masculinities*, edited by Harry Brod and Michael Kaufman, (1994), by permission of Sage Publications, Inc. Copyright © 1994 by Sage Publications, Inc.

successfully completed an arduous initiation ritual. In the words of poet Robert Bly (1990), "the structure at the bottom of the male psyche is still as firm as it was twenty thousand years ago" (p. 230).

In this chapter, I view masculinity as a constantly changing collection of meanings that we construct through our relationships with ourselves, with each other, and with our world. Manhood is neither static nor timeless; it is historical. Manhood is not the manifestation of an inner essence; it is socially constructed. Manhood does not bubble up to consciousness from our biological makeup; it is created in culture. Manhood means different things at different times to different people. We come to know what it means to be a man in our culture by setting our definitions in opposition to a set of "others"—racial minorities, sexual minorities, and, above all, women.

Our definitions of manhood are constantly changing, being played out on the political and social terrain on which the relationships between women and men are played out. In fact, the search for a transcendent, timeless definition of manhood is itself a sociological phenomenon—we tend to search for the timeless and eternal during moments of crisis, those points of transition when old definitions no longer work and new definitions are yet to be firmly established.

This idea that manhood is socially constructed and historically shifting should not be understood as a loss, that something is being taken away from men. In fact, it gives us something extraordinarily valuable—agency, the capacity to act. It gives us a sense of historical possibilities to replace the despondent resignation that invariably attends timeless, ahistorical essentialisms. Our behaviors are not simply "just human nature," because "boys will be boys." From the materials we find around us in our culture—other people, ideas, objects—we actively create our worlds, our identities. Men, both individually and collectively, can change.

In this chapter, I explore this social and historical construction of both hegemonic masculinity and alternate masculinities, with an eye toward offering a new theoretical model of American manhood.[1] To accomplish this I first uncover some of the hidden gender meanings in classical statements of social and political philosophy, so that I can anchor the emergence of contemporary manhood in specific historical and social contexts. I then spell out the ways in which this version of masculinity emerged in the United States, by tracing both psychoanalytic developmental sequences and a historical trajectory in the development of marketplace relationships.

◉ Classical Social Theory as a Hidden Meditation of Manhood

Begin this inquiry by looking at four passages from that set of texts commonly called classical social and political theory. You will, no doubt, recognize them, but I invite you to recall the way they were discussed in your undergraduate or graduate courses in theory:

> The bourgeoisie cannot exist without constantly revolutionizing the instruments of production, and thereby the relations of production, and with them the whole relations of society. Conservation of the old modes of production in unaltered form, was, on the contrary, the first condition of existence for all earlier industrial classes. Constant revolutionizing of production, uninterrupted disturbance of all social conditions, everlasting uncertainty and agitation distinguish the bourgeois epoch from all earlier ones. All fixed, fast-frozen relations, with their train of ancient and venerable prejudices and opinions are swept away, all new-formed ones become antiquated before they can ossify. All that is solid melts into air, all that is holy is profaned, and man is at last compelled to face with sober senses, his real conditions of life, and his relation with his kind (Marx & Engels, 1848/1964)

> An American will build a house in which to pass his old age and sell it before the roof is on; he will plant a garden and rent it just as the trees are coming into bearing; he will clear a field and leave others to reap the harvest; he will take up a profession and leave it, settle in one place and soon go off elsewhere with his changing desires. . . . At first sight there is something astonishing in this spectacle of so many lucky men restless in the midst of abundance. But it is a spectacle as old as the world; all that is new is to see a whole people performing in it. (Tocqueville, 1835/1967)

> Where the fulfillment of the calling cannot directly be related to the highest spiritual and cultural values, or when, on the other hand, it need not be felt simply as economic compulsion, the individual generally abandons the attempt to justify it at all. In the field of its highest development, in the United States, the pursuit of wealth, stripped of its religious and ethical meaning, tends to become associated with purely mundane passions, which often actually give it the character of sport. (Weber, 1905/1966)

> We are warned by a proverb against serving two masters at the same time. The poor ego has things even worse: it serves three severe masters and does what it can to bring their claims and demands into harmony with one

another. These claims are always divergent and often seem incompatible. No wonder that the ego so often fails in its task. Its three tyrannical masters are the external world, the super ego and the id. . . . It feels hemmed in on three sides, threatened by three kinds of danger, to which, if it is hard pressed, it reacts by generating anxiety. . . . Thus the ego, driven by the id, confined by the super ego, repulsed by reality, struggles to master its economic task of bringing about harmony among the forces and influences working in and upon it; and we can understand how it is that so often we cannot suppress a cry: "Life is not easy!" (Freud, "The Dissection of the Psychical Personality," 1933/1966)

If your social science training was anything like mine, these were offered as descriptions of the bourgeoisie under capitalism, of individuals in democratic societies, of the fate of the Protestant work ethic under the ever rationalizing spirit of capitalism, or of the arduous task of the autonomous ego in psychological development. Did anyone ever mention that in all four cases the theorists were describing men? Not just "man" as in generic mankind, but a particular type of masculinity, a definition of manhood that derives its identity from participation in the marketplace, from interaction with other men in that marketplace—in short, a model of masculinity for whom identity is based on homosocial competition? Three years before Tocqueville found Americans "restless in the midst of abundance," Senator Henry Clay had called the United States "a nation of self-made men."

What does it mean to be "self-made"? What are the consequences of self-making for the individual man, for other men, for women? It is this notion of manhood—rooted in the sphere of production, the public arena, a masculinity grounded not in landownership or in artisanal republican virtue but in successful participation in marketplace competition—this has been the defining notion of American manhood. Masculinity must be proved, and no sooner is it proved that it is again questioned and must be proved again—constant, relentless, unachievable, and ultimately the quest for proof becomes so meaningless than it takes on the characteristics, as Weber said, of a sport. He who has the most toys when he dies wins.

Where does this version of masculinity come from? How does it work? What are the consequences of this version of masculinity for women, for other men, and for individual men themselves? These are the questions I address in this chapter.

❧ /Masculinity as /History and the /History of /Masculinity

The idea of masculinity expressed in the previous extracts is the product of historical shifts in the grounds on which men rooted their sense of themselves as men. To argue that cultural definitions of gender identity are historically specific goes only so far; we have to specify exactly what those models were. In my historical inquiry into the development of these models of manhood[2] I chart the fate of two models for manhood at the turn of the 19th century and the emergence of a third in the first few decades of that century.

In the late 18th and early 19th centuries, two models of manhood prevailed. The *Genteel Patriarch* derived his identity from landowner ship. Supervising his estate, he was refined, elegant, and given to casual sensuousness. He was a doting and devoted father, who spent much of his time supervising the estate and with his family. Think of George Washington or Thomas Jefferson as examples. By contrast, the *Heroic Artisan* embodied the physical strength and republican virtue that Jefferson observed in the yeoman farmer, independent urban craftsman, or shopkeeper. Also a devoted father, the Heroic Artisan taught his son his craft, bringing him through ritual apprenticeship to status as master craftsman. Economically autonomous, the Heroic Artisan also cherished his democratic community, delighting in the participatory democracy of the town meeting. Think of Paul Revere at his pewter shop, shirtsleeves rolled up, a leather apron—a man who took pride in his work.

Heroic Artisans and Genteel Patriarchs lived in casual accord, in part because their gender ideals were complementary (both supported participatory democracy and individual autonomy, although patriarchs tended to support more powerful state machineries and also supported slavery) and because they rarely saw one another: Artisans were decidedly urban and the Genteel Patriarchs ruled their rural estates. By the 1830s, though, this casual symbiosis was shattered by the emergence of a new vision of masculinity, *Marketplace Manhood.*

Marketplace Man derived his identity entirely from his success in the capitalist marketplace, as he accumulated wealth, power, status. He was the urban entrepreneur, the businessman. Restless, agitated, and anxious, Marketplace Man was an absentee landlord at home and an absent father with his children, devoting himself to his work in an increasingly homosocial environment—a male-only world in which he pits himself against other men. His efforts at self-making transform the political and economic spheres, casting

223

aside the Genteel Patriarch as an anachronistic feminized dandy—sweet, but ineffective and outmoded, and transforming the Heroic Artisan into a dispossessed proletarian, a wage slave.

As Tocqueville would have seen it, the coexistence of the Genteel Patriarch and the Heroic Artisan embodied the fusion of liberty and equality. Genteel Patriarchy was the manhood of the traditional aristocracy, the class that embodied the virtue of liberty. The Heroic Artisan embodied democratic community, the solidarity of the urban shopkeeper or craftsman. Liberty and democracy, the patriarch and the artisan, could, and did, coexist. But Marketplace Man is capitalist man, and he makes both freedom and equality problematic, eliminating the freedom of the aristocracy and proletarianizing the equality of the artisan. In one sense, American history has been an effort to restore, retrieve, or reconstitute the virtues of Genteel Patriarchy and Heroic Artisanate as they were being transformed in the capitalist marketplace.

Marketplace Manhood was a manhood that required proof, and that required the acquisition of tangible goods as evidence of success. It reconstituted itself by the exclusion of "others"—women, nonwhite men, nonnative-born men, homosexual men—and by terrified flight into a pristine mythic homosocial Eden where men could, at last, be real men among other men. The story of the ways in which Marketplace Man becomes American Everyman is a tragic tale, a tale of striving to live up to impossible ideals of success leading to chronic terrors of emasculation, emotional emptiness, and a gendered rage that leave a wide swath of destruction in its wake.

❧ Masculinities as Power Relations

Marketplace Masculinity describes the normative definition of American masculinity. It describes his characteristics—aggression, competition, anxiety—and the arena in which those characteristics are deployed—the public sphere, the marketplace. If the marketplace is the arena in which manhood is tested and proved, it is a gendered arena, in which tensions between women and men and tensions among different groups of men are weighted with meaning. These tensions suggest that cultural definitions of gender are played out in a contested terrain and are themselves power relations.

All masculinities are not created equal; or rather, we are all *created* equal, but any hypothetical equality evaporates quickly because our definitions of masculinity are not equally valued in our society. One definition of manhood continues to remain the standard against which other forms of manhood are measured and evaluated. Within the dominant culture, the masculinity that defines white, middle class, early middle-aged, heterosexual men is the masculinity that sets the standards for other men, against which other men are measured and, more often than not, found wanting. Sociologist Erving Goffman (1963) wrote that in America, there is only "one complete, unblushing male":

> a young, married, white, urban, northern heterosexual, Protestant father of college education, fully employed, of good complexion, weight and height, and a recent record in sports. Every American male tends to look out upon the world from this perspective. . . . Any male who fails to qualify in any one of these ways is likely to view himself . . . as unworthy, incomplete, and inferior. (p. 128)

This is the definition that we will call "hegemonic" masculinity, the image of masculinity of those men who hold power, which has become the standard in psychological evaluations, sociological research, and self-help and advice literature for teaching young men to become "real men" (Connell, 1987). The hegemonic definition of manhood is a man *in* power, a man *with* power, and a man *of* power. We equate manhood with being strong, successful, capable, reliable, in control. The very definitions of manhood we have developed in our culture maintain the power that some men have over other men and that men have over women.

Our culture's definition of masculinity is thus several stories at once. It is about the individual man's quest to accumulate those cultural symbols that denote manhood, signs that he has in fact achieved it. It is about those standards being used against women to prevent their inclusion in public life and their consignment to a devalued private sphere. It is about the differential access that different types of men have to those cultural resources that confer manhood and about how each of these groups then develop their own modifications to preserve and claim their manhood. It is about the power of these definitions themselves to serve to maintain the real-life power that men have over women and that some men have over other men.

This definition of manhood has been summarized cleverly by psychologist Robert Brannon (1976) into four succinct phrases:

1. "No Sissy Stuff!" One may never do anything that even remotely suggests femininity. Masculinity is the relentless repudiation of the feminine.

2. "Be a Big Wheel." Masculinity is measured by power, success, wealth, and status. As the current saying goes, "He who has the most toys when he dies wins."

3. "Be a Sturdy Oak." Masculinity depends on remaining calm and reliable in a crisis, holding emotions in check. In fact, proving you're a man depends on never showing your emotions at all. Boys don't cry.

4. "Give 'em Hell." Exude an aura of manly daring and aggression. Go for it. Take risks.

These rules contain the elements of the definition against which virtually all American men are measured. Failure to embody these rules, to affirm the power of the rules and one's achievement of them is a source of men's confusion and pain. Such a model is, of course, unrealizable for any man. But we keep trying, valiantly and vainly, to measure up. American masculinity is a relentless test.[3] The chief test is contained in the first rule. Whatever the variations by race, class, age, ethnicity, or sexual orientation, being a man means "not being like women." This notion of anti-femininity lies at the heart of contemporary and historical conceptions of manhood, so that masculinity is defined more by what one is not rather than who one is.

❧ Masculinity as the Flight From the Feminine

Historically and developmentally, masculinity has been defined as the flight from women, the repudiation of femininity. Since Freud, we have come to understand that developmentally the central task that every little boy must confront is to develop a secure identity for himself as a man. As Freud had it, the oedipal project is a process of the boy's renouncing his identification with and deep emotional attachment to his mother and then replacing her with the father as the object of identification. Notice that he reidentifies but never reattaches. This entire process, Freud argued, is set in motion by the boy's sexual desire for his mother. But the father stands in the son's path and will not yield his sexual property to his puny son. The boy's first emotional experience, then, the one that inevitably follows his experience of desire, is fear—fear of the bigger, stronger, more sexually powerful father. It is this fear, experienced symbolically as the fear of castration, Freud argues, that forces the young boy to renounce his identification with mother and seek to identify with the being who is the actual source of his fear, his father. In so doing, the boy is now symbolically capable of sexual union with a motherlike substitute, that is, a woman. The boy becomes gendered (masculine) and heterosexual at the same time.

Masculinity, in this model, is irrevocably tied to sexuality. The boy's sexuality will now come to resemble the sexuality of his father (or at least the way he imagines his father)—menacing, predatory, possessive, and possibly punitive. The boy has come to identify with his oppressor; now he can become the oppressor himself. But a terror remains, the terror that the young man will be unmasked as a fraud, as a man who has not completely and irrevocably separated from mother. It will be other men who will do the unmasking. Failure will de-sex the man, make him appear as not fully a man. He will be seen as a wimp, a Mama's boy, a sissy.

After pulling away from his mother, the boy comes to see her not as a source of nurturance and love, but as an insatiably infantalizing creature, capable of humiliating him in front of his peers. She makes him dress up in uncomfortable and itchy clothing, her kisses smear his cheeks with lipstick, staining his boyish innocence with the mark of feminine dependency. No wonder so many boys cringe from their mothers' embraces with groans of "Aw, Mom! Quit it!" Mothers represent the humiliation of infancy, helplessness, dependency. "Men act as though they were being guided by (or rebelling against) rules and prohibitions enunciated by a moral mother," writes psychohistorian Geoffrey Gorer (1964). As a result, "all the niceties of masculine behavior—modesty, politeness, neatness, cleanliness—come to be regarded as concessions to feminine demands, and not good in themselves as part of the behavior of a proper man" (pp. 56, 57).

The flight from femininity is angry and frightened, because mother can so easily emasculate the young boy by her power to render him dependent, or at least to remind him of dependency. It is relentless; manhood becomes a lifelong quest to demonstrate its achievement, as if to prove the unprovable to others, because we feel so unsure of it ourselves. Women don't often feel compelled to "prove their womanhood"—the phrase itself sounds ridiculous. Women have different kinds of gender identity crises; their anger and frustration, and their own symptoms of depression, come more from being excluded than from questioning whether they are feminine enough.[4]

The drive to repudiate the mother as the indication of the acquisition of masculine gender identity has three consequences for the young boy. First, he pushes away his real mother, and with her the traits of nurturance, compassion, and tenderness she may have embodied. Second, he suppresses those traits in himself, because they will reveal his incomplete separation from mother. His life becomes a lifelong project to demonstrate that he possesses none of his mother's traits. Masculine identity is born in the renunciation of the feminine, not in the direct affirmation of the masculine, which leaves masculine gender identity tenuous and fragile.

Third, as if to demonstrate the accomplishment of these first two tasks, the boy also learns to devalue all women in his society, as the living embodiments of those traits in himself he has learned to despise. Whether or not he was aware of it, Freud also described the origins of sexism—the systematic devaluation of women—in the desperate efforts of the boy to separate from mother. We may *want* "a girl just like the girl that married dear old Dad," as the popular song had it, but we certainly don't want to *be like* her.

This chronic uncertainty about gender identity helps us understand several obsessive behaviors. Take, for example, the continuing problem of the school-yard bully. Parents remind us that the bully is the *least* secure about his manhood, and so he is constantly trying to prove it. But he "proves" it by choosing opponents he is absolutely certain he can defeat; thus the standard taunt to a bully is to "pick on someone your own size." He can't, though, and after defeating a smaller and weaker opponent, which he was sure would prove his manhood, he is left with the empty gnawing feeling that he has not proved it after all, and he must find another opponent, again one smaller and weaker, that he can again defeat to prove it to himself.[5]

One of the more graphic illustrations of this lifelong quest to prove one's manhood occurred at the Academy Awards presentation in 1992. As aging, tough guy actor Jack Palance accepted the award for Best Supporting Actor for his role in the cowboy comedy *City Slickers,* he commented that people, especially film producers, think that because he is 71 years old, he's all washed up, that he's no longer competent. "Can we take a risk on this guy?" he quoted them as saying, before he dropped to the floor to do a set of one-armed push-ups. It was pathetic to see such an accomplished actor still having to prove that he is virile enough to work and, as he also commented at the podium, to have sex.

When does it end? Never. To admit weakness, to admit frailty or fragility, is to be seen as a wimp, a sissy, not a real man. But seen by whom?

❧ /Masculinity as a ℋomosocial ℰnactment

Other men: We are under the constant careful scrutiny of other men. Other men watch us, rank us, grant our acceptance into the realm of manhood. Manhood is demonstrated for other men's approval. It is other men who evaluate the performance. Literary critic David Leverenz (1991) argues that "ideologies of manhood have functioned primarily in relation to the gaze of male peers and male authority" (p. 769). Think of how men boast to one another of their accomplishments—from their latest sexual conquest to the size of the fish they caught—and how we constantly parade the markers of manhood—wealth, power, status, sexy women—in front of other men, desperate for their approval.

That men prove their manhood in the eyes of other men is both a consequence of sexism and one of its chief props. "Women have, in men's minds, such a low place on the social ladder of this country that it's useless to define yourself in terms of a woman," noted playwright David Mamet. "What men need is men's approval." Women become a kind of currency that men use to improve their ranking on the masculine social scale. (Even those moments of heroic conquest of women carry, I believe, a current of homosocial evaluation.) Masculinity is a *homosocial* enactment. We test ourselves, perform heroic feats, take enormous risks, all because we want other men to grant us our manhood.

Masculinity as a homosocial enactment is fraught with danger, with the risk of failure, and with intense relentless competition. "Every man you meet has a rating or an estimate of himself which he never loses or forgets," wrote Kenneth Wayne (1912) in his popular turn-of-the-century advice book. "A man has his own rating, and instantly he lays it alongside of the other man" (p. 18). Almost a century later, another man remarked to psychologist Sam Osherson (1992) that "[b]y the time you're an adult, it's easy to think you're always in competition with men, for the attention of women, in sports, at work" (p. 291).

❧ /Masculinity as ℋomophobia

If masculinity is a homosocial enactment, its overriding emotion is fear. In the Freudian model, the fear of the father's power terrifies the young boy to renounce his desire for his mother and identify with his father. This model links gender identity with sexual orientation: The little boy's identification with father (becoming masculine) allows him to now engage in sexual relations with women (he becomes heterosexual). This is the origin of how we can "read" one's sexual orientation through the successful performance of gender identity. Second, the fear that the little boy feels does not send him scurrying into the arms of his mother to protect him from his father. Rather, he believes he will overcome his fear by identifying with its source. We become masculine by identifying with our oppressor.

But there is a piece of the puzzle missing, a piece that Freud, himself, implied but did not follow up.[6] If the pre-oedipal boy identifies with mother, he *sees the world through mother's eyes.* Thus, when he confronts father during his great oedipal crisis, he experiences a split vision: He sees his father as his mother sees his father, with a combination of awe, wonder, terror, *and desire.* He simultaneously sees the father as he, the boy, would like to see him—as the object not of desire but of emulation. Repudiating mother and identifying with father only partially answers his dilemma. What is he to do with that homoerotic desire, the desire he felt because he saw father the way that his mother saw father?

He must suppress it. Homoerotic desire is cast as feminine desire, desire for other men. Homophobia is the effort to suppress that desire, to purify all relationships with other men, with women, with children of its taint, and to ensure that no one could possibly ever mistake one for a homosexual. Homophobic flight from intimacy with other men is the repudiation of the homosexual within—never completely successful and hence constantly reenacted in every homosocial relationship. "The lives of most American men are bounded, and their interests daily curtailed by the constant necessity to prove to their fellows, and to themselves, that they are not sissies, not homosexuals," writes psychoanalytic historian Geoffrey Gorer (1964). "Any interest or pursuit which is identified as a feminine interest or pursuit becomes deeply suspect for men" (p. 129).

Even if we do not subscribe to Freudian psychoanalytic ideas, we can still observe how, in less sexualized terms, the father is the first man who evaluates the boy's masculine performance, the first pair of male eyes before whom he tries to prove himself. Those eyes will follow him for the rest of his life. Other men's eyes will join them—the eyes of role models such as teachers, coaches, bosses, or media heroes; the eyes of his peers, his friends, his workmates; and the eyes of millions of other men, living and dead, from whose constant scrutiny of his performance he will never be free. "The tradition of all the dead generations weighs like a nightmare on the brain of the living," was how Karl

Marx put it over a century ago (1848/1964, p. 11). "The birthright of every American male is a chronic sense of personal inadequacy," is how two psychologists describe it today (Woolfolk & Richardson, 1978, p. 57).

That nightmare from which we never seem to awaken is that those other men will see that sense of inadequacy, they will see that in our own eyes we are not who we are pretending to be. What we call masculinity is often a hedge against being revealed as a fraud, an exaggerated set of activities that keep others from seeing through us, and a frenzied effort to keep at bay those fears within ourselves. Our real fear "is not fear of women but of being ashamed or humiliated in front of other men, or being dominated by stronger men" (Leverenz, 1986, p. 451).

This, then, is the great secret of American manhood: *We are afraid of other men.* Homophobia is a central organizing principle of our cultural definition of manhood. Homophobia is more than the irrational fear of gay men, more than the fear that we might be perceived as gay. "The word 'faggot' has nothing to do with homosexual experience or even with fears of homosexuals," writes David Leverenz (1986). "It comes out of the depths of manhood: a label of ultimate contempt for anyone who seems sissy, untough, uncool" (p. 455). Homophobia is the fear that other men will unmask us, emasculate us, reveal to us and the world that we do not measure up, that we are not real men. We are afraid to let other men see that fear. Fear makes us ashamed, because the recognition of fear in ourselves is proof to ourselves that we are not as manly as we pretend, that we are, like the young man in a poem by Yeats, "one that ruffles in a manly pose for all his timid heart." Our fear is the fear of humiliation. We are ashamed to be afraid.

Shame leads to silence—the silences that keep other people believing that we actually approve of the things that are done to women, to minorities, to gays and lesbians in our culture. The frightened silence as we scurry past a woman being hassled by men on the street. That furtive silence when men make sexist or racist jokes in a bar. That clammy-handed silence when guys in the office make gay-bashing jokes. Our fears are the sources of our silences, and men's silence is what keeps the system running. This might help to explain why women often complain that their male friends or partners are often so understanding when they are alone and yet laugh at sexist jokes or even make those jokes themselves when they are out with a group.

The fear of being seen as a sissy dominates the cultural definitions of manhood. It starts so early. "Boys among boys are ashamed to be unmanly," wrote one educator in 1871 (cited in Rotundo, 1993, p. 264). I have a standing bet with a friend that I can walk onto any playground in America where

6-year-old boys are happily playing and by asking one question, I can provoke a fight. That question is simple: "Who's a sissy around here?" Once
posed, the challenge is made. One of two things is likely to happen. One boy
will accuse another of being a sissy, to which that boy will respond that he is
not a sissy, that the first boy is. They may have to fight it out to see who's
lying. Or a whole group of boys will surround one boy and all shout "He is!
He is!" That boy will either burst into tears and run home crying, disgraced,
or he will have to take on several boys at once, to prove that he's not a sissy.
(And what will his father or older brothers tell him if he chooses to run home
crying?) It will be some time before he regains any sense of self-respect.

Violence is often the single most evident marker of manhood. Rather it is
the willingness to fight, the desire to fight. The origin of our expression that
one has a chip on one's shoulder lies in the practice of an adolescent boy in
the country or small town at the turn of the century, who would literally walk
around with a chip of wood balanced on his shoulder—a signal of his readi-
ness to fight with anyone who would take the initiative of knocking the chip
off (see Gorer, 1964, p. 38; Mead, 1965).

As adolescents, we learn that our peers are a kind of gender police, constantly threatening to unmask us as feminine, as sissies. One of the favorite
tricks when I was an adolescent was to ask a boy to look at his fingernails. If
he held his palm toward his face and curled his fingers back to see them, he
passed the test. He'd looked at his nails "like a man." But if he held the back of
his hand away from his face, and looked at his fingernails with arm out-
stretched, he was immediately ridiculed as a sissy.

As young men we are constantly riding those gender boundaries, checking the fences we have constructed on the perimeter, making sure that nothing even remotely feminine might show through. The possibilities of being
unmasked are everywhere. Even the most seemingly insignificant thing can
pose a threat or activate that haunting terror. On the day the students in my
course "Sociology of Men and Masculinities" were scheduled to discuss
homophobia and male-male friendships, one student provided a touching
illustration. Noting that it was a beautiful day, the first day of spring after a
brutal northeast winter, he decided to wear shorts to class. "I had this really
nice pair of new Madras shorts," he commented. "But then I thought to
myself, these shorts have lavender and pink in them. Today's class topic is
homophobia. Maybe today is not the best day to wear these shorts."

Our efforts to maintain a manly front cover everything we do. What we
wear. How we talk. How we walk. What we eat. Every mannerism, every
movement contains a coded gender language. Think, for example, of how

you would answer the question: How do you "know" if a man is homosexual? When I ask this question in classes or workshops, respondents invariably provide a pretty standard list of stereotypically effeminate behaviors. He walks a certain way, talks a certain way, acts a certain way. He's very emotional; he shows his feelings. One woman commented that she "knows" a man is gay if he really cares about her; another said she knows he's gay if he shows no interest in her, if he leaves her alone.

Now alter the question and imagine what heterosexual men do to make sure no one could possibly get the "wrong idea" about them. Responses typically refer to the original stereotypes, this time as a set of negative rules about behavior. Never dress that way. Never talk or walk that way. Never show your feelings or get emotional. Always be prepared to demonstrate sexual interest in women that you meet, so it is impossible for any woman to get the wrong idea about you. In this sense, homophobia, the fear of being perceived as gay, as not a real man, keeps men exaggerating all the traditional rules of masculinity, including sexual predation with women. Homophobia and sexism go hand in hand.

The stakes of perceived sissydom are enormous—sometimes matters of life and death. We take enormous risks to prove our manhood, exposing ourselves disproportionately to health risks, workplace hazards, and stress-related illnesses. Men commit suicide three times as often as women. Psychiatrist Willard Gaylin (1992) explains that it is "invariably because of perceived social humiliation," most often tied to failure in business:

> Men become depressed because of loss of status and power in the world of men. It is not the loss of money, or the material advantages that money could buy, which produces the despair that leads to self-destruction. It is the "shame," the "humiliation," the sense of personal "failure." . . . A man despairs when he has ceased being a man among men. (p. 32)

In one survey, women and men were asked what they were most afraid of. Women responded that they were most afraid of being raped and murdered. Men responded that they were most afraid of being laughed at (Noble, 1992, pp. 105–106).

☺ Homophobia as a Cause of Sexism, Heterosexism, and Racism

Homophobia is intimately interwoven with both sexism and racism. The fear—sometimes conscious, sometimes not—that others might perceive us as homosexual propels men to enact all manner of exaggerated masculine behaviors and attitudes to make sure that no one could possibly get the wrong idea about us. One of the centerpieces of that exaggerated masculinity is putting women down, both by excluding them from the public sphere and by the quotidian put-downs in speech and behaviors that organize the daily life of the American man. Women and gay men become the "other" against which heterosexual men project their identities, against whom they stack the decks so as to compete in a situation in which they will always win, so that by suppressing them, men can stake a claim for their own manhood. Women threaten emasculation by representing the home, workplace, and familial responsibility, the negation of fun. Gay men have historically played the role of the consummate sissy in the American popular mind because homosexuality is seen as an inversion of normal gender development. There have been other "others." Through American history, various groups have represented the sissy, the non-men against whom American men played out their definitions of manhood, often with vicious results. In fact, these changing groups provide an interesting lesson in American historical development.

At the turn of the 19th century, it was Europeans and children who provided the contrast for American men. The "true American was vigorous, manly, and direct, not effete and corrupt like the supposed Europeans," writes Rupert Wilkinson (1986). "He was plain rather than ornamented, rugged rather than luxury seeking, a liberty loving common man or natural gentleman rather than an aristocratic oppressor or servile minion" (p. 96). The "real man" of the early 19th century was neither noble nor serf. By the middle of the century, black slaves had replaced the effete nobleman. Slaves were seen as dependent, helpless men, incapable of defending their women and children, and therefore less than manly. Native Americans were cast as foolish and naive children, so they could be infantilized as the "Red Children of the Great White Father" and therefore excluded from full manhood.

By the end of the century, new European immigrants were also added to the list of the unreal men, especially the Irish and Italians, who were seen as too passionate and emotionally volatile to remain controlled sturdy oaks, and Jews, who were seen as too bookishly effete and too physically puny to truly measure up. In the mid-20th century, it was also Asians—first the Japanese during the Second World War, and more recently, the Vietnamese during the Vietnam War—who have served as unmanly templates against which American men have hurled their gendered rage. Asian men were seen as small, soft, and effeminate—hardly men at all.

Such a list of "hyphenated" Americans—Italian-, Jewish-, Irish-, African-, Native-, Asian-, gay—composes the majority of American men. So manhood is only possible for a distinct minority, and the definition has been constructed to prevent the others from achieving it. Interestingly, this emasculation of one's enemies has a flip side—and one that is equally gendered. These very groups that have historically been cast as less than manly were also, often simultaneously, cast as hypermasculine, as sexually aggressive, violent rapacious beasts, against whom "civilized" men must take a decisive stand and thereby rescue civilization. Thus black men were depicted as rampaging sexual beasts, women as carnivorously carnal, gay men as sexually insatiable, southern European men as sexually predatory and voracious, and Asian men as vicious and cruel torturers who were immorally disinterested in life itself, willing to sacrifice their entire people for their whims. But whether one saw these groups as effeminate sissies or as brutal uncivilized savages, the terms with which they were perceived were gendered. These groups become the "others," the screens against which traditional conceptions of manhood were developed.

Being seen as unmanly is a fear that propels American men to deny manhood to others, as a way of proving the unprovable—that one is fully manly. Masculinity becomes a defense against the perceived threat of humiliation in the eyes of other men, enacted through a "sequence of postures"—things we might say, or do, or even think, that, if we thought carefully about them, would make us ashamed of ourselves (Savran, 1992, p. 16). After all, how many of us have made homophobic or sexist remarks, or told racist jokes, or made lewd comments to women on the street? How many of us have translated those ideas and those words into actions, by physically attacking gay men, or forcing or cajoling a woman to have sex even though she didn't really want to because it was important to score?

❧ Power and Powerlessness in the Lives of Men

I have argued that homophobia, men's fear of other men, is the animating condition of the dominant definition of masculinity in America, that the reigning definition of masculinity is a defensive effort to prevent being emasculated. In our efforts to suppress or overcome those fears, the dominant culture exacts a tremendous price from those deemed less than fully manly: women, gay men, nonnative-born men, men of color. This perspective may help clarify a paradox in men's lives, a paradox in which men have virtually all the power and yet do not feel powerful (see Kaufman, 1993).

Manhood is equated with power—over women, over other men. Everywhere we look, we see the institutional expression of that power—in state and national legislatures, on the boards of directors of every major U.S. corporation or law firm, and in every school and hospital administration. Women have long understood this, and feminist women have spent the past three decades challenging both the public and the private expressions of men's power and acknowledging their fear of men. Feminism as a set of theories both explains women's fear of men and empowers women to confront it both publicly and privately. Feminist women have theorized that masculinity is about the drive for domination, the drive for power, for conquest.

This feminist definition of masculinity as the drive for power is theorized from women's point of view. It is how women experience masculinity: But it assumes a symmetry between the public and the private that does not conform to men's experiences. Feminists observe that women, as a group, do not hold power in our society. They also observe that individually, they, as women, do not feel powerful. They feel afraid, vulnerable. Their observation of the social reality and their individual experiences are therefore symmetrical. Feminism also observes that men, as a group, *are* in power. Thus, with the same symmetry, feminism has tended to assume that individually men must feel powerful.

This is why the feminist critique of masculinity often falls on deaf ears with men. When confronted with the analysis that men have all the power, many men react incredulously. "What do you mean, men have all the power?" they ask. "What are you talking about? My wife bosses me around. My kids boss me around. My boss bosses me around. I have no power at all! I'm completely powerless!"

Men's feelings are not the feelings of the powerful, but of those who see themselves as powerless. These are the feelings that come inevitably from the discontinuity between the social and the psychological, between the aggregate analysis that reveals how men are in power as a group and the psychological fact that they do not feel powerful as individuals. They are the feelings of men who were raised to believe themselves entitled to feel that power, but do not feel it. No wonder many men are frustrated and angry.

This may explain the recent popularity of those workshops and retreats designed to help men to claim their "inner" power, their "deep manhood," or their "warrior within." Authors such as Bly (1990), Moore and Gillette (1991, 1992, 1993a, 1993b), Farrell (1986, 1993), and Keen (1991) honor and respect men's feelings of powerlessness and acknowledge those feelings to be both true and real. "They gave white men the semblance of power," notes John Lee, one of the leaders of these retreats (quoted in *Newsweek,* p. 41). "We'll let you run the country, but in the meantime, stop feeling, stop talking, and continue swallowing your pain and your hurt." (We are not told who "they" are.)

Often the purveyors of the mythopoetic men's movement, that broad umbrella that encompasses all the groups helping men to retrieve this mythic deep manhood, use the image of the chauffeur to describe modern man's position. The chauffeur appears to have the power—he's wearing the uniform, he's in the driver's seat, and he knows where he's going. So, to the observer, the chauffeur looks as though he is in command. But to the chauffeur himself, they note, he is merely taking orders. He is not at all in charge.[7]

Despite the reality that everyone knows chauffeurs do not have the power, this image remains appealing to the men who hear it at these weekend workshops. But there is a missing piece to the image, a piece concealed by the framing of the image in terms of the individual man's experience. That missing piece is that the person who is giving the orders is also a man. Now we have a relationship *between* men—between men giving orders and other men taking those orders. The man who identifies with the chauffeur is entitled to be the man giving the orders, but he is not. ("They," it turns out, are other men.)

The dimension of power is now reinserted into men's experience not only as the product of individual experience but also as the product of relations with other men. In this sense, men's experience of powerlessness is *real*—the men actually feel it and certainly act on it—but it is not *true,* that is, it does not accurately describe their condition. In contrast to women's lives, men's lives are structured around relationships of power and men's differential access to power, as well as the differential access to that power of men as a group. Our imperfect analysis of our own situation leads us to believe that we men need *more* power, rather than leading us to support feminists' efforts to rearrange power relationships along more equitable lines.

Philosopher Hannah Arendt (1970) fully understood this contradictory experience of social and individual power:

> Power corresponds to the human ability not just to act but to act in concert. Power is never the property of an individual; it belongs to a group and remains in existence only so long as the group keeps together. When we say of somebody that he is "in power" we actually refer to his being empowered by a certain number of people to act in their name. The moment the group, from which the power originated to begin with . . . disappears, "his power" also vanishes. (p. 44)

Why, then, do American men feel so powerless? Part of the answer is because we've constructed the rules of manhood so that only the tiniest fraction of men come to believe that they are the biggest of wheels, the sturdiest of oaks, the most virulent repudiators of femininity, the most daring and aggressive. We've managed to disempower the overwhelming majority of American men by other means—such as discriminating on the basis of race, class, ethnicity, age, or sexual preference.

Masculinist retreats to retrieve deep, wounded, masculinity are but one of the ways in which American men currently struggle with their fears and their shame. Unfortunately, at the very moment that they work to break down the isolation that governs men's lives, as they enable men to express those fears and that shame, they ignore the social power that men continue to exert over women and the privileges from which they (as the middle-aged, middle-class white men who largely make up these retreats) continue to benefit—regardless of their experiences as wounded victims of oppressive male socialization.[8]

Others still rehearse the politics of exclusion, as if by clearing away the playing field of secure gender identity of any that we deem less than manly— women, gay men, nonnative-born men, men of color—middle-class, straight, white men can reground their sense of themselves without those haunting fears and that deep shame that they are unmanly and will be exposed by other men. This is the manhood of racism, of sexism, of homophobia. It is the manhood that is so chronically insecure that it trembles at the idea of lifting the ban on gays in the military, that is so threatened by women in the workplace that women become the targets of sexual harassment, that is so deeply frightened of equality that it must ensure that the playing field of male competition remains stacked against all newcomers to the game.

Exclusion and escape have been the dominant methods American men have used to keep their fears of humiliation at bay. The fear of emasculation by other men, of being humiliated, of being seen as a sissy, is the leitmotif in my reading of the history of American manhood. Masculinity has become a relentless test by which we prove to other men, to women, and ultimately to ourselves, that we have successfully mastered the part. The restlessness that men feel today is nothing new in American history; we have been anxious and restless for almost two centuries. Neither exclusion nor escape has ever brought us the relief we've sought, and there is no reason to think that either will solve our problems now. Peace of mind, relief from gender struggle, will come only from a politics of inclusion, not exclusion, from standing up for equality and justice, and not by running away.

*E*ndnotes

[1]Of course, the phrase "American manhood" contains several simultaneous fictions. There is no single manhood that defines all American men; "America" is meant to refer to the United States proper, and there are significant ways in which this "American manhood" is the outcome of forces that transcend both gender and nation, that is, the global economic development of industrial capitalism. I use it, therefore, to describe the specific hegemonic version of masculinity in the United States, that normative constellation of attitudes, traits, and behaviors that became the standard against which all other masculinities are measured and against which individual men measure the success of their gender accomplishments.

[2]Much of this work is elaborated in *Manhood: The American Quest* (in press).

[3]Although I am here discussing only American masculinity, I am aware that others have located this chronic instability and efforts to prove manhood in the particular cultural and economic arrangements of Western society. Calvin, after all, inveighed against the disgrace "for men to become effeminate," and countless other theorists have described the mechanics of manly proof. (See, for example, Seidler, 1994.)

[4]I do not mean to argue that women do not have anxieties about whether they are feminine enough. Ask any woman how she feels about being called aggressive; it sends a chill into her heart because her femininity is suspect. (I believe that the reason for the enormous recent popularity of sexy lingerie among women is that it enables women to remember they are still feminine underneath their corporate business suit—a suit that apes masculine styles.) But I think the stakes are not as great for women and that women have greater latitude in defining their identities around these questions than men do. Such are the ironies of sexism: The powerful have a narrower range of options than the powerless, because the powerless can *also* imitate the powerful and get away with it. It may even enhance status, if done with charm and grace—that is, is not threatening. For the powerful, any hint of behaving like the powerless is a fall from grace.

[5]Such observations also led journalist Heywood Broun to argue that most of the attacks against feminism came from men who were shorter than 5 ft. 7 in. "The man who, whatever his physical size, feels secure in his own masculinity and in his own relation to life is rarely resentful of the opposite sex" (cited in Symes, 1930, p. 139).

[6]Some of Freud's followers, such as Anna Freud and Alfred Adler, did follow up on these suggestions. (See especially, Adler, 1980.) I am grateful to Terry Kupers for his help in thinking through Adler's ideas.

[7]The image is from Warren Farrell, who spoke at a workshop I attended at the First International Men's Conference, Austin, Texas, October 1991.

[8]For a critique of these mythopoetic retreats, see Kimmel and Kaufman, Chapter 14, this volume.

❧ ❧ ❧

Questions

1. Delineate the characteristics of Marketplace Man and Marketplace Masculinity.

2. What is "hegemonic" masculinity and what are its defining features?

3. What does Kimmel mean when he writes, "Masculinity is a *homosocial* enactment"? What are some consequences of this fact?

4. Explain the relationship Kimmel posits between masculinity and homophobia. What evidence does he use to make his argument?

5. Do you think the benefits of proving masculinity outweigh the costs? Explain why or why not.

6. How can men's experience of powerlessness be "real" without being "true"?

❧ References

Adler, A. (1980). *Cooperation between the sexes: Writings on women, love and marriage, sexuality and its disorders* (H. Ansbacher & R. Ansbacher, Eds. & Trans.). New York: Jason Aronson.

Arendt, H. (1970). *On revolution.* New York: Viking.

Bly, R. (1990). *Iron John: A book about men.* Reading, MA: Addison-Wesley.

Brannon, R. (1976). The male sex role—and what it's done for us lately. In R. Brannon & D. David (Eds.), *The forty-nine percent majority* (pp. 1–40). Reading, MA: Addison-Wesley.

Connell, R. W. (1987). *Gender and power.* Stanford, CA: Stanford University Press.

Farrell, W. (1986). *Why men are the way they are.* New York: McGraw-Hill.

Farrell, W. (1993). *The myth of male power: Why men are the disposable sex.* New York: Simon & Schuster.

Freud, S. (1993/1966). *New introductory lectures on psychoanalysis* (L. Strachey, Ed.). New York: Norton.

Gaylin, W. (1992). *The male ego.* New York: Viking.

Goffman, E. (1963). *Stigma.* Englewood Cliffs, NJ: Prentice Hall.

Gorer, G. (1964). *The American people: A study in national character.* New York: Norton.

Kaufman, M. (1993). *Cracking the armour: Power and pain in the lives of men.* Toronto: Viking Canada.

Keen, S. (1991). *Fire in the belly.* New York: Bantam.

Kimmel, M. S. (in press). *Manhood: The American quest.* New York: HarperCollins.

Leverenz, D. (1986). Manhood, humiliation and public life: Some stories. *Southwest Review, 71,* Fall.

Leverenz, D. (1991). The last real man in America: From Natty Bumppo to Batman. *American Literary Review, 3.*

Marx, K., & F. Engels. (1848/1964). The communist manifesto. In R. Tucker (Ed.), *The Marx-Engels reader.* New York: Norton.

Mead, M. (1965). *And keep your powder dry.* New York: William Morrow.

Moore, R., & Gillette, D. (1991). *King, warrior, magician lover.* New York: HarperCollins.

Moore, R., & Gillette, D. (1992). *The king within: Accessing the warrior in the male psyche.* New York: William Morrow.

Moore, R., & Gillette, D. (1993a). *The warrior within: Accessing the warrior in the male psyche.* New York: William Morrow.

Moore, R., & Gillette, D. (1993b). *The magician within: Accessing the magician in the male psyche.* New York: William Morrow.

Noble, V. (1992). A helping hand from the guys. In K. L. Hagan (Ed.), *Women respond to the men's movement.* San Francisco: HarperCollins.

Osherson, S. (1992). *Wrestling with love: How men struggle with intimacy, with women, children, parents, and each other.* New York: Fawcett.

Rotundo, E. A. (1993). *American manhood: Tranformations in masculinity from the revolution to the modern era.* New York: Basic Books.

Savran, D. (1992). *Communists, cowboys and queers: The politics of masculinity in the work of Arthur Miller and Tennessee Williams.* Minneapolis: University of Minnesota Press.

Seidler, V. J. (1994). *Unreasonable men: Masculinity and social theory.* New York: Routledge.

Symes, L. (1930). The new masculinism. *Harper's Monthly, 161,* January.

Tocqueville, A. de. (1835/1967). *Democracy in America.* New York: Anchor.

Wayne, K. (1912). *Building the young man.* Chicago: A. C. McClurg.

Weber, M. (1905/1966). *The Protestant ethic and the spirit of capitalism.* New York: Charles Scribner's.

What men need is men's approval. (1993, January 3). *The New York Times,* p. C-11.

Wilkinson, R. (1986). *American tough: The tough-guy tradition and American character.* New York: Harper & Row.

Woolfolk, R. L. & Richardson, F. (1978). *Sanity, stress and survival.* New York: Signet.

"Don't Ask, Don't Tell, Don't Pursue": Military Policy and the Construction of Heterosexual Masculinity

DANA M. BRITTON, PHD AND
CHRISTINE L. WILLIAMS, PHD
University of Texas at Austin

Many people have an opinion on whether gays and lesbians belong in the military. In this article, the authors review common themes in arguments made by people who support the "don't ask, don't tell, don't pursue" policy that is currently in force in the U.S. military. However, by drawing on feminist theory, the authors add a new level to the debate. They contend that the military's resistance to full participation by gays and lesbians reflects its implicit support of a particular image of the perfect soldier—one that is based on a heterosexual, masculine ideal.

*J*n 1993, newly elected President Bill Clinton announced his intention to follow through on his promise to lift the ban on gays

"'Don't Ask, Don't Tell, Don't Pursue': Military Policy and the Construction of Heterosexual Masculinity," by Dana M. Britton and Christine L. Williams, reprinted from *Journal of Homosexuality*, vol. 30, no. 1, 1995, pp. 1-22.

and lesbians serving in the U.S. military. A firestorm of controversy engulfed the President, who ultimately agreed to what he has described as an "honorable compromise," his "don't ask, don't tell, don't pursue" policy. Recently, however, the previous Pentagon policy has been struck down by a federal appeals court. While this court was clear that their decision did not apply to the new rules, many believe that the same grounds can be applied in challenging the new policy as well. Thus, while the fate of the military policy is still very much in the air, Clinton's plan took effect in February 1994.

• • •

In this paper, we will review the most common themes in the arguments of those who support restrictions on the participation of gays and lesbians in the military. After reviewing the arguments in support of the policy and the criticisms of them, we offer an alternative analysis. We contend that the military's resistance to the full participation of both women and gay men and lesbians reflects an institutional privileging of a certain type of soldier—the heterosexual male.

❧ Policies of Exclusion

The compromise agreed to by the Clinton administration and passed by Congress reads as follows:

> Applicants for military service will no longer be asked or required to reveal if they are homosexual or bisexual. . . . Sexual orientation will not be a bar to service unless manifested by homosexual conduct. The military will discharge members who engage in homosexual conduct, which is defined as a homosexual act, a statement that the member is homosexual or bisexual, or a marriage or attempted marriage to someone of the same gender. (draft Department of Defense Policy, 7/19/93)

For the purposes of separation under this policy, the minimum which may be considered a homosexual act is "bodily contact between service members of the same sex that a reasonable person would understand to demonstrate a propensity or intent to engage in homosexual acts (e.g., hand-holding or kissing in most circumstances) will be sufficient to initiate separation" (draft Department of Defense Policy, 7/19/93).

The new policy does contain some provisions to discourage "witchhunts" (mass investigations of homosexuality by the military, most commonly used in the discharge of women accused of lesbianism),[1] but does allow investigations of service members if there is any reason to suspect homosexual behavior.[2] The bill also includes a stipulation that would allow a future Defense Secretary to reinstate the practice of questioning recruits and service members about their sexual orientation, and provides for the discharge of a service member who openly acknowledges that he or she is a "person who engages in, attempts to engage in, has a propensity to engage in, or intends to engage in homosexual acts" (Senate Bill 1337, Section 546, Subsection F).

Though much has been made of the new policy's focus on behavior, rather than orientation per se, in reality, Clinton's policy actually represents little change from the rules it supersedes (Department of Defense Directive 1332.14, 1982. Part 1, Section H).

· · ·

Until the recent public furor over the topic, military officials had been reluctant to state their reasons for supporting the exclusion of lesbians and gay men, arguing only that "homosexuality is incompatible with military service." However, since the change in policy was proposed by the Clinton administration, official discourse in support of continuing restrictions on gays in the military has concentrated on two main lines of argument. The first group of objections to repealing the ban center around "prejudice-based" arguments, the second, around concern over sexual privacy.

In the context of what follows, it is important to remember that though arguments in support of the exclusionary policy apply in theory to both gay men and lesbians, most of the debate about the ban has concerned only men. . . . [L]esbians have been almost invisible in both official and popular discourse around this issue.

❧ Prejudice-Based Arguments

One of the most commonly articulated rationales for maintaining restrictions on the military service of gay men and lesbians concerns bias within the armed forces and in the public at large. The presence of homosexuals is perceived as a threat to effective individual and unit performance because gay and lesbian soldiers will be targets for harassment by heterosexual soldiers and, if they are officers, will not command respect. Furthermore, the presence of homosexuals in the military is asserted to impair morale and teamwork, also due to prejudices held by other soldiers (Department of Defense, quoted in General Accounting Office, 1992a, p. 58; Sarbin & Karols, 1988, p. 28; Snyder & Nyberg, 1980. . . .). . . .

Prejudice in the larger society is also a rationale for supporting the ban: the military excludes gay men and lesbians because it does not want to offend the public at large, which views homosexuality negatively. . . .

Echoing the official view, Snyder and Nyberg argue that the presence of acknowledged homosexuals could lead to a "perception of the military as a gay organization" (1980, p. 81), which would adversely affect the prestige of the military and hamper recruiting efforts.

In response to the "prejudice" arguments, critics have drawn on evidence demonstrating that gay men and lesbians have always served in the military, without creating significant breaches of morale, teamwork, and discipline, or provoking widespread public rejection of the military—even when they have been open about their sexual orientation (Williams & Weinberg, 1971; Humphrey, 1990; Bérubé, 1990; Shilts, 1993). The military's statistics on rates of discharge for homosexuality seem to support this assertion: in times of national emergency the military tends to relax enforcement of the exclusionary policy. This occurred most recently during Operation Desert Storm; under a "stop loss" policy, the military delayed discharging homosexual soldiers sent to the Persian Gulf until after the war was over (Shilts, 1991). . . . Clinton's policy continues this practice: . . .

A second, and ultimately much more controversial, argument made by those in support of lifting the ban has likened the exclusion of gays and lesbians from the military to the former exclusion of African-American men (comparisons have also been made to limitations on the exclusion of women; more on this below). Those who support lifting the ban contend that to the extent that the military relies on prejudices held by other soldiers to justify its policy, the situation of lesbians and gay men may be compared to the prejudice which was used by the military to justify the exclusion of African-American men. Indeed, prior to the Korean War, racial segregation was mandated on this basis in order to maintain troop cohesion (Segal, 1989, p. 113). . . .

This analogy has drawn fire, especially from some in the African-American community, as a comparison which is both insensitive and inappropriate, like comparing "apples and oranges" (Waller, quoted in Duke, 1993, p. 1) . . . Critics have argued that homosexuality is a behavioral characteristic, which has little in common with skin color. The success of "closeted" homosexuals in serving their country bears this assertion out; gay men and lesbians can "pass" in a way that most African-American men and women cannot. Colin Powell underlined this focus on behavior recently, contending that "Homosexuality is not a benign . . . characteristic such as skin color. . . . It goes to one of the most fundamental aspects of human behavior" (quoted in Duke, 1993, p. 1).

As a political strategy, the kind of reasoning by analogy that has characterized this debate is obviously inappropriate, and to some extent, the controversy has been fueled by the positing of "natural alliances" between gays and lesbians and African-Americans, rather than by an effort to build coalitions. The analytic point, however, at which heterosexism and racism intersect is an important one, and to ignore this interaction is to neglect a crucial way in which the privilege of some groups over others is maintained by military policy.

In terms of historical context, Powell's objection, that skin color is a "benign" characteristic, while sexual orientation *is* not, is simply not accurate in terms of the perceptions of white military leaders in 1948 (the year that President Truman integrated the military). At that time, African-American soldiers were argued to have a number of characteristics which made them unable to serve in the Armed Forces on an equal basis with white men. Skin color carried (and continues to carry in the perceptions of some) a host of implications about fundamental aspects of human behavior (Eskridge, 1993). Much as gay men are perceived to be effeminate or sexually uncontrollable, and thus incapable of military service, so too were African-Americans perceived as possessing qualities which made them unfit. Though this does not mean that the historical situation of African-Americans in integrating the U.S. military is "the same as" the experience of gay men and lesbians, the focus of policy makers on behavioral characteristics which unfit a particular group for the Armed Forces is clearly an important strategy that has been used in restricting the right of military service.

In addition, Powell's objection frames the debate such that the issue is one of sexuality versus skin color. This creates a false dichotomy, whose danger lies in the assumption that racism and heterosexism have little in common. Both are forms of domination which rely to some degree upon specifically *sexual* anxieties (J. P Butler, 1993; Eskridge, 1993; West, 1993). In this regard, it is instructive to compare the concern about the sexually unrestrained black woman manifested in discourse about "welfare mothers," or in notions about the danger to white women posed by sexually uncontrollable black men (Collins, 1991; Harper, 1993) to the worry that allowing openly gay men on Naval vessels is analogous to "leaving an alcoholic in charge of a liquor store" (Deputy Chaplain of the Marine Corps, quoted in Schmitt, 1992, p. A16). In both cases, notions about the sexuality of subordinated groups is instrumental in perpetuating systems of oppression whose beneficiaries are white, heterosexual men.

Finally, the actual experiences of service members belie any neat separation of the issues of race and sexuality. In the Navy's 1988 investigation of women aboard the U.S.S. Yellowstone, every African-American woman on board was accused (Benecke & Dodge, 1990). Though statistics released by the military do not show that African-Americans are more likely than white service members to be discharged for homosexuality (GAO, 1992b), the example of the Yellowstone points to the ways in which racism and heterosexism are conflated in the daily lives of women and men serving in the military.

☺ Sexual Privacy

The second argument in support of the restrictions on gay military service is based on privacy (Moskos, 1992). The revised policy recently passed by Congress specifically cites this condition, noting:

> The worldwide deployment of United States Military Forces . . . routinely makes it necessary for members of the Armed Forces involuntarily to accept living conditions and working conditions that are often spartan, primitive, and characterized by forced intimacy with little or no privacy. (Senate Bill 1337, Section A, Subsection 12)

This rationale has achieved considerable prominence of late; no contemporary discussion is complete without the requisite "shower scene" in which gay men (and lesbians, though they are invisible in this context) gaze licentiously at unsuspecting heterosexuals. Rather than relying on the prejudice of heterosexual service members, this argument focuses on "pragmatic" conditions, like those requiring separate living quarters for men and women.

Opponents have been quick to point out that this is a rationale which only applies to openly gay members of the Armed Forces. Undoubtedly, many heterosexuals *have* showered in the presence of gay men or lesbians—but they were unaware of this because most gays and lesbians are closeted. Indeed, this is the condition that the "don't ask, don't tell" policy explicitly seeks to maintain. Opponents have also noted that the issue is one of conduct; unwanted homosexual as well as heterosexual advances are barred by military policy.

At another level, however, this debate lays bare the problematic of sexual exploitation and desire upon which much homophobia rests. There is a great deal in the current discussion of the policy to suggest that part of the resistance to the presence of openly gay men in the military comes fairly directly from a fear of sexual exploitation. . . . While there appears to be room in the military to accommodate the "male gaze" so long as it is directed at women (witness the "Tailhook" scandal) such a gaze directed at men by men is clearly perceived as threatening and objectifying. The fear seems to be that the gaze of the male homosexual will turn heterosexual men from subjects with desire to objects of desire (Bordo, 1993).

• • •

Also at work is a fear of seduction. A recurrent theme in the policy debate has been the need for the protection of young military recruits from seduction by gay service members. . . . This fear is heightened by the sex-segregation of military units, a context in which homoerotic relationships are both encouraged (in the name of male bonding and unit cohesion) and prohibited (in the name of social control). The possibility that seduction or attraction may occur is even provided for in the current policy, which mandates separation for homosexual conduct unless "such conduct is a departure from the member's usual and customary behavior" or if "such conduct, under-the circumstances, is unlikely to recur" (Senate Bill 1337, Section 546, Subsection B).

Overall, the arguments of those in support of retaining restrictions on the military participation of gay men and lesbians have relied, in the main, on grounds which highlight either the prejudices of heterosexual soldiers or the need for sexual privacy. We have begun to highlight the ways in which both of these rationales work to support a system in which the main beneficiaries are white, heterosexual soldiers. Below, we will propose a more systematic framework for understanding the military's resistance to lesbian and gay soldiers.

❧ Compulsory Heterosexuality in the Military

Thus far, our discussion of the military's defense of its exclusionary policy has focused on gays and lesbians themselves. We now submit that a better way to understand this policy is to examine its flipside: The military's refusal to admit gay men and lesbians is an implicit sanctioning of heterosexuality. This will shift the question away from asking "Why does the military disdain gay men and lesbians?" to "Why does the military prefer heterosexual soldiers?"

Restrictions on the participation of lesbians and gay men is but one of many ways that the military has institutionalized a preference for heterosexuals. This preference is reflected in the military's support for the traditional family among officers and career enlisted men (Kohen, 1984; Payne, Warner, and Little, 1992; Segal, 1986). Until fairly recently, official policy penalized officers who did not have dependent spouses. It was only in 1988 that the Department of Defense formally announced that wives' participation in volunteer activities would no longer be considered in officer promotions for any branch of the service (Stiehm, 1989, p. 215).

This institutionalization of sexual norms in the military is a form of what Adrienne Rich (1980) has called "compulsory heterosexuality." Rich argues that heterosexuality should be viewed as a political institution, which has a material and an ideological base. Heterosexuality becomes compulsory through the use of force, sanctions, and control of consciousness to ensure its perpetuation. The military's exclusion of homosexual men and lesbians is more understandable in light of an institutionalized sanctioning of heterosexuality. In the remainder of the paper, we will address the social control interests and ideological interests which are served by limiting the participation of lesbians and gay men in the military.

❧ "Social Control" Interests

Continuing restrictions on the service of gay men and lesbians serve important social control functions for the military. The recently revised policy still stipulates that homosexual conduct is detrimental to "good order and discipline." However, it is important to note in this context that the military does not repress all sexuality in the interests of good order—only homosexuality. In many ways, the military condones heterosexuality of a particularly violent and virulent form. Among male enlisted soldiers and junior officers, the expectation of heterosexuality is reflected in the tolerance (some would say encouragement) of prostitution (Enloe, 1983, 1989, 1993) and other forms of objectification and exploitation of women. This attitude towards women is institutionalized in the military through practices such as sexist cadence ("I don't know but I've been told, Eskimo pussy is mighty cold") and through the use of symbols glorifying a very violent male heterosexuality (Arkin, 1978; Burke, 1992).

The 1991 Tailhook Convention is only the most recent example of the way that these attitudes and practices are articulated in the military. At this annual convention of Naval aviators, 26 women, more than half of them naval officers, reported that they were sexually molested by male service members. Women also described how they had to run a nightly "gauntlet" in a hotel hallway; an ordeal that sometimes involved up to 200 men. A Naval Investigative Service report on the incident disclosed that similar activities have taken place at the annual conventions since 1986, with the knowledge of senior Navy officials. Though charges were filed against many of the men alleged to be involved, so far, none has been convicted, and several men have had the charges against them dismissed.

If homosexuality is believed to interfere with "good order and discipline," then it is important to understand how heterosexuality promotes social order. This may be the case in two ways. There is evidence that married soldiers have fewer disciplinary problems than single ones, and married soldiers with dependent wives are more likely to reenlist (Segal, 1986). The military may view heterosexually married soldiers as more docile and tractable than gay and lesbian soldiers for this reason. But there may be other, less tangible ways that the social control function is realized through heterosexuality.

Hearn and Parkin (1987) argue that total institutions, such as the military, have an interest in controlling and directing the release of sexuality. Hearn writes that "rules on sexuality are . . . characteristic of those organizations that subordinate sexuality yet are explicitly physical and implicitly sexual" (1987, p. 70. . . .) From this perspective, excluding homosexuals and lesbians can be seen as an attempt to suppress the homoerotic elements of "buddy bonding" and other highly sexualized elements of military life. Even a cursory examination of war narratives reveals the subjectively felt importance of such bonds between soldiers. These personal accounts are replete with glowing descriptions of camaraderie, brotherhood, and the forging of universal bonds between men under the constant threat of death. This kind of bonding and solidarity is encouraged by military leaders and is seen as essential in forging effective fighting units.

Given an underlying framework of compulsory heterosexuality, however, these bonds are viable only in a highly gendered context. Such ties are defined in opposition to women and may even be cemented through the exchange of women's bodies (Britton, 1990; Jeffords, 1989; Sedgwick, 1985; Theweleit, 1987. . . .) The armed forces, with their combat exclusionary policies for women and ban on homosexuality, are one of the last remaining refuges for the affirmation of solidarity between men.

. . .

Presumably, bonding would become suspect if soldiers knew that there were gay men in the ranks. In a setting in which connections between men are seen as crucial in achieving the military mission and in which masculinity is synonymous with heterosexuality the presence of openly gay men appears intolerable.

253

❧ *Ideological* Interests

A second interest served by compulsory heterosexuality in the military is ideological. By institutionalizing heterosexual masculinity, the armed forces bestow status advantages to men as a group over women. The military perpetuates an almost mythological form of masculinity: the soldier is aggressive, macho, bloodthirsty. Recruiters advertise that they are looking for "a few good men"; and popular movies proclaim that "war at its worst" inspires "men at their best" (*Hamburger Hill,* 1987). Though few "real life" soldiers live up to this image, the myth has great cultural vitality and serves as a reward for military service available only to men. As the Persian Gulf War demonstrated, status advantages accrue to the combat soldier even, in this age of high-tech, sanitized warfare.

The hegemonic masculine ideal perpetuated by the military conflates soldierliness, masculinity, and heterosexuality.

. . .

Homosexual men and lesbians challenge this ideological interest, though in different ways. Gay men pose a direct threat to the hegemonic masculine ideal. Their distinguished service exposes the myth that soldiers are hypermasculine "he-men," thus depreciating the status rewards that all military men reap from their service. Their exclusion from the service preserves the status of military men in a more indirect way as well. By imposing a ban on homosexuality, the military insures that soldiers retain the status inherent in heterosexuality (Britton, 1990). As noted above, the exclusion of (openly) homosexual men obscures the homoeroticism already present in the military context. Conjuring visions of leering homosexual men in the showers elides the prospect of leering (hetero)sexual men in those same showers.

The threat posed by the presence of lesbians is more complicated than that posed by male homosexuality because lesbians are women. The military has always been extremely reluctant to integrate any women into the services—straight or lesbian. Women's roles in the military are still constrained by combat exclusionary policies, which impose limits on their recruitment and their access to top military jobs (Williams, 1989). . . .

Policies restricting women's participation in the military are also based on the organization's desire to protect and project its masculine image. Like gay men, all women threaten the viability of this popular image when they successfully accomplish the feats defined as masculine. The organization and its rituals are devalued if "even a girl" can do them (Karst, 1991; Williams, 1989). Consequently, to protect the masculinity of the military, successful military women tend to be stereotyped as "unfeminine" and, quite frequently, lesbian as well. This places women in a complex catch-22 situation: The fact that they are women presumably makes them incapable of meeting the demands of military service: yet if they distinguish themselves through their military service (which is viewed as masculine behavior), they are labelled lesbians, therefore also unsuitable for military service (Benecke & Dodge, 1990; Gay and Lesbian Military Freedom Project, 1989). . . .

Thus, while a man who succeeds in the military *negates* the stereotype of a homosexual man, a woman who succeeds *confirms* the stereotype of a lesbian. The effects of these stereotypes can be seen in discharge statistics: women are nearly three times more likely to be persecuted and discharged for homosexuality than are men. Lesbians are more frequently court-martialed for their sexuality; they more frequently serve prison sentences for homosexuality; and women in general receive more convictions for sex crimes (including sodomy) than men (Brownworth, 1993). . . . Women are subject to this closer scrutiny because their very presence to the military raises suspicions that they are not "real" (i.e., truly feminine) women (Benecke & Dodge, 1990). The differential enforcement of the ban on homosexuality reserves status positions for men. Even closeted homosexual men accrue status advantages over women.

Furthermore, the more rigid enforcement of a ban on lesbians creates a situation in which male bonding is explicitly encouraged by military policy, but solidarity between women is immediately suspect. Both lesbian and heterosexual women are intimidated by frequent investigations of lesbianism, which often take on the character of a "witchhunt" (Faderman, 1991; Stiehm, 1988). The constant threat of these investigations inhibits military women from forming close social relationships and support networks with each other, which are essential for surviving in a hostile male environment (Gay and Lesbian Military Freedom Project, 1989).

Finally, the simultaneous encouragement of aggressive heterosexuality and limitation of the participation of women has created a situation in the military in which situations like Tailhook and witchhunts are almost inevitable. A woman recently discharged from the military for homosexuality makes the link between these factors:

> The same attitude that made rapes in Saudi Arabia possible during Desert Storm and made it possible for over a hundred men involved in Tailhook to get off is what makes it possible to terrorize lesbians in the military, purge them and have nobody bat an eye. (Blakely, quoted in Brownworth, 1993)

Given an institutional context intimately tied to the construction and reproduction of this particular kind of hegemonic masculinity, it seems unlikely that this climate will change markedly for women. . . .

☻ Conclusion

. . .

We have argued in this paper that the military's exclusion of gay men and lesbians can be seen as a way of privileging the male heterosexual soldier. Through its policies restricting the participation of all women and gay men, the military privileges the contributions of these soldiers, and the "don't ask, don't tell" policy ensures that the accomplishments of actual lesbian and gay service members will never be able to contradict the arguments of the military establishment.

Endnotes

[1]These provisions are, in part: "Activities such as association with known homosexuals, presence at a gay bar, possessing or reading homosexual publications or marching in a gay rights rally in civilian clothes will not, in and of themselves, constitute credible information that would provide a basis for initiating an investigation or serve as a basis for an administrative discharge under this policy" (draft Department of Defense policy, 7/19/93).

[2]These new regulations have, understandably, created some confusion among those responsible for enforcing them. For this reason, the Pentagon has recently issued a handbook to guide field officers in their investigations. For example, while visiting a gay bar is not sufficient cause to initiate an investigation under the new policy, photographs which show service members engaged in homosexual behavior would constitute grounds to investigate.

References

Arkin, W. (1978). Military socialization and masculinity. *Journal of Social Issues, 34,* 151–68.

Benecke, M., & Dodge, K. (1990). Military women in nontraditional fields: Casualties of the armed forces' war on homosexuals. *Harvard Women's Law Journal, 13,* 215–250.

Bordo, S. (1993, September). Reading the male body. *Michigan Quarterly Review,* pp. 696–737.

Britton, D. M. (1990). Homophobia and homosociality: An analysis of boundary maintenance. *Sociological Quarterly, 31,* 423–439.

Brownworth, V. (1993). Invisible soldier: Lesbians in the military. *Deneuve, 3*(6), 14–17.

Burke, C. (1992). Dames at Sea. *The New Republic, 207*(8/9), 16–20.

Butler, J. S. (1993). Homosexuals and the military establishment. *Society, 31*(1), 13–21.

Butler, J. P (1993). Endangered/Endangering: Schematic racism and white paranoia. In Robert Gooding-Williams (Ed.), *Reading Rodney King/Reading urban uprising* (pp. 15–22). New York: Routledge.

Collins, P H. (1991). *Black feminist thought: Knowledge, consciousness, and the politics of empowerment.* New York: Routledge.

Duke, L. (1993, February 15). Opponents of military ban liken fight to that of Blacks. *Washington Post*, p. 3.

Enloe, C. (1983). *Does khaki become you? The militarization of women's lives.* Boston: South End Press.

Enloe, C. (1989). *Bananas, beaches and bases: Making feminist sense of international politics.* Berkeley: University of California Press.

Enloe C. (1993). *The morning after: Sexual politics at the end of the cold war.* Berkeley: University of California Press.

Eskridge, W. N. (1993). Race and sexual orientation in the military: Ending the apartheid of the closet. *Reconstruction*, 2(2), 52–57.

Faderman, L. (1991). *Odd girls and twilight lovers: A history of lesbian life in twentieth-century America.* New York: Penguin Books.

Gay and Lesbian Military Freedom Project. (1989). Backgrounder on homosexuality and the military. Washington, DC: Author.

General Accounting Office. (1992a). Defense force management: DOD's policy on homosexuality. Washington, DC: Government Printing Office.

General Accounting Office. (1992b). Defense force management: Statistics related to DOD's policy on homosexuality. Washington, DC: Government Printing Office.

Harper, S. (1993). *The brotherhood: Race and gender ideologies in the white supremacist movement.* Unpublished doctoral dissertation. University of Texas at Austin.

Hearn, J., & Parkin, W. (1987). *'Sex' at 'work': The power and paradox of organization sexuality.* New York: St. Martin's Press.

Humphrey, M. A. (1990). *My country, my right to serve: Experiences of gay men and women in the military, World War II to the present.* New York: Harper Collins.

Jeffords, S. (1989). *The remasculinization of America: Gender and the Vietnam War.* Bloomington: Indiana University Press.

Karst, K. L. (1991). The pursuit of manhood and the desegregation of the armed forces. *UCLA Law Review*, 38, 499–581.

Kohen, J. A. (1984). The military career is a family affair. *Journal of Family Issues. 5,* 401–418.

Moskos, C. (1992, March 16). Don't ignore good reasons for homosexual ban. *Army Times,* p. 31.

Payne, D. M., Warner, J. T., & Little, R. D. (1992). Tied migration and returns to human capital: The case of military wives. *Social Science Quarterly, 73,* 324–339.

Rich, A. (1980). Compulsory heterosexuality and lesbian existence. *Signs, 5,* 631–660.

Sarbin, T. R., & Karols, K. E. (1988). Nonconforming sexual orientations and military suitability. Monterey, CA: Defense Personnel Security Research and Education Center.

Schmitt, E. (1992, August 26). Marine Corps chaplain says homosexuals threaten military. *The New York Times,* p. A 16.

Sedgwick, E. K. (1985). *Between men: English literature and male homosocial desire.* New York: Columbia University Press.

Segal, D. R. (1989). *Recruiting for Uncle Sam: Citizenship and military manpower policy.* Lawrence: University Press of Kansas.

Segal, M. W. (1986). The military and the family as greedy institutions. *Armed Forces and Society, 13,* 9–38.

Shilts, R. (1991, August 5). In wake of war, military again targets gays. *San Francisco Chronicle,* p. Al.

Shilts, R. (1993). *Conduct unbecoming: Lesbians and gays in the U.S. military: Vietnam to the present.* New York: St. Martin's Press.

Snyder, W. P, & Nyberg, K. L. (1980). Gays and the military: An emerging policy issue. *Journal of Political and Military Sociology, 8,* 71–84.

Stiehm, J. H. (1988). The effect of myths about military women on the waging of war. In E. Isaksson (Ed.), *Women and the military system* (pp. 94–106). New York: Harvester-Wheatsheaf.

Stiehm, J. H. (1989). *Arms and the enlisted woman.* Philadelphia: Temple University Press.

Theweleit, K. (1987). *Male fantasies, Volume 1: Women, floods, bodies, history.* Cambridge: Polity Press.

West, C. (1993). *Race matters.* Boston: Beacon Press.

Williams, C. L. (1989). *Gender differences at work: Women and men in non-traditional occupations.* Berkeley: University of California Press.

Williams, C. J., & Weinberg, M. S. (1971). *Homosexuals and the military: A study of less than honorable discharge.* New York: Harper and Row.

☻ ☻ ☻

Questions

1. Under the "don't ask, don't tell, don't pursue" policy, on what basis can people be excluded from the U.S. military?

2. Explain how societal prejudice is used to support the ban of gays and lesbians from the military, just as it has been used to exclude African-Americans.

3. How do gay men, lesbians, and heterosexual women challenge the image of the perfect soldier?

4. Ask 10 people whether they believe gays and lesbians should be allowed to openly serve in the military. Then ask them why they feel this way. Compare these explanations with those in the article. In what ways are their arguments similar or dissimilar to those reviewed in this article? Bring your results to class and share them with your classmates.

The Globalization of Sexual Identities

Dennis Altman

While it is difficult to generalize across societies, it appears that traditional notions of sexuality and sexual identity are being challenged through processes associated with globalization. For example, think about the implications of e-mail and the World Wide Web for people who, less than a generation ago, might have felt isolated as sexual minorities, thinking there was no one else who felt like they did. Today, these individuals—if they have computer access—can communicate with others across the globe who share their desires/behaviors/identities. Or they can simply find information about sexuality that not long ago would have been difficult to access in many parts of the world. Yet, not surprisingly, the effects of globalization on sexuality are not entirely positive. This chapter is from Dennis Altman's Global Sex.

*M*ost of the literature about globalization and identity is concerned with the rebirth of nationalist, ethnic, and religious fundamentalism, or the decline of the labor movement.[1] (I am using "identity" to suggest a socially constructed myth about shared characteristics, culture, and history which comes to have real meaning for those who espouse it.)[2] Here I concentrate on the identity politics born of sexuality and gender, and the new social movements which arise from these, already foreshadowed in the previous chapter. These new identities are closely related to the larger changes of globalization: consider the globalization of "youth," and the role of international capitalism in creating a teenage identity in almost every country, with specific music, language, fashion, and mores.[3] In recent years this is expressed in terms of "boy" and "girl" cultures, as in references to "boy bands" or "a booming girl culture worldwide,"[4] which suggests the invention of an intermediate generational identity between "children" and "youth."

Over the past decade I've been researching and thinking about the diffusion of certain sorts of "gay/lesbian" identities, trying to trace the connections between globalization and the preconditions for certain sexual subjectivities.[5]

My examples are drawn predominantly from Southeast Asia because this is the part of the "developing" world I know best, but they could even more easily be drawn from Latin America, which has a particularly rich literature exploring these questions.[6] The question is not whether homosexuality exists—it does in almost every society of which we know—but how people incorporate homosexual behavior into their sense of self. Globalization has helped create an international gay/lesbian identity, which is by no means confined to the western world: there are many signs of what we think of as "modern" homosexuality in countries such as Brazil, Costa Rica, Poland, and Taiwan. Indeed the gay world—less obviously the lesbian, largely due to marked differences in women's social and economic status—is a key example of emerging global "subcultures," where members of particular groups have more in common across national and continental boundaries than they do with others in their own geographically defined societies.

It is worth noting that even within the "first world" there is a range of attitudes toward the assertion of gay/lesbian identities. While they have flourished in the English-speaking countries and in parts of northern Europe, there is more resistance to the idea in Italy and France, where ideas of communal rights—expressed through the language of multiculturalism in Australia and Canada, and through a somewhat different tradition of religious pluralism in the Netherlands and Switzerland—seem to run counter to a universalist rhetoric of rights, which are not equated with the recognition of separate group identities.[7] The United States shares both traditions, so that its gay and lesbian movement argues for recognition of "civil rights" on the basis of being just like everyone else, and in some cases deserving of special protection along the lines developed around racial and gender discrimination.

At the same time the United States has gone farthest in the development of geographically based gay and lesbian communities, with defined areas of its large cities—the Castro in San Francisco, West Hollywood, Halsted in Chicago, the West Village in New York—becoming urban "ghettos," often providing a base to develop the political clout of the community. (In almost all large American cities politicians now recognize the importance of the gay vote.) This model has been replicated in a number of western countries, whether it is the Marais in Paris ox Darlinghurst in Sydney. There is some irony in the fact that, while homosexual rights have progressed much further in the countries of northern Europe, the United States remains the dominant cultural model for the rest of the world.

This dominance was symbolized in accounts in Europe of "gay pride" events in the summer of 1999, which often ignored national histories and attributed the origins of gay political activism to the Stonewall riots of 1969, ignoring the existence of earlier groups in countries such as Germany, the Netherlands, Switzerland, and France, and the radical gay groups which grew out of the 1968 student movements in both France and Italy. (Stonewall was a gay bar in New York City which was raided by the police, leading to riots by angry homosexuals and the birth of the New York Gay Liberation Front.) In cities as diverse as Paris, Hamburg, and Warsaw the anniversary of Stonewall was celebrated with Christopher Street Day, and the dominance of American culture is summed up by the press release from the Lisbon Gay, Lesbian, Bisexual, and Transgender Pride committee boasting of the performances of a "renowned DJ from New York City" and "Celeda—the Diva Queen from Chicago."

Thinking and writing about these questions, it became clear to me that observers, indigenous and foreign alike, bring strong personal investments to how they understand what is going on, in particular whether (in words suggested to me by Michael Tan) we are speaking of "ruptures" or "continuities." For some there is a strong desire to trace a continuity between precolonial forms of homosexual desire and its contemporary emergence, even where the latter might draw on the language of (West) Hollywood rather than indigenous culture. Such views are argued strenuously by those who cling to an identity based on traditional assumptions about the links between gender performance and sexuality, and deny the relevance of an imported "gay" or "lesbian" identity for themselves. Thus the effeminate *bakkla* in the Philippines or the *kathoey* in Thailand might see those who call themselves "gay" as hypocrites, in part because they insist on their right to behave as men, and to desire others like them.[8] For others there is a perception that contemporary middle-class self-proclaimed gay men and lesbians in, say, New Delhi, Lima, or Jakarta have less in common with "traditional" homosexuality than they do with their counterparts in western countries. As Sri Lankan author Shaym Selvadurai said of his novel *Funny Boy,* which is in part about "coming out" as gay: "The people in the novel are in a place that has been colonized by Western powers for 400 years. A lot of Western ideas—bourgeois respectability, Victorian morality—have become incorporated into the society, and are very much part of the Sri Lankan society."[9]

"Modern" ways of being homosexual threaten not only the custodians of "traditional" morality, they also threaten the position of "traditional" forms of homosexuality, those which are centered around gender nonconformity and transvestism. The title of the Indonesian gay/lesbian journal *Gaya Nusantara,* which literally means "Indonesian style," captures this ambivalence nicely with its echoes of both "traditional" and "modern" concepts of nation and sexuality, but at the same time it is clearly aimed at "modern" homosexuals rather than the "traditional" transvestite *waria*.[10]

It is often assumed that homosexuals are defined in most "traditional" societies as a third sex, but that too is too schematic to be universally useful. As Peter Jackson points out, the same terms in Thailand can be gender *and* sexual categories.[11] Here, again, we are confronted by considerable confusion, where similar phenomena can be viewed as either culturally specific or as universal. Insofar as there is a confusion between sexuality and gender in the "traditional" view that the "real" homosexual is the man who behaves like a woman (or, more rarely, vice versa) this is consistent with the dominant understanding of homosexuality in western countries during the hundred years or so before the birth of the contemporary gay movement. The idea of a "third sex" was adopted by people like Ulrichs and Krafft-Ebing as part of an apologia for homosexuality (giving rise to Carpenter's "intermediate sex").[12] In the 1918 novel *Despised and Rejected* the hero laments: "What had nature been about, in giving him the soul of a woman in the body of a man?"[13] Similar views can be found in Radclyffe Hall's novel *The Well of Loneliness* (1928), whose female hero calls herself Stephen. Today many people who experience homosexual desires in societies which do not allow space for them will see themselves as "men trapped in women's bodies" or vice versa.

In popular perceptions something of this confusion remains today—and persists in much popular humor, such as the remarkably successful play/film *La cage aux folles (The Birdcage)* or the film *Priscilla, Queen of the Desert.* George Chauncey argues that the very idea of a homosexual/heterosexual divide became dominant in the United States only in the mid-twentieth century: "The most striking difference between the dominant sexual culture of the early twentieth century and that of our own era is the degree to which the earlier culture permitted men to engage in sexual relations with other men, often on a regular basis, without requiring them to regard themselves—or be regarded by others—as gay . . . Many men . . . neither understood nor organised their sexual practices along a hetero-homosexual axis."[14] John Rechy's landmark novel *City of Night* (1963) captures the transition to "modern" concepts: his world is full of "hustlers," "queens," "masculine" or "butch" homosexuals," whom he sometimes calls "gay."[15]

If one reads or views contemporary accounts of homosexual life in, say, Central America, Thailand, and Côte d'Ivoire,[16] one is immediately struck by the parallels. It is of course possible that the observers, all of whom are trained m particular ethnographic and sociological methods, even where, as in the case of Schifter, they are indigenous to the country of study, are bringing simi-lar—and one assumes unconscious—preconceptions with them. Even so, it is unlikely that this itself would explain the degree of similarity they identify. In the same way, the Dutch anthropologist Saskia Wieringa has pointed to the similarities of butch-femme role-playing in Jakarta and Lima, and how they echo that of preliberation western lesbian worlds.[17] In many "traditional" soci-eties there were complex variations across gender and sex lines, with "trans-gender" people (Indonesian *waria,* Thai *kathoey,* Moroccan *hassas,* Turkish *kocek,* Filipino *bayot,* Luban *kitesha* in parts of Congo) characterized by both transvestite and homosexual behavior. These terms are usually—not always—applied to men, but there are other terms sometimes used of women, such as *mati* in Suriname, which also disrupt simplistic assumptions about sex and gender.[18] As Gilbert Herdt says: "Sexual orientation and identity are not the keys to conceptualizing a third sex and gender across time and space."[19] In many societies there is confusion around the terms—for example the *hijras* of India, who were literally castrated, are sometimes considered equivalent to homosexuals even though the reality is more complex.[20]

Different people use terms such as *bayot* or *waria* in different ways, depending on whether the emphasis is on gender—these are men who wish in some way to be women—or on sexuality—these are men attracted to other men. Anthropology teaches us the need to be cautious about any sort of binary system of sex/gender; Niko Besnier uses the term "gender liminality" to avoid this trap[21] and it should also alert us against the sort of romanticized assumptions that some Americans have brought to understanding the Native American *bedarche.*[22] Besnier also stresses that such "liminality" is not the same as homosexuality: "Sexual relations with men are seen as an optional consequence of gender liminality, rather than its determiner, prerequisite or primary attribute."[23] The other side of this distinction is that there are strong pressures to define *fa'afafine* (the Samoan term) or other such groups in Pacific countries as asexual, thus leading to a particular denial in which both Samoans and outsiders are complicit.[24]

Certainly most of the literature about Latin America stresses that a homo-sexual *identity* (as distinct from homosexual practices) is related to rejection of dominant gender expectations, so that "a real man" can have sex with other men and not risk his heterosexual identity. As Roger Lancaster put it: "What-ever else a *cochon* might or might not do, he is tacitly understood as one who assumes the receptive role in anal intercourse. His partner, defined as 'active' in the terms of their engagement, is not stigmatized, nor does he acquire a special identity of any sort."[25] Thus the *nature* rather than the *object* of the

265

sexual act becomes the key factor. However, there is also evidence that this is changing, and a more western concept of homosexual identity is establishing itself; especially among the middle classes.

Sexuality becomes an important arena for the production of modernity, with "gay" and "lesbian" identities acting as markers for modernity.[26] There is an ironic echo of this in the Singapore government's bulldozing of Bugis Street, once the center of transvestite prostitution in the city—and its replacement by a Disneyland-like simulacrum where a few years ago I was taken to see a rather sanitized drag show presented to a distinctly yuppie audience.[27] There is an equal irony in seeing the decline of a homosexuality defined by gender nonconformity as a "modern" trend just when transsexuals and some theorists in western countries are increasingly attracted by concepts of the malleability of gender.[28] From one perspective the fashionable replica of the stylized "lipstick lesbian" or "macho" gay man is less "postmodern" than the *waria* or the Tongan *fakaleiti*.[29]

Perhaps the reality is that androgyny is postmodern when it is understood as performance, not when it represents the only available way of acting out certain deep-seated beliefs about one's sexual and gender identity. Even so, I remain unsure just why "drag," and its female equivalents, remains a strong part of the contemporary homosexual world, even where there is increasing space for open homosexuality and a range of acceptable ways of "being" male or female. Indeed there is evidence that in some places there is a simultaneous increase in both gay/lesbian identities *and* in transgender performance, as in recent developments in Taiwan where drag shows have become very fashionable, and some of the performers, known as "third sex public relations officers," insist that they are not homosexual even when their behavior would seem to contradict this.[30] Similar comments could probably be made about *onnabe*, Japanese women who dress as men and act as the equivalent of geishas for apparently heterosexual women, and Jennifer Robertson describes the incorporation of androgyny into the "'libidinal' economy of the capitalist market" as "gender-bending" performers are turned into marketable commodities.[31] In the west it has become increasingly fashionable to depict transvestism in unmistakably heterosexual terms; what was daring (and possibly ambiguous) in the 1959 film *Some Like It Hot* becomes farce in the 1993 film *Mrs. Doubtfire*.[32] But at the same time there is, particularly in the United States, the emergence of a somewhat new form of transgender politics, in which the concern of an older generation to be accepted the woman or man they "really" are is replaced by an assertion of a transgender identity and the malleability of gender.[33] (Western writers tend to be reasonably careful to distinguish between *transsexual* and *transvestite*. However, this distinction is often not made in parts of Asia and, I assume, other parts of the world.)

Speaking openly of homosexuality and transvestism, which is often the consequence of western influence, can unsettle what is accepted but not acknowledged. Indeed there is some evidence in a number of societies that those who proclaim themselves "gay" or "lesbian," that is, seek a public identity based on their sexuality, encounter a hostility which may not have been previously apparent. But there is a great deal of mythology around the acceptance of gender/sexual nonconformity outside the west, a mythology to which for different reasons both westerners and nonwesterners contribute. Romanticized views about homoeroticism in many nonwestern cultures, often based on travel experiences, disguise the reality of persecution, discrimination, and violence, sometimes in unfamiliar forms. Firsthand accounts make it clear that homosexuality is far from being universally accepted—or even tolerated—in such apparent "paradises" as Morocco, the Philippines, Thailand, or Brazil: "Lurking behind the Brazilians' pride of their flamboyant drag queens, their recent adulation of a transvestite chosen as a model of Brazilian beauty, their acceptance of gays and lesbians as leaders of the country's most widely practised religion and the constitutional protection of homosexuality, lies a different truth. Gay men, lesbians and transvestites face widespread discrimination, oppression and extreme violence."[34]

Just as the most interesting postmodern architecture is found in cities like Shanghai or Bangkok, so too the emphasis of postmodern theory on pastiche, parody, hybridity, and so forth is played out in a real way by women and men who move, often with considerable comfort, from apparent obedience to official norms to their own sense of gay community. The dutiful Confucian or Islamic Malaysian son one weekend might appear in drag at Blueboy, Kuala Lumpur's gay bar, the next—and who is to say which is "the real" person? Just as many Malaysians can move easily from one language to another, so most urban homosexuals can move from one style to another, from camping it up with full awareness of the latest fashion trends from Castro Street to playing the dutiful son at a family celebration.

To western gay liberationists these strategies might seem hypocritical, even cowardly (and some westerners expressed surprise at the apparent silence from Malaysian gay men after the arrest of Anwar on sodomy charges). But even the most politically aware Malaysians may insist that there is no need to "come out" to their family while explaining that in any case their lover is accepted as one of the family—though not so identified. (The Malaysian situation is further complicated by the fact that Muslims are subject to both civil and *sharia* laws, and the latter have been used quite severely, against transvestites in particular.) Some people have suggested that everything is possible *as long as it is not stated,* but it is probably more complex than that. For many men I have met in Southeast Asia being gay does mean a sense of communal identity, and even a sense of "gay pride," but this is not necessarily experienced in the vocabulary of the west.

Middle-class English-speaking homosexuals in places like Mexico City, Istanbul, and Mumbai will speak of themselves as part of a gay (sometimes "gay and lesbian") community, but the institutions of such a community will vary considerably depending on both economic resources and political space. Thus in Kuala Lumpur, one of the richer cities of the "developing" world, there are no gay or lesbian bookstores, restaurants, newspapers, or businesses—at least not in the open way we would expect them in comparable American or European cities. There is, however, a strong sense of gay identity around the AIDS organization Pink Triangle—its name is emblematic—and sufficient networks for a gay sauna to open and attract customers. Yet when a couple of years ago I gave some copies of the Australian gay magazine *Outrage* to the manager of the Kuala Lumpur sauna, I was told firmly there could be no display of something as overtly homosexual as these magazines—which are routinely sold by most Australian newsagents. In the same way there is also a strong lesbian network in the city, and many women use office faxes and email to arrange meetings and parties.

At that same sauna I met one man who told me he had heard of the place through a friend now living in Sydney. In conversations I have had with middle-class gay men in Southeast Asia there are frequent references to bars in Paris and San Francisco, to Sydney's Gay and Lesbian Mardi Gras, to American gay writers. Those who take on gay identities often aspire to be part of global culture in all its forms, as suggested by this quote from a Filipino anthology of gay writing: "I met someone in a bar last Saturday . . . He's a bank executive. He's mestizo (your type) and . . . loves Barbra Streisand, Gabriel Garcia Marquez, Dame Margot Fonteyn, Pat Conroy, Isabel Allende, John Williams, Meryl Streep, Armistead Maupin, k. d. lang, Jim Chappell, Margaret Atwood and Luciano Pavarotti."[35]

Similarly magazines like *G & L* in Taiwan—a "lifestyle" magazine launched in 1996—mixes local news and features with stories on international, largely American, gay and lesbian icons. As mobility increases, more and more people are traveling abroad and meeting foreigners at home. It is as impossible to prevent new identities and categories traveling as it is to prevent pornography traveling across the Internet.

As part of the economic growth of south and east Asia the possibilities of computer-based communications have been grasped with enormous enthusiasm, and have created a new set of possibilities for the diffusion of information and the creation of (virtual) communities. Whereas the gay movements of the 1970s in the west depended heavily on the creation of a gay/lesbian press, in countries such as Malaysia, Thailand, and Japan the Internet offers the same possibilities, with the added attraction of anonymity and instant contact with overseas, thus fostering the links with the diaspora already discussed. Work by Chris Berry and Fran Martin suggests that the Internet has become a crucial way for young homosexuals to meet each other in Taiwan and Korea—and in the process to develop a certain, if privatized, form of community.[36] In Japan the Internet has become a central aid to homosexual cruising.

It is precisely this constant dissemination of images and ways of being, moving disproportionately from north to south, which leads some to savagely criticize the spread of sexual identities as a new step in neocolonialism: "The very constitution of a subject entitled to rights involves the violent capture of the disenfranchised by an institutional discourse which inseparably weaves them into the textile of global capitalism."[37] This position is argued with splendid hyperbole by Pedro Bustos-Aguilar, who attacks both "the gay ethnographer . . . [who] kills a native with the charm of his camera" and "the union of the New World Order and Transnational Feminism" which asserts neocolonialism and western hegemony in the name of supposed universalisms.[38]

Bustos-Aguilar's argument is supported by the universalist rhetoric which surrounded the celebration of the twenty-fifth anniversary of Stonewall, but he could have had great fun with a 1993 brochure from San Francisco which offered "your chance to make history . . . [at] the first ever gay & lesbian film festival in India & parallel queer tour"—and even more with the reporter from the *Washington Blade* who wrote of Anwar's "ostensibly being gay."[39] It finds a troubling echo in the story of an American, Tim Wright, who founded a gay movement in Bolivia, and after four years was found badly beaten and amnesiac: "And things have gone back to being what they were."[40]

A more measured critique comes from Ann Ferguson, who has warned that the very concept of an international lesbian *culture* is politically problematic, because it would almost certainly be based upon western assumptions, even though she is somewhat more optimistic about the creation of an international *movement,* which would allow for self-determination of local lesbian communities.[41] While western influences were clearly present, it is as true to see the emergence of groups in much of Latin America, in Southeast Asia, and among South African blacks as driven primarily by local forces.

It is certainly true that the assertion of gay/lesbian identity can have neo-colonial implications, but given that many anti/postcolonial movements and governments deny existing homosexual traditions it becomes difficult to know exactly whose values are being imposed on whom. Both the western outsider and the local custodians of national culture are likely to ignore existing realities in the interest of ideological certainty. Those outside the west tend to be more aware of the difference between traditional homosexualities and contemporary gay identity politics, a distinction sometimes lost by the international gay/lesbian movement in its eagerness to claim universality.[42] New sexual identities mean a loss of certain traditional cultural comforts while offering new possibilities to those who adopt them, and activists in non-western countries will consciously draw on both traditions. In this they may be inconsistent, but no more than western gay activists who simultaneously deploy the language of universal rights and special group status.

In practice most people hold contradictory opinions at the same time, reminding us of Freud's dictum that "it is only in logic that contradictions cannot exist." There are large numbers of men and fewer women in non-western countries who will describe themselves as "gay" or "lesbian" in certain circumstances, while sometimes claiming these labels are inappropriate to their situation. It is hardly surprising that people want both to identify with and to distinguish themselves from a particular western form of homosexuality, or that they will call upon their own historical traditions to do so. This ambivalence is caught in this account by a Chinese-Australian: "[Chinese] gays were determined to advance their cause but in an evolutionary rather than revolutionary way. They seized on issues such as gayness, gay culture, gay lifestyle, equal rights for gays and so on. In romantic poems the gay dreams of our ancestors were represented by two boys sharing a peach and the emperor who cut his sleeves of his gown rather than disturb his lover sleeping in his arms. To revive this dream, and enable millions of Chinese-born gays to choose their lifestyle, is a huge task. But it has happened in Taiwan, as it did in Hong Kong, and so it will in China."[43]

There are of course examples of Asian gay groups engaging in political activity of the sort associated with their counterparts in the west. Indonesia has a number of gay and lesbian groups, which have now held three national meetings. The best-known openly gay figure in Indonesia, Dede Oetomo, was a candidate of the fledgling Democratic People's Party in the 1999 elections, which followed the overthrow of Suharto. There have been several small radical gay political groups established in the Philippines in recent years, and gay demonstrations have taken place in Manila. ProGay (the Progressive Organization of Gays in the Philippines), as its name suggests, is concerned to draw links between specifically gay issues and larger questions of social justice.[44] The first lesbian conference was held in Japan in 1985,[45] and there have been lesbian organizations in Taiwan since 1990 and the Philippines since 1992.[46] The international lesbigay press carried reports of a national conference of lesbians in Beijing in late 1998 and in Sri Lanka the following year. There have been several *tongzhi* gatherings in Hong Kong (a term adopted to cover "lesbians, bisexuals, gays and transgendered people"), and a manifesto adopted by the 1996 meeting argued that "[c]ertain characteristics of confrontational politics, such as through coming out and mass protests and parades may not be the best way of achieving *tongzhi* liberation in the family-centred, community-oriented Chinese societies which stress the importance of social harmony."[47] (An odd myth, given the revolutionary upheavals in twentieth-century China.) None of these groups have the history or the reach of gay/lesbian movements in Latin America, where Brazil, Argentina, Chile, and Mexico all have significant histories of a politicized homosexuality.

In many cases homosexual identities are asserted without an apparent gay/lesbian movement. In 1998 there was a move by bar owners in Kuala Lumpur to organize a gay-pride party which was canceled after a protest by the Malaysian Youth Council. The best example of a nonpolitical gay world can probably be found in Thailand, where there is a growing middle-class gay world, based neither on prostitution nor on traditional forms of gender nonconformity (as in the person of the *kathoey*), but only a small lesbian group, Anjaree, and no gay male groups at all since the collapse of a couple of attempts to organize around HIV in the late 1980s.[48] In late 1996 controversy erupted in Thailand after the governing body of the country's teacher-training colleges decreed that "sexual deviants" would be barred from entering the colleges. While there was considerable opposition to the ban (subsequently dropped), other than Anjaree most of this came from nongay sources. In the ensuing public debate one could see contradictory outside influences at work—both an imported fear of homosexuals and a more modern emphasis on how such a ban infringed human rights. As Peter Jackson concluded: "A dynamic gay scene has emerged . . . in the complete absence of a gay rights movement."[49]

Indeed it may be that a political movement is the least likely part of western concepts of homosexual identity to be adopted in many parts of the world, even as some activists enthusiastically embrace the mores and imagery of western queerdom. The particular form of identity politics which allowed for the mobilization of a gay/lesbian electoral pressure in countries like the United States, the Netherlands, and even France may not be appropriate elsewhere, even if western-style liberal democracy triumphs. The need of western lesbian/gays to engage in identity politics as a means of enhancing self-esteem may not be felt in other societies. Even so, one should read Jackson's comment about Thailand with some caution. Already when he wrote it there was an embryonic group in Bangkok around an American-owned and -run gay bookstore. At the end of 1999 one of the country's gay papers organized a gay festival and twilight parade in the heart of Bangkok, announcing it as "the first and biggest gay parade in Asia where Asian gay men have a basic human right to be who they want to be and love who they want to love."[50] Similarly, accounts of homosexual life in Japan alternate between assuming a high degree of acceptance—and therefore no reason for a political movement—and severe restrictions on the space to assert homosexual identity, though the gay group OCCUR has recently gained a certain degree of visibility.

The western gay/lesbian movement emerged in conditions of affluence and liberal democracy, where despite other large social issues it was possible to develop a politics around sexuality, which is more difficult in countries where the basic structures of political life are constantly contested.[51] Writing of contemporary South Africa Mark Gevisser notes: "Race-identification overpowers everything else—class, gender and sexuality."[52] In the same way basic questions of political economy and democratization will impact the future development of gay/lesbian movements in much of Asia and Africa. Yet in Latin America and eastern Europe gay/lesbian movements have grown considerably in the past decade, and there are signs of their emergence in some parts of Africa, for example in Botswana and in Zimbabwe, where President Mugabe has consistently attacked homosexuality as the product of colonialism.[53] Similar rhetoric has come from the leaders of Kenya,[54] Namibia, and Uganda, whose President Museveni has denounced homosexuality as "western"—using the rhetoric of the Christian right to do so.[55] Anglican bishops from Africa—though not South Africa—were crucial in defeating moves to change the Church of England's attitudes toward homosexuality at the 1998 decennial Lambeth Conference. South Africa is a crucial exception, perhaps because apartheid's denunciation of homosexuality made it easier for the African National Congress to develop a policy of acceptance as part of their general support for "a rainbow nation." Even so, some elements of the ANC are strongly homophobic, revealed in the rhetoric of many of Winnie Mandela's supporters.[56]

While many African officials and clergy maintain that homosexuality is not part of precolonial African culture, the evidence for its existence—and the slow acknowledgment of its role in African life—is emerging across the continent. One might speculate that the strong hostility from some African political and religious leaders toward homosexuality as a "western import" is an example of psychoanalytic displacement, whereby anxieties about sexuality are redirected to continuing resentment against colonialism and the subordinate position of Africa within the global economy. Western-derived identities can easily become markers of those aspects of globalization which are feared and opposed. Similarly a 1994 conference for gay/MSMs (men who have sex with men) in Bombay was opposed by the National Federation of Indian Women, an affiliate of the Communist party of India, as "an invasion of India by decadent western cultures and a direct fallout of our signing the GATT agreement."[57] Whether the federation was aware of how close its rhetoric was to right-wing Americans such as Patrick Buchanan is unknown.

Part of the appearance of modernity is the use of western languages. Rodney Jones has noted the importance of English as part of the cultural capital of Hong Kong homosexuals,[58] and when I attended an AIDS conference in Morocco in 1996 participants complained that despite an attempt to ensure equal use of Arabic it was "easier" to talk about sexuality in French. A similar emphasis on English is noted by James Farrar in presumably heterosexual discos in Shanghai, where ironically the Village People song "YMCA" has now become "a globalized dance ritual in which the dancers are encouraged to use their hands to make shapes of the English letters, identifying themselves momentarily with a boundless global ecumene of sexy happy youth 'at the YMCA.'"[59] One assumes the Shanghai dancers are unaware of the clearly gay overtones to both the song and the group. I admit to particular pleasure in reading this piece; an early proposal for my book *The Homosexualization of America* was rejected by an editor who complained (this was in 1982) that in a year no one would remember the Village People, the image with which I began that book.

A common language is essential for networking, and the past twenty years have seen a rapid expansion of networks among lesbian and gay groups across the world. In 1978 the International Lesbian and Gay Association (ILGA) was formed at a conference in Coventry, England.[60] While ILGA has largely been driven by northern Europeans, it now has member groups in more than seventy countries and has organized international meetings in several southern cities. Other networks, often linked to feminist and AIDS organizing, have been created in the past two decades, and emerging lesbian and gay movements are increasingly likely to be in constant contact with groups across the world. The inspiration from meeting with other lesbians at international women's conferences has been a powerful factor in the creation of lesbian groups in a number of countries. Thus the Asian Lesbian Network, which now includes women from twelve or thirteen countries, began at an International Lesbian Information Service conference in Geneva in 1986.[61]

In recent years there has been some attempt to promote international networking among transgendered people—or, as Americans now call them, transfolk—with both the British-based International Gender Transient Affinity and the U.S.-based Gender Freedom International lobbying to protect transgendered people across the world from what seems to be routine harassment and persecution. The paradox of globalization is played out in constructions of sex/gender which combine the premodern with the modern, so that people identifying with "traditional" forms of transgender identity will employ modern techniques of surgery and hormone therapy to alter their bodies.

The two largest international gay/lesbian institutions are probably those based around the Metropolitan Community Church and the Gay Games. The MCC is a Protestant sect founded by the Reverend Troy Perry in Los Angeles in 1968, whose congregations and ministers are largely homosexual, with an estimated congregation of more than 40,000 in some sixteen countries. Similar gay churches have emerged somewhat independently in several other societies such as South Africa and Mexico.[62] The Gay Games, modeled on the Olympics, which refused the use of its name, were first held in San Francisco in 1982, and have since become a major international event every four years, for which cities contend very bitterly They also generate considerable international publicity, much of it of a somewhat voyeuristic nature.[63] Both of these "networks," it is worth stressing, originated in the United States.

Homosexuality becomes a particularly obvious measure of globalization, for the transformation of local regimes of sexuality and gender is often most apparent in the emergence of new sorts of apparently "gay" and "lesbian," even "queer," identities. Yet we must beware reading too much into these scripts. What is happening in Bangkok, Rio, and Nairobi is the creation of new forms of understanding and regulating the sexual self, but it is unlikely that they will merely repeat those forms which were developed in the Atlantic world. Walking through the "gay" area of Tokyo's Shinjuku you will see large numbers of young men in sneakers and baseball caps (or whatever happens to be the current "gay" look) but this does not mean they will behave or view themselves in the same way as equivalent young men in North America or northern Europe.

❧ Prostitute Versus Sex Worker

A growing globalization of both identities and human rights is reflected in the growth of sex-worker groups and the regulation of prostitution. In recent years there have been legislative attempts in a number of first-world countries to decriminalize prostitution and at the same time to control certain forms of sex work, especially that involving enforced prostitution or children.[64] There is a bitter division between those who argue that human rights should mean the end of prostitution (understood as "sex-slavery" to use Kathleen Barry's phrase)[65] and those who argue that adults should have the right to use their bodies to make money, and should be protected from exploitation and danger in making use of that right. Indeed the use of the term "sex worker" is a deliberate ploy to demystify the category of "prostitute," and the terms "sex work" and "sex worker" "have been coined by sex-workers themselves to redefine commercial sex, not as the social or psychological characteristic of a class of women, but as an income-generating activity or form of employment for women and men."[66] One of the most eloquent statements comes from the Indian group Durbar Mahila Samanwaya Committee, even if the language clearly reflects western academic discourse.

> The "prostitute" is rarely used to refer to an occupational group of women earning their livelihood through providing sexual services, rather it is deployed as a descriptive term denoting a homogenised category, usually of women, which poses threats to public health, sexual morality, social stability and civic order. Within this discursive boundary we systematically find ourselves to be targets of moralising impulses of dominant social groups through missions of cleansing and sanitising both materially and symbolically. If and when we figure in political or development agenda we are enmeshed in discursive practices and practical projects which aim to rescue, rehabilitate, improve, discipline, control or police us.[67]

The first sex-worker organization seems to have been COYOTE (standing for Call Off Your Old Tired Ethics), which was established by Margo St. James in San Francisco in 1973 with support from the Glide Memorial Church and the Playboy Foundation.[68] Apparently unconnected to this a group emerged in France in the mid-1970s, following the murder of several prostitutes in Lyons in which the police showed little interest. Out of this group, and the subsequent English Collective of Prostitutes, came the formation of the International Committee for Prostitutes' Rights. COYOTE organized the First World Meeting of Prostitutes in Washington in 1976,

following which other groups emerged, such as Red Thread in the Netherlands. At the Second World Whores' Congress in Brussels in 1986 delegates
demanded that "[p]rostitution should be redefined as legitimate work and the
prostitutes should be redefined as legitimate citizens."[69]

This shift toward seeing prostitution as work is reflected in the development of "sex-work" organizations in some developing countries, the first of
which seems to have been in Ecuador, followed by groups in a number of
other Latin American countries[70] and a couple in Southeast Asia such as
Talikala in Davao City, the Philippines. The women who founded Talikala
were concerned from the outset to empower sex workers, and were attacked
by conservative Catholics for "promoting prostitution," ironic as the initial
funding for the project came from the Maryknoll Fathers. In 1995 sex workers in the Sonagachi area of Calcutta organized the Durbar Mahila Samanwaya Committee, which claims to be the registered organization of more than
40,000 female, male, and transsexual sex workers of West Bengal[71] and with
the Usha Co-operative runs its own STI clinics, a cooperative credit union,
literacy classes, and a crèche. One report suggested 3,000 people attended
the first national prostitution conference in India in 1997.[72] Even if this sort
of organizing was in part inspired by western ideas, does that make it less significant? One might remember that the Indian independence movement was
also influenced by western concepts of nation and democracy—and itself
became a major inspiration for the American and South African civil rights
movements. In the same way the Durbar Mahila Samanwaya Committee has
taken the mobilization of sex workers to a scale beyond that reached in any
western country.

During the 1990s an international network of sex-work projects (NSWP)
has sought to link sex-worker groups in both rich and poor countries, often
organizing around international HIV/AIDS conferences. By the end of the
decade the network linked groups in forty countries, but was limited by huge
difficulty in getting resources, and the dependence on a handful of dedicated
volunteers.[73] Gaining acceptance for sex-worker groups has been a tough
ongoing struggle, with only a few governments being willing to accord any
recognition at all. In both Australia and New Zealand the national organizations have at times played a role in national AIDS advisory bodies, but this is
rare, nor have better-established community AIDS organizations always been
particularly supportive. Guenter Frankenberg's comment about Germany
applies elsewhere: "The gay dominated AIDS-Hilfen have effectively colonized junkies, prostitutes and prisoners, speaking for them instead of
enabling them to be their own advocates."[74] The recognition of representa-

tives of both sex workers and lesbians in the 1998 Indonesian Women's Congress which followed the downfall of Suharto was therefore particularly significant,[75] as was the inclusion of lesbianism on the official agenda of the 1998 All National Women's Conference in India.

Most people who engage in sex for money have no sense of this comprising their central identity, and they may well be repelled by attempts to organize around an identity they would strongly reject. It is a fact that money will be involved in a great many sexual encounters in almost any cash economy, and that the great majority of such transactions will not involve people who identify themselves as professional sex workers, but see it rather as one among a number of strategies to survive.[76] This is true of young African girls who find "sugar daddies" (sometimes known as "spare tyres") to help with their school fees, as it is of American beach bums who accept hospitality and gifts in exchange for sexual favors. We should be skeptical of those studies which claim to tell us that 36% of sex workers are positive/negative/use condoms or whatever: this assumes a fixed population, which is a dangerous fiction. It seems useful to think of prostitution not as a fixed state or identity, but rather as a continuum ranging from organized prostitution, through brothels, escort agencies, and so forth, to unpremeditated transactions resulting from chance encounters.

This does not mean that organization around conditions of employment and protection from abuse may not be successful. Speaking of drug users, Chris Jones suggested the idea of a "pragmatic community . . . a community in action affected by various forces producing potentially pro-active responses to various situations."[77] We need to know more about organizations which may well include sex workers without making this a central definition, as in the example of the Ghana Widows' Association, which according to at least one account includes large numbers of women in Accra working in commercial sex.[78] In early 1998 a group known as the Henao Sisters was established in Port Moresby (Papua New Guinea) for women known as *raun-raun* girls, those who move in and out of prostitution. While the group grew out of a peer-education program established by a government-supported program for HIV-prevention education, the initiative for its development appears to have come from the women themselves who are faced with ongoing issues of survival, violence, and police harassment.

As both the examples of gay/lesbian and sex-worker identities show, socioeconomic change will produce new ways of understanding ourselves and our place in the world. The breakdown of the extended family household as both an economic and social unit was one of the most important conse-

quences of industrialization in the western world. In turn the growth of affluence, and the shifting emphasis from production to consumption, has meant
a steady shrinking in households as even the nuclear family is replaced by
large numbers of unmarried couples, of single-parent families, of people living large parts of their lives alone or in shared households. With this has
come a new range of identities, as people seek to make sense of their lives as
divorced, single, unmarried, or sole parents. Both commercial pressures to
target specific "demographics" and the personal need to define one's identity
in psychological terms means the growth of new sorts of support and social
groups for, say, divorcées, single fathers, people living in multiple relationships (for which the word "polyandry" has been revived).

Unlike identities based on sexuality such as "lesbian" or "transvestite,"
these are identities based on relationship status and can in fact cross over definitions of sexuality. In Harvey Fierstein's play *Torch Song Trilogy* there is an
angry argument where Arnold tries to make his mother accept that the loss of
his lover is equivalent to her loss of her husband. There are small signs that
this emphasis on relationship identities is spreading beyond the rich world,
such as a report of an attempt to found "the Divorced Women's Teahouse" in
Beijing in 1995. The association foundered on Chinese government restrictions on the creation of nongovernmental organizations.[79]

Underlying all these developments is an increasing stress on ideas of
individual identity and satisfaction, and the linking of these concepts to sexuality. One of the dominant themes in post-Freudian western thinking sex has
been to explain why sexuality is so central to our sense of self, and thus the
basis of both psychological and political identity. These assumptions about
sexuality are far from universal; as Heather Montgomery warned; speaking of
children in the sex industry in Thailand: "Sexuality was never identified with
personal fulfilment or individual pleasure . . . Prostitution was an incidental
way of constructing their identities."[80] Similarly Lenore Manderson wrote,
also of Thailand: "For women, commercial sex is the mechanism by which
many women today fulfill their obligations as mothers and daughters. For
them, the body and its sexual expression in work are a means of production
rather than a mirror to the self."[81]

That last phrase is crucial, for it sums up the dominant script by which
westerners have interpreted sexuality for the past century, whether they have
sought genetic and biological explanations or, like the radical Freudian
school derived from thinkers like Wilhelm Reich and Herbert Marcuse, have
sought to develop concepts of repression and sublimation to explain political
attitudes and behavior.[82] In some ways Frantz Fanon also belongs to this tra-

dition, and the fact that he wrote from the position of a colonized Algerian has made him particularly attractive to postcolonial theorists, who tend to ignore his strong homophobia.[83] This attempt to link sexuality with the political is far less fashionable today, where sexuality is more commonly linked with contemporary capitalism, and we increasingly think of ourselves as consumers rather than citizens. Indeed it is the Right who seem to set the agenda for sexual politics, through attacks on abortion, contraception, and homosexuality which they link clearly to dissatisfaction with the whole tenor of modern life, yet refusing, except for a small group of religious thinkers, to see the connection between contemporary capitalism and the changes in the sex/gender order they so abhor.

ℰnotes

[1] E.g., Frances Fox Piven, "Globalizing Capitalism and the Rise of Identity Politics," in L. Panitch, ed., *Socialist Register* (London: Merlin, 1995), 102–16; Leslie Sklair, "Social Movements and Global Capitalism," in F. Jameson and M. Miyoshi, eds., *The Cultures of Globalization* (Durham: Duke University Press, 1998), 291–311; Kaldor, *New and Old Wars,* 76–86.

[2] For a clear exposition of this view of social constructionism see Jeffrey Weeks, *Sexuality and Its Discontents* (London: Routledge & Kegan Paul, 1985).

[3] E.g., Beverley Hooper, "Chinese Youth: The Nineties Generation," *Current History* 90:557 (1991): 264–69.

[4] See Sherrie Inness, ed., *Millennium Girls* (Lanham, MD: Rowman & Littlefield, 1999); Marion Leonard, "Paper Planes: Travelling the New Grrrl Geographies," in T. Skelton and G. Valentine, eds., *Cool Places: Geographies of Youth Cultures* (London: Routledge, 1998), 101–18.

[5] Much of this section draws on work originally published in the mid-1990s. See especially Dennis Altman, "Rupture or Continuity? The Internationalization of Gay Identities," *Social Text* 14:3 (1996): 77–94; Altman, "On Global Queering," *Australian Humanities Review,* no. 2, July 1996 (electronic journal, www.lib.latrobe.edu.au); Altman, "Global Gaze/Global Gays," *GLQ* 3 (1997): 417–36.

[6] See the bibliography in Balderston and Guy, *Sex and Sexuality in Latin America,* 259–77; the chapters on Brazil and Argentina in B. Adam, J. W. Duyvendak, and A. Krouwel, eds., *The Global Emergence of Gay and Lesbian Politics* (Philadelphia: Temple University Press, 1999); and the special issue of *Culture, Health, and Society* (1:3 [1999]) on "alternative sexualities and changing identities among Latin American men," edited by Richard Parker and Carlos Carceres.

[7]For a discussion of the French position see David Caron, "Liberté, Egalité, Sero-positivité: AIDS, the French Republic, and the Question of Community," in Boule and Pratt, "AIDS in France," 281–93. On the Netherlands see Judith Schuyf and Andre Krouwel, "The Dutch Lesbian and Gay Movement: The Politics of Accommodation," in Adam, Duyvendak, and Krouwel, *Global Emergence of Gay and Lesbian Politics,* 158–83. On Australia see Dennis Altman, "Multiculturatism and the Emergence of Lesbian/Gay Worlds," in R. Nile, ed., *Australian Civilisation* (Melbourne: Oxford University Press, 1994), 110–24.

[8]I owe thanks to a long list of people who over the years have discussed these issues with me, including Ben Anderson, Eufracio Abaya, Hisham Hussein, Lawrence Leong, Shivananda Khan, Peter Jackson, Julian Jayaseelan, Ted Nierras, Dede Oetomo, and Michael Tan.

[9]Jim Marks, "The Personal Is Political: An Interview with Shaym Selvadurai," *Lambda Book Report* (Washington) 5:2 (1996): 7.

[10]The original Indonesian term was *banci.* The term *waria* was coined in the late 1970s by combining the words for "woman" and "man." See Dede Oetomo, "Masculinity in Indonesia," in R. Parker, R. Barbosa, and P. Aggleton, eds., *Framing the Sexual Subject* (Berkeley: University of California Press, 2000), 58–59 n. 2.

[11]See Peter Jackson, "Kathoey><Gay><Man: The Historical Emergence of Gay Male Identity in Thailand," in Manderson and Jolly, *Sites of Desire,* 166–90.

[12]See Jeffrey Weeks, *Coming Out* (London: Quartet, 1977); John Lauritsen and David Thorstad, *The Early Homosexual Rights Movement* (New York: Times Change Press, 1974).

[13]A. T. Fitzroy, *Despised and Rejected* (London: Gay Men's Press, 1988; originally published 1918), 223.

[14]George Chauncey, *Gay New York* (New York: Basic Books, 1994), 65.

[15]John Rechy, *City of Night* (New York: Grove, 1963).

[16]E.g., Annick Prieur, *Mema's House, Mexico City* (Chicago: University of Chicago Press, 1998); Jacobo Schifter, *From Toads to Queens* (New York: Haworth, 1999); Peter Jackson and Gerard Sullivan, eds., *Lady Boys, Tom Boys, Rent Boys* (New York: Haworth, 1999); *Woubi Cheri,* (1998), directed by Philip Brooks and Laurent Bocahut.

[17]Saskia Wieringa, "Desiring Bodies or Defiant Cultures: Butch-Femme Lesbians in Jakarta and Lima," in E. Blackwood and S. Wieringa, eds., *Female Desires: Same-Sex Relations and Transgender Practices across Cultures* (New York: Columbia University Press, 1999), 206–29.

[18]Gloria Wekker, "What's Identity Got to Do with It? Rethinking Identity in Light of the Mati Work in Suriname," in Blackwood and Wieringa, *Female Desires,* 119–38. Compare the very complex typologies of "same-sex" groups in Murray

and Roscoe, *Boy-Wives and Female Husbands,* 279–82, and the chapter by Rudolph Gaudio on "male lesbians and other queer notions in Hausa," 115–28.

[19]Herdt, *Third Sex, Third Gender,* 47.

[20]See Serena Nanda, "The Hijras of India: Cultural and Individual Dimensions of an Institutionalized Third Gender Role," in E. Blackwood, ed., *The Many Face of Homosexuality* (New York: Harrington Park Press, 1986), 35–54. And read her comments in light of Shivananda Khan, "Under the Blanket: Bisexualities and AIDS in India," in Aggleton, *Bisexualities and AIDS,* 161–77.

[21]See Niko Besnier, "Polynesian Gender Liminality through Time and Space," in Herdt, *Third Sex, Third Gender,* 285–328. Note that the subtitle of Herdt's book is "Beyond Sexual Dimorphism in Culture and History."

[22]See Ramon Gutierrez, "Must We Deracinate Indians to Find Gay Roots?" *Outlook* (San Francisco), winter 1989, 61–67.

[23]Besnier, "Polynesian Gender Liminality," 300.

[24]See Lee Wallace, "*Fa'afafine: Queens of Samoa* and the Elision of Homosexuality, *GLQ* 5:1 (1999): 25–39.

[25]Roger Lancaster, "'That We Should All Turn Queer?' Homosexual Stigma in the Making of Manhood and the Breaking of Revolution in Nicaragua," in Parker and Gagnon, *Conceiving Sexuality,* 150.

[26]See Henning Bech, *When Men Meet: Homosexuality and Modernity* (Chicago: University of Chicago Press, 1997); Kenneth Plummer, *The Making of the Modern Homosexual* (London: Hutchinson, 1981); Seidman, *Difference Troubles.*

[27]See Laurence Wai-teng Leong, "Singapore," in West and Green, *Sociolegal Control of Homosexuality,* 134; and the remarkable Singapore film *Bugis Street* (1995), directed by Yon Fan—remarkable for having been made at all.

[28]E.g., Sandy Stone, "The Empire Strikes Back: A Posttranssexual Manifesto," in P. Treichler, L. Cartwright, and C. Penley, eds., *The Visible Woman* (New York: New York University Press, 1998), 285–309.

[29]See Niko Besnier, "Sluts and Superwomen: The Politics of Gender Liminality in Urban Tonga," *Ethnos* 62:1–2 (1997): 531.

[30]Thanks to Arthur Chen of the AIDS Prevention and Research Center, Taipei, for this information.

[31]Jennifer Robertson, *Takarazuka: Sexual Politics and Popular Culture in Modern Japan* (Berkeley: University of California Press, 1998), 207.

[32]For some of the complications in reading cinematic versions of cross-dressing see Marjorie Garber, *Vested Interests* (New York: Routledge, 1992).

[33]See Leslie Feinberg, *Transgender Warriors* (Boston: Beacon, 1996); Kate Bornstein, *Gender Outlaw* (New York: Routledge, 1993)

[34]Sereine Steakley, "Brazil Can Be Tough and Deadly for Gays," *Bay Windows* (Boston), June 16, 1994.

[35]Jerry Z. Torres, "Coming Out," in N. Garcia and D. Remoto, eds., *Ladlad: An Anthology of Philippine Gay Writing* (Manila: Anvil, 1994), 128.

[36]Chris Berry and Fran Martin, "Queer'n'Asian on the Net: Syncretic Sexualities in Taiwan and Korean Cyberspaces," *Inqueeries* (Melbourne), June 1998, 67–93.

[37]Pheng Cheah, "Posit(ion)ing Human Rights in the Current Global Conjuncture," *Public Culture* 9 (1997): 261.

[38]Pedro Bustos-Aguilar, "Mister Don't Touch the Banana," *Critique of Anthropology* 15:2 (1995): 149–70.

[39]Kai Wright, "Industrializing Nations Confront Budding Movement," *Washington Blade,* October 23, 1998.

[40]Pedro Albornoz, "Landlocked State," *Harvard Gay and Lesbian Review* 6:1 (1999): 17.

[41]Ann Ferguson "Is There a Lesbian Culture?" in J. Allen, ed., *Lesbian Philosophies and Cultures* (Albany: State University of New York Press, 1990), 63–88.

[42]See, e.g., the interview by William Hoffman with Mumbai activist Ashok Row Kavi, *Poz,* July 1998, which proclaims him "the Larry Kramer of India."

[43]Bing Yu, "Tide of Freedom," *Capital Gay* (Sydney), May 1, 1998.

[44]In July 1999 the paper ManilaOUT listed over twenty gay, lesbian, and "gay and lesbian-friendly" organizations in Manila.

[45]Naeko, "Lesbian = Woman," in B. Summerhawk et al., eds., *Queer Japan* (Norwich, VT: New Victoria Publishers, 1998), 184–87.

[46]Malu Marin, "Going beyond the Personal," *Women in Action* (ISIS International Manila) 1 (1996): 58–62.

[47]Manifesto of Chinese Tongzhi Conference, Hong Kong, December 1996. Thanks to Graham Smith for providing this source.

[48]See Andrew Matzner, "Paradise Not," *Harvard Gay and Lesbian Review* 6:1 (winter 1999): 42–44.

[49]Peter Jackson, "Beyond Bars and Boys: Life in Gay Bangkok," *Outrage* (Melbourne), July 1997, 61–63.

[50]Statement from *Male* magazine, quoted in *Brother/Sister* (Melbourne), September 16, 1999, 51.

[51]There is a similar argument in Barry Adam, Jan Willem Duyvendak, and Andre Krouwel, "Gay and Lesbian Movements beyond Borders?" in Adam, Duyvendak, and Krouwel, *Global Emergence of Gay and Lesbian Politics,* 344–71.

[52]Mark Gevisser, "Gay Life in South Africa," in Drucker, *Different Rainbows:* 116.

[53]Dean Murphy, "Zimbabwe's Gays Go 'Out' at Great Risk," *Los Angeles Times,* July 27, 1998.

[54]For one view of the situation in Kenya see Wanjira Kiama, "Men Who Have Sex with Men in Kenya," in Foreman, *AIDS and Men,* 115–26.

[55]Chris McGreal, "Gays Are Main Evil, Say African Leaders," *Guardian Weekly,* October 7–13, 1999, 4.

[56]See Carl Stychin, *A Nation by Rights* (Philadelphia: Temple University Press, 1998), chap. 3.

[57]*Times of India,* November 9, 1994, quoted by Sherry Joseph and Pawan Dhall, "No Silence Please, We're Indians!" in Drucker, *Different Rainbows:* 164.

[58]Rodney Jones, "'Potato Seeking Rice': Language, Culture, and Identity in Gay Personal Ads in Hong Kong," *International Journal of the Sociology of Language* 143 (2000): 31–59.

[59]James Farrar, "Disco 'Super-Culture': Consuming Foreign Sex in the Chinese Disco," *Sexualities* 2:2 (1999): 156.

[60]John Clark, "The Global Lesbian and Gay Movement," in A. Hendriks, R. Tielman, and E. van der Veen, eds., *The Third Pink Book* (Buffalo: Prometheus Books, 1993), 54–61.

[61]"The Asian Lesbian Network," *Breakout* (newsletter of Can't Live in the Closet, Manila) 4:3–4 (1998): 13.

[62]On South Africa see Graeme Reid, "'Going Back to God, Just as We Are': Contesting Identities in the Hope and Unity Metropolitan Community Church," *Development Update* (Johannesburg) 2:2 (1998): 57–65. For a discussion of a gay church in Azcapotzalco, on the outskirts of Mexico City, see "Living la Vida Local," *Economist,* December 18, 1999, 85–87.

[63]Coverage of the 1994 games in New York by the Brazilian press is discussed in Charles Klein, "The Ghetto Is Over, Darling': Emerging Gay Communities and Gender and Sexual Politics in Contemporary Brazil," *Culture, Health, and Society* 1:3 (1999): 239–41.

[64]This legislation, it might be argued, is another form of western discourse being deployed to counter a largely western-generated phenomenon. See Eliza Noh, "Amazing Grace, Come Sit on My Face,' or Christian Ecumenical Representations of the Asian Sex Tour Industry," *Positions* 5:2 (1997): 439–65.

[65]Kathleen Barry, *Female Sexual Slavery* (New York: New York University Press, 1984). This should be read alongside the very different views of G. Phetersen, ed., *A Vindication of the Rights of Whores* (Seattle: Seal Press, 1989). A more contemporary statement drawing on Barry's work is Sheila Jeffreys, *The Idea of Prostitution* (Melbourne: Spinifex, 1997). For an overview of some of the relevant literature see Lynn Sharon Chancer, "Prostitution, Feminist Theory, and

Ambivalence," *Social Text,* no. 37 (1993): 143–71; Wendy Chapkis, *Live Sex Acts* (London: Cassell, 1997).

[66]Jo Bindman with Jo Doezema, *Redefining Prostitution as Sex Work on the International Agenda* (London: Anti-Slavery International, 1997), 1. See also Cheryl Overs and Paulo Longo, *Making Sex Work Safe* (London: Network of Sex Work Projects, 1997).

[67]*Sex Workers' Manifesto,* theme paper of the First National Conference of Sex Workers organized by Durbar Mahila Samanwaya Committee, Calcutta, November 14–16, 1997. Compare Wendy Chapkis's statement that "[t]here is no such thing as The Prostitute; there are only competing versions of prostitution" (*Live Sex Acts,* 211).

[68]See Valerie Jenness, *Making It Work: The Prostitutes' Rights Movement in Perspective* (New York: Aldine de Gruyter, 1993).

[69]Cecilie Hoigard and Liv Finstad, *Backstreets: Prostitution, Money, and Love,* translated by K. Hanson, N. Sipe, and B. Wilson (Cambridge: Polity, 1992), 181.

[70]See Kemala Kempadoo, "Introduction: Globalizing Sex Workers' Rights," and Angelita Abad et al., "The Association of Autonomous Women Workers, Ecuador," in K. Kempadoo and J. Doezema, eds., *Global Sex Workers* (New York: Routledge, 1998), 1–28, 172–77.

[71]"The 'Fallen' Learn to Rise," and "Sex Worker's Co-operative," publications of Durbar Mahila Samanwaya Committee, Calcutta, 1998–99.

[72]"Prostitutes Seek Workmen Status," *Statesman Weekly,* November 22, 1997.

[73]There is an interview with the central figure in the development of NSWP, Cheryl Overs, in Kempadoo and Doezema, *Global Sex Workers,* 204–9. Overs here pays tribute both to her "mates in the global village" and to her Australian background.

[74]Guenter Frankenberg, "Germany: The Uneasy Triumph of Pragmatism," in D. Kirp and R. Bayer, eds., *AIDS in the Industrialized Democracies* (New Brunswick: Rutgers University Press, 1992), 121.

[75]"Sex Appeal," *Far Eastern Economic Review,* February 4, 1999, 29–31.

[76]This sort of "transactional sex" is discussed in Lori Heise and Chris Elias, "Transforming AIDS Prevention to Meet Women's Needs," *Social Science and Medicine* 40 (1995): 931–43.

[77]Chris Jones, "Making a Users Voice," paper presented at the Fifth International Conference on Drug-Related Harm, Toronto, March 1994, 7.

[78]See Alfred Neequaye, "Prostitution in Accra," in M. Plant, ed., *AIDS, Drugs, and Prostitution* (London: Routledge, 1993), 178–79.

[79]Matt Forney, "Voice of the People," *Far Eastern Economic Review,* May 7, 1998, 10.

[80]Heather Montgomery, "Children, Prostitution, and Identity," in Kempadoo and Doezema, *Global Sex Workers,* 147.

[81]Lenore Manderson, "Public Sex Performances in Patpong and Explorations of the Edges of Imagination," *Journal of Sex Research* 29:4 (1992): 473. See also Barbara Zalduondo, "Prostitution Viewed Cross-Culturally: Toward Recontextualizing Sex Work in AIDS Intervention Research," *Journal of Sex Research* 28:2 (1991): 232–48.

[82]On the sexual radicals see Paul Robinson, *The Freudian Left* (New York: Harper & Row, 1969).

[83]See Frantz Fanon, *Black Skin, White Masks* (London: Pluto, 1986), and the introduction to that volume by Homi Bhabha, vii–xxvi.

❧ ❧ ❧

Questions

1. How has communication—both electronic and in terms of language itself—influenced the globalization of sexual identities?

2. What kinds of differences exist between "traditional" and "modern" conceptualizations of (homo)sexual identity?

3. What is the difference between "prostitution" and "sex work"?

4. Name some of the problems associated with political organizing around sex work.

5. Give some examples of Western influence on global sexual identities.

6. How it is possible for homosexual identity to be asserted/accepted without an accompanying political movement?